THOMAS KEN
BISHOP AND NON-JUROR

BISHOP KEN
AN ENGRAVING FROM A CONTEMPORARY
PORTRAIT

THOMAS KEN

BISHOP AND NON-JUROR

By

HUGH A. L. RICE

LONDON

S · P · C · K

1958

First published in 1958 by
S.P.C.K.
Holy Trinity Church, Marylebone Road, London, N.W.1
Made and printed in Great Britain by
William Clowes and Sons, Limited
London and Beccles
© Hugh A. L. Rice, 1958

CONTENTS

ILLUSTRATIONS

PREFACE

BISHOP KEN was one who believed that a man's word ought to be his bond; that an undertaking given, whether to commoner or king, should be honoured though it be to one's own hindrance and material loss. From this belief he never wavered, in this belief he played his not inconsiderable part in the great public controversies and happenings of his time. The *political* issues so imperative then no longer concern us to any great extent, though they are still of importance as indicating vital steps in our constitutional evolution. The *spiritual* problems of his day have their modern echoes and counterparts, and Ken's approach to them can be studied with profit as well as interest by modern Christians.

But it is, first and foremost, *as a man* that this gentle pastor of souls must make his appeal to this generation, as he has to those which have gone before. A man in whom was the love of God abundantly; a man to whom principle was all, and expediency nothing; whose life, lived so largely in the fierce light of public affairs, exemplifies to perfection the apostolic injunction to "Honour all men; love the brotherhood; fear God, and honour the King." To ponder the life of such a one can do much to counteract the prevailing cynicism of an age which believes that every man has his price, which says in its haste that all men are liars.

This book, then, has been written for the general reader, who is neither afraid nor sceptical of the sentiments expressed in Longfellow's hackneyed lines about the lives of great men. It makes no claim to original scholarship, a claim which in any case would not be easy to sustain where the ground to be covered has been so well worked and over so long a period of time.

There has been no biography of Bishop Ken published for over fifty years and those published in the nineteenth century are, of course, out of print. With the exception of F. A. Clarke's *Life*, they are of the somewhat diffuse, heavily documented Victorian style in two volumes, and while invaluable as sources (to which the present author gladly acknowledges his indebtedness), they are neither readily accessible nor written in a manner particularly attractive to modern readers. If this be considered insufficient excuse for adding to their number, it can only be pleaded that the writing of the present volume has been undertaken in a spirit of humble homage to a great Englishman, and in the earnest hope that it may materially increase the number of those to whom its subject is more than merely a name.

I should like to express my gratitude to the Dean of Winchester and the Honorary Librarian of the Lyttelton Library for their generous assistance, and to the Warden of St Deiniol's Library, Hawarden, for kindly allowing me to inspect the early editions of Bishop Ken's Works which form part of the Glynne collection.

H.A.L.R.

1

EARLY LIFE

WINCHESTER College, founded by William of
Wykeham in 1382, has for many centuries occupied
a position of prominence among the great schools
of England of which it is very largely the epitome and
prototype. Its proper style is "The College of St Mary at
Winchester", and to remind the visitor of this a figure of the
Blessed Virgin with the Holy Child looks down upon him
from a niche above the Middle Gate leading into the
medieval Chamber Court.

This statue miraculously survived the iconoclastic attentions of Cromwell's Puritans, who played such havoc with
the Castle and Cathedral. Perhaps it owes its escape to the
loyalty and determination of that young ex-Wykehamist
Roundhead, Colonel Fiennes, who is reputed to have stood
with drawn sword at the entrance to the Founder's Chantry
in the Cathedral and thus to have saved it from the dese-
crating hands of the Cromwellian soldiery. To this statue of
our Lady Wykehamists used to raise their hats as they passed
through the gateway—a pleasing courtesy exemplifying the
College's famous motto, "Manners Makyth Man".

Through the centuries many boys destined to high place
in Church or State have passed beneath the steady gaze of
the Holy Mother into the medieval austerity of the College's
ancient precincts; men who have left their mark on the life
of the nation as one young Wykehamist of a bygone century

left his mark on a stone buttress in the cloisters. Here the curious visitor may read, rudely carved, "Tho. Ken 1656".

The stones of England's historical architectural treasures up and down the country have for long suffered defacement as a consequence of the addiction to name and initial carving to which our fellow countrymen are so peculiarly prone. Generally speaking, it is a habit which cannot be too strongly reprehended. No ancient building has its appearance enhanced by the indelible autographs of vulgar-minded nonentities, and every effort ought surely to be made to stamp out this particular form of exhibitionism. At the same time, to come across the self-recorded name of a Wordsworth in Hawkshead Grammar School, of a Philip Sidney in the old Schools at Shrewsbury, or of a Thomas Ken at Winchester, is to catch a glimpse of the schoolboy who was father to a famous man.

Thomas Ken was 13 years old when he was admitted as a Scholar of Winchester on 30 January 1651.[1] He was the youngest son of an attorney in the Court of Common Pleas, a member of an ancient Somerset family. When the boy was only 4 years old his mother died, but his father had been twice married and by his first wife he had a daughter Anne, who was in 1641 about 30 years of age and who devoted herself to the upbringing of her motherless half-brother. Five years later Anne Ken married no less a person than Izaak Walton, who upon the death of Thomas's father in 1651 became the boy's guardian.

To have as his mentor the gentle, God-fearing author of *The Compleat Angler* was a considerable compensation for the loss of both parents at so tender an age, and although there is no evidence that Thomas absorbed any of his brother-in-law's enthusiasm for the fisherman's art, there can be little doubt that he was trained up in a truly Christian atmosphere

[1] He was born at Berkhamsted, in the county of Hertford, in July 1637, but as the parish registers were destroyed in the eighteenth century, no record of his baptism exists.

and taught to hold in highest esteem the Church of the English people and the sacred office of its ministers.

For loyal members of that Church the years of Thomas's boyhood were sad and difficult ones. He was only 12 years old when, after seven years of Civil War, Charles I was judicially done to death and Cromwell's military dictatorship was forced upon the country. During the next eleven years the Church of England was to pass through the severest trials and sorrows. The Prayer Book was proscribed and its use made an indictable offence, while Anglican parish priests were deprived of their benefices and Puritan clergymen intruded in their places. A book of worship called the Directory was brought into use throughout the land, the festivals of the Church were abolished, and, as a substitute, Parliament from time to time authorized Days of Thanksgiving or Humiliation. For Anglicans at least, there was little or no cause for thanksgiving and plenty of grounds for humiliation. Many of those who were able to do so fled to France, where the English Embassy chapel in Paris became a spiritual Cave of Adullam for exiled Churchmen, and where notable divines such as the saintly George Morley, later Bishop of Winchester, Dr Stewart, Dean of St Paul's and John Cosin, later Bishop of Durham, preached and ministered.

Here and there in England scattered groups still gathered together on occasion, to keep the Church Holy Days and to hear the Prayer Book services read, cluding the Cromwellian soldiery and braving the wrath of the military junta which ruled the country. John Evelyn in his diary, under Christmas Day 1657, has left us a vivid account of the Eucharist celebrated on that day at the Exeter Chapel in London by Peter Gunning, Master of St John's College, Cambridge and later Bishop of Ely. Evelyn himself was present and describes how the worshippers were surprised by the Puritan soldiers as they were about to communicate. "As we went up to receive the Sacrament the miscreants held their muskets against us as if they would have shot us at the Altar, but yet suffering us to finish the Office of Communion, as perhaps not having instructions what to do in case they found us in that action." He was taken to Whitehall for interrogation and was asked to explain how "contrarie to an Ordinance made that none should any longer observe the superstitious time of the Nativity, I durst offend, and particularly be at Common Prayers, which they told me was but the Masse in English".

Against this background of Puritan supremacy and persecution Thomas Ken's schooldays at Winchester were passed. In an introduction to the *Manual of Prayers* which he drew up in 1675 for the use of the Scholars of Winchester College, the author tells us something of the religious life of the school as he knew it. It would appear that even during the Commonwealth and under the Wardenship of the Puritan-minded Dr John Harris, the Church festivals were observed and the Daily Offices performed in the College Chapel. "So much care is taken", he says, "to make the youths good Christians, as well as good scholars, and they go so frequently to prayers, every day in the Chapel and in the school, singing hymns and psalms to God so frequently in their chamber, and in the Chapel, and in the Hall, that they are in a manner brought up in a perpetuity of prayer."

Nor were these devotional exercises the only austerities which gave to the College its air of monastic asceticism. The discipline was strict, the fare at table was sparse and plain, while the scholars slept on mattresses of straw in unheated, stone-floored chambers. The boys rose at half-past five in winter and summer alike, and before early morning school were required to make their beds and clean out their rooms. This, on an empty stomach and without benefit of central heating or electric light, must have constituted a chilling prelude to the day's academic pursuits.

There is little to indicate what Ken's intellectual attainments were at Winchester, but he seems to have made steady progress to the top of the school during the five years he was there, in company with his close friend, Francis Turner, who was in later years to become Bishop of Ely and, with Ken, one of the famous seven prelates who defied James II and were sent to the Tower as a consequence. Their schoolboy friendship was to continue into adult life, and together they were to bear courageous witness to the Church principles which they shared. Turner left Winchester for New College, Oxford in the autumn of 1655, but Ken had to wait another year before he could follow his friend to William of Wykeham's foundation in the University and assume his *toga virilis* in the shape of a freshman's gown.

His election to New College took place on 5 September 1656. The examiners from Oxford were welcomed at the College gate, according to immemorial custom, by a speech in Latin from one of the candidates, who were then invited to parade their learning more formally in Hall. As a result of the examination Thomas Ken's name stood second on the roll of those "elected", next to those of two of the "Founder's Kin" who were always privileged to occupy the first place. As there were no immediate vacancies at New College, however, Ken's name was entered on the students' roll at Hart Hall (later to be absorbed in Hertford College) in the hope of a vacancy occurring within the ensuing year.

And so, leaving his name on the cloister buttress, "Tho. Ken" bade farewell to Wykeham's College, though not to Winchester, which was destined yet again to provide the setting for his activities. Meanwhile he shed the schoolboy for the undergraduate and took his journey, as has many a Wykehamist before and since, from Winchester to Oxford.

In the seventeenth century poor men, and most University students came within this category, travelled on foot, the better-off on horseback; only the rich by coach—and they in the summer only, when the roads were passable. It was probably on foot, therefore, that young Thomas Ken came to Oxford, to seek out his friend Francis Turner and to enter upon the freer life of an undergraduate.

Like the Church of England, the University of Oxford was passing through its own particular purgatory. Its colleges and halls had not escaped the attentions of the Puritans and, as a result of the activities of the Parliamentary Visitors sent to "reform" the University, hundreds of Fellows, tutors, and chaplains had been expelled from their posts to make room for men politically and doctrinally acceptable to the republican government. Many of the college buildings had been neglected and allowed to fall into serious disrepair, while some of the smaller halls had been suppressed altogether. Endowments had been embezzled, libraries ruthlessly pillaged, and one of the "Visitors", a certain Sir Nathaniel Brent, is said to have torn down the altar hangings from Merton College Chapel and to have had them converted into curtains for his bedroom.

The University Church of St Mary the Virgin was under Parliamentary control, its clergy excluded, its pulpit used for the ceaseless dissemination of Puritan political and religious propaganda. Nor had the Cathedral, churches, and college chapels of the city escaped the fury of the iconoclasts. Altars were cast down, windows of coloured glass destroyed, chancels levelled, and organs dismantled. The use of the surplice was forbidden, the simplest ceremonies sweepingly condemned as "a heap of atheistical Roman rubbish", and loyalist clergymen denounced as "scandalous ministers, fancy Jacks and brazen-faced fellows". Even the Lord's Prayer was abhorred as formal and prelatical, and if ever he happened to be present when it was said, Mr John Owen, the Puritan Vice-Chancellor of the University (Cromwell himself was Chancellor) would ostentatiously put on his hat and sit down.

There was little or no discipline among the students, many of whom were Royalist sympathizers. Some of them as boys had even taken part, on the King's side, in the Civil War. The ignorance of many of the intruded dons, the strange ejaculations, dronings, and lachrymosities of the Puritan preachers, were the causes of much ribaldry and derision on the part of the students who frequently punctuated lectures and sermons alike with whistles, groans, and cat-calls. This barracking provoked the Puritans into providing armed escorts for their lecturers and preachers, and when these storm-troopers drew their swords on the students the latter fought back with cudgels and any other weapon that came to hand. Anthony Wood, the Oxford historian and antiquary, has left us a rather censorious description of the typical undergraduate of that period, declaring him to be guilty of "noctivagation, intemperance, perturbation of the peace, and especially of offering intolerable affronts to the soldiery of the garrison".[1] All of which, being interpreted, tells us that the students were given to wandering about at night, over-imbibing, and rowdiness, and that they were openly "agin the Government" and its militaristic rule.

This, then, was the state of Oxford when Thomas Ken went up in September 1656. During all these troubles and confusions New College remained loyal to its Church and Royalist principles under the courageous Wardenship of Dr Pink who, during the siege of Oxford, had raised a militia, largely composed of undergraduates, to defend the city against the Roundheads. These volunteers he trained, sometimes in the quadrangle of New College, sometimes in Christ Church Meadow. A trench was dug at the corner of Magdalen College, and on the Tower, from whose summit the choristers sang their May morning carol, were placed "three or four loads of stones" with which to welcome the enemy upon their appearance. Guards were mounted nightly and, in short, the local defence volunteers, though as inadequately armed as their counterparts of 1940, prepared with equal valour to oppose a well-equipped and highly-trained foe.

After Naseby, however, when Fairfax laid siege to Oxford, the King, who had had his headquarters there, slipped away in disguise and the town surrendered on honourable terms,

[1] *Annals of Oxford*, Vol. II.

the Royalist garrison (but not, of course, the militia) march-
ing out with flying colours and beating drums. After the
Roundheads occupied the town, so Anthony Wood tells us,
"hell was broke loose—nothing but sectarianism, blasphemy
and hypocrisy". In spite of the fact, however, that a Puritan
minister who had been a chaplain with Fairfax's army was
made Warden in place of Dr Pink, when John Evelyn visited
Oxford five years later he found New College less affected by
Puritanism that some of the others. "I found the glass windows of the Cathedral much abused, and in Magdalen
College Chapel the altar turned tablewise, and the famous
Independent, Dr Owen [the Vice-Chancellor] preached at
St Mary's perstringing[1] Episcopacy." The Chapel of New
College, however, he found adorned "in its ancient garb,
notwithstanding the scrupulosity of the times: and at
Magdalen the Chapel was in pontifical order, and that
abomination (as now esteemed and almost universally
abolished), the double organ, still existed, and the famous
musician, Dr Gibbon gave them a taste of his skill and talents
on that instrument."

Thus by the time Ken arrived in Oxford the worst of the
violence was over and the city and university had more or
less settled down to endure, with what fortitude it could
muster, a régime which for the time being it was powerless
to resist or overthrow. In Oxford, too, although no official
post or preferment was open to them, resided such true
scholars and philosophers as Dr Wilkins, Seth Ward, William
Petty, Ralph Bathurst, Christopher Wren (father of the
architect of St Paul's), and the learned thinker, scientist, and
Orientalist, Robert Boyle. These men, meeting for discussion
and mutual consultation in private houses, formed a scholarly
coterie towards which many young men gravitated, eager for
more solid instruction than could be had from the intruded
lecturers and tutors. After the Restoration this group of
savants, who during those dark days had done so much to

[1] I.e., denouncing.

keep alight in Oxford the flame of knowledge and scientific research, were granted by King Charles II a Charter of Incorporation as "The Royal Society of London"; thus was born out of tribulation and distress what has for three centuries endured and flourished as one of the foremost learned institutions of Europe.

The influence of these men upon the youth of the University was profound. To them must no small amount of the credit be given for disseminating among that generation of undergraduates to which Thomas Ken and his friend Francis Turner belonged the traditional Oxford respect for classical culture allied to a lively spirit of inquiry and progress.

Ken at Oxford also made friends with two undergraduates of Christ Church whose tastes and outlook were congenial to him. These were Thomas Thynne, in later years elevated to the peerage as Viscount Weymouth, and George Hooper, of whom a contemporary wrote that he was "the best scholar, the finest gentleman, and would make the best bishop that was ever educated at Westminster School". He became one of the foremost Greek and Hebrew scholars of his time and Evelyn, after recording in his diary that Hooper had preached before the King, was to write of him, "This is one of the first rank of pulpit men in the nation".

The paths of Ken and Lord Weymouth lay somewhat far apart after Oxford days—until the closing years of the former's life when his old friend offered him a haven and a home. Hooper and Ken, on the other hand, were thrown together at various stages of their ecclesiastical careers, one of them on more than one occasion succeeding the other.

It is difficult to discover many details about Ken's years at Oxford. His great-nephew and earliest biographer, William Hawkins, has little to say about it; Thomas Hearne, the antiquary, records only that "he was, even then when young, very pious and charitable"; while Anthony Wood contents himself with the equally formal observation that "his

2

towardliness towards good Letters and Virtue was observed by the Seniors". From such meagre tributes little is to be gleaned of Ken's personality, his habits, manners, bearing, or of his impact upon his fellow undergraduates.

In 1657, after a probationary year at Hart Hall, he was elected to a vacancy at New College, where to his joy he was able to share rooms with Francis Turner.

Living in a house near Merton College was one Thomas Willis, brother-in-law to that redoubtable Churchman, Dr John Fell (later Dean of Christ Church and Bishop of Oxford), whom Thomas Brown of Shifnal professed himself, in a famous quatrain, unaccountably unable to love.[1] At this house assembled weekly a band of loyal Oxford Anglicans, under the leadership of Fell himself, of John Dolben, later Bishop of Rochester, and of Richard Allestry, who subsequently became Regius Professor of Divinity and then Provost of Eton. Like the persecuted Christians of the Primitive Church, they met under conditions of secrecy and peril to celebrate the Prayer Book Liturgy and to receive Communion according to its proscribed and prohibited rite. The Offices were recited, festivals, fasts, and vigils observed, and mutual support and comfort provided for those who waited for the Church of England's Babylonish Captivity to be brought to its long-prayed-for end. Vice-Chancellor Owen's biographer, Orme, mentions that there were frequently as many as three hundred present at these gatherings and, implying that they were known at the time to the University authorities, quotes them as instances of his hero's tolerance and forbearance. But perhaps he was merely being

---

[1] This quatrain:

> "I do not love thee, Dr Fell,
> The reason why I cannot tell;
> But this I know and know full well,
> I do not love thee, Dr Fell"

was said to have been an extempore translation from an epigram of the Latin poet Martial, by which its author saved himself from expulsion for idleness.

wise after the event. At all events, their principles and courage being what they were later shown to be, it is hardly to be doubted that Ken and his friends were sometimes, at least, to be found at these gatherings. Here, perhaps, were laid the foundations of that firm faith in Anglicanism and the Anglican Church which was to be their guiding light and motive force throughout their earthly lives.

Hawkins tells us that Ken had "an excellent genius for music" and was an accomplished lute player. Musical parties were as popular a form of amusement and of relaxation at Oxford as in Pepys's London, and were largely promoted and encouraged by the considerable number of unemployed church organists and choir-masters who awaited better days amid Oxford's bare, if not altogether ruined, choirs. Anthony Wood himself took a leading part in these musical activities and has left us a full account of them, seasoned with many a sly reference to his fellow enthusiasts and of their respective talents as performers. His earliest biographer tells of a visit to Oxford, as Chancellor, of Cromwell himself, and incidentally reveals the man of iron as possessing a softer side to his generally flinty nature.

He would, it seems, play a game of bowls with General Fairfax on the lawn at Magdalen after dinner on a summer evening. The game finished, musicians would be summoned to entertain the Lord Protector, who "loved a good voice and instrumental music well". Among the vocalists on one such occasion was a certain James Quin, a former Student (i.e., Fellow) of Christ Church who had been ejected from his post as a suspected Royalist sympathizer. Quin had a good voice and his singing greatly pleased Oliver, who "heard him with delight, liquored him with sack, and in conclusion said, 'Mr Quin, you have done very well; what shall I do for you?' To which Quin made answer, 'I desire that your Highness would be pleased to restore me to my Student's place'; which he did accordingly, and so he kept it to his dying day."

Such distinguished and alarming auditors, however, were

doubtless rare at the tuneful gatherings which gave such delight to Anthony Wood, from whom we learn that "Thomas
Ken, of New College, a Junior, would be sometimes among
them and sing his part".

Thus agreeably, and no doubt profitably, young Ken
passed his student days, while University, Church, and
Nation sullenly, and ever less submissively, bore the yoke of
a joyless, authoritarian régime. Then Oliver died, and John
Evelyn watched them take his remains to Westminster for
burial—with royal robes, regalia, and every princely pomp.
"But", says the diarist, "it was the joyfullest funeral that
ever I saw, for there were none that cried but dogs, which
the soldiers hooted away with a barbarous noise."

Oliver's son, Richard, who reigned in his stead was no
man of destiny; only poor "Tumble-down Dick" who preferred horse-racing to ruling. With the Dictator's strong hand
removed, England began to stir beneath her shackles, while
across the cold, grey North Sea waters a crownless King
awaited the outcome of General Monk's meticulous search-
ings of heart.

Then at last, on a fresh spring morning and after a breakfast of peas, pork and boiled beef, a tall young man was rowed
ashore at Dover from a ship of war, knelt for a moment in
silent thanksgiving, kissed General Monk and accepted a
Bible from the Mayor, declaring it to be the thing which he
loved above all else in the world. These surprising ob-
servances over, the tall young man entered a coach and,
amidst a roar of cheers, a clashing of bells, and a thundering
of guns, departed for Canterbury on his way to London. It
was 26 May 1660, and the King had come into his own. The
reign of the saints was ended.

2

ORDINATION AND EARLY
MINISTRY

AS SOON as the news reached Oxford that Charles II
had landed and was on his way to Whitehall, the
faithful city, which had suffered and endured so much
for the cause of the House of Stuart, gave itself up to un-
confined rejoicing after the fashion of seventeenth-century
England, with church bells, bonfires, a great public concert,
and all-night tavernings and toastings, the like of which had
not been known for ten godly but mirthless years.

The new régime quickly began to make itself felt and to
undo some of the more harmful measures of the Commonwealth. It was not long before orders came from London that
all who had been unjustly ejected from their posts in the
University were to be restored forthwith. Men like Morley,
Dolben, Fell, Sanderson, and countless others who had been
deprived as "malignant and scandalous recusants", were now
reinstated. The Book of Common Prayer and the use of the
surplice were restored in all the churches and college
chapels; extempore prayers and services, together with those
who had concocted them, disappeared with discretion and
unlamented by most. The Church of England returned from
her Babylonish exile with her faith unimpaired, the loyalty
of many of her sons immeasurably fortified and, after the
Savoy Conference of 1661, with her Liturgy revised and
beautified. Minority rule in religion was at an end and if, in

the hour of triumphant Restoration, some of her members—notoriously in the newly-elected "Cavalier" Parliament—showed little tolerance towards those who had so recently shown none towards them, twelve years of proscription and persecution could be pleaded in mitigation of all but the severest counter-measures.

In the happier atmosphere now prevailing in Oxford Thomas Ken proceeded with his studies, and on 3 May 1661 took his degree of Bachelor of Arts. He at once undertook teaching work in the College, the Bursar's accounts for the year revealing that he was paid twenty-five shillings a term for three terms as Lecturer in Logic, a similar sum for one term as Mathematical Tutor, and ten shillings for each of two terms as Junior Moderator in Logic. Thus, while continuing to reside in Oxford, he was able to prepare for the Anglican priesthood to which he felt himself truly called.

No small self-sacrifice was called for in these early days of Restoration from men who offered themselves for ordination, for the Church of England had by no means recovered from her long years of oppression. Diocesan organization had to be set up again and this, for a variety of reasons, could only be done by slow degrees. All the pre-Commonwealth bishops had been deprived, and there were only nine of them still alive at the Restoration. Had Cromwell lived for another ten years, the Apostolic Succession might well have died out altogether in the English Church. Furthermore, many of the Church's revenues had been alienated, and although the new Parliament in 1661 passed an Act restoring all the property she had enjoyed prior to the Civil War, financial stability could not be secured overnight. The prohibition of the Prayer Book for so many years rendered its immediate restoration a matter of some difficulty. A generation had grown up to whom its phrases and ordered proceedings were wholly unfamiliar. Six months after the Restoration, on 4 November 1660, Samuel Pepys recorded in that indispensable diary of his: "In the morning to our own Church,

when Mr Mills did begin to nibble at the Common Prayer
by saying 'Glory be to the Father' etc. after he had read the
two Psalms; but the people had been so little used to it, that
they could not tell what to answer. After dinner I went to
Westminster Abbey, where the first time that ever I heard
the organs in a Cathedral."

To the service of the Church of England, in this hour of
her need, Ken had decided to devote his life, and Oxford,
liberated from Puritan control and with discipline and
decorum replacing licence and disorder, afforded him the
quiet and academic amenities which he needed in his
spiritual and theological preparation for the ministry. His
College library and the Bodleian were at his disposal, rich
in the works of the Catholic Fathers of the Primitive Church.
Here he plunged deep into the writings passed down from
the heroic period of early Christianity—the age of persecution and martyrdom, the age of the great Councils and the
hammering out of the historic Creeds, the age which saw the
rise of monasticism and the spiritual conquest of the
Roman Empire, the age of Cyprian, Athanasius, Chrysostom,
Ambrose, Augustine, Jerome, and Gregory the Great. These
were the pastures upon which he browsed; here he laid the
foundations of that sound scholarship and deep spirituality
which never ceased to distinguish him throughout his long
and eventful ministry.

There is little contemporary evidence to help us in form-
ing a mental picture of Ken as he must have been at this
stage of his career, though Thomas Hearne, the antiquary,
has left a recollection of the far from wealthy young student's
habitual generosity: "He [Ken] was even then, when young
and a B.A. of New College, very pious and charitable, and
used always to have small money to give away constantly, as
he walked the streets, in pence or twopences, or more, at a
time as he saw proper objects."

While he was still up at New College Ken suffered a
grievous personal loss in the sudden death of his sister, Anne

Walton, while on a visit with her husband to Dr Morley, Bishop of Worcester. After the early deaths of his parents Anne had mothered the orphan boy and had doubtless, by her gentle loving influence, done much to mould his character during those formative years. Her death at the early age of 52 must have occasioned Ken a deep sorrow and sense of bereavement. He was now very much alone in the world, sustained only by the compelling power of his priestly vocation.

The precise date and place of his ordination are not known, nor do any diocesan records throw any light upon it. He took his Bachelor's degree in 1661 and it was probably in the following year, when he was 25 years of age, that he was admitted to Holy orders. In view of the prevailing shortage of clergymen, it is likely that no long period of time elapsed between his receiving the diaconate and the priesthood. The first few months of his ministry are lost in equal obscurity; it is possible that they were passed in Oxford, perhaps as acting chaplain of New College of which he was now a Fellow.

On 20 August 1663, however, he was instituted to the Rectory of Little Easton, near Dunmow in Essex. Here his patron was Lord Maynard of Easton Lodge, who, with his wife, Margaret, set a noble example of Christian devotion and piety. Preaching twenty years later at the funeral of Lady Maynard, Ken speaks of her deep spirituality, her life of prayer and penitence, her "daily frequenting . . . morning and evening, of the public services"—an indication that the young parish priest knew what the Prayer Book required of him in the daily public recitation of the Church's Offices. Later, as a diocesan bishop, Ken issued a Lenten Pastoral to his clergy in which he admonished them to "be sure to offer up to God, every day, the Morning and Evening Prayer; offer it up in your family at least; or rather, as far as your circumstances will possibly permit, offer it up in the Church. Go, though you go alone, or with but one besides yourself;

and there, as God's remembrancer, 'keep not silence, and give Him no rest, till He establish, till He make Jerusalem a praise in the earth'."

Here the precepts of the bishop are undoubtedly fortified by the faithful practice of the country parish priest, and their wisdom and force are in no wise diminished with the passage of time. Many a lonely rural incumbent has found a deep sense of spiritual fellowship in the company of all faithful people everywhere, as he loyally obeys the rubric which requires him to say the Daily Offices and adds his contribution, morning and evening, to the world-wide oblation of penitence and praise. Many a parish priest has in this way won the respect of his people, as George Herbert won that of the Bemerton farm workers "who did so love and reverence him, that they would let their plough rest when his Saints-bell rung to prayers, that they might also offer their devotions to God with him; and would then return back to their plough. And his most holy life was such, that it begot such reverence to God and to him, that they thought themselves the happier when they carried Mr Herbert's blessing back with them to their labour."[1]

Herbert's *Life*, written by Izaak Walton, was not published until 1670, but it is unlikely that the gentle priest poet's career and habits were unknown to Walton's brother-in-law, and it is not improbable that the young Rector of Little Easton drew from them encouragement and inspiration.

Ken's stay at Little Easton Rectory was not to be a long one, in spite of his friendship and admiration for Lord and Lady Maynard. In January 1664 he took his Master of Arts degree and in April of the following year he resigned his benefice in order to become chaplain to George Morley, formerly Bishop of Worcester and since 1662 Bishop of Winchester. This appointment Ken probably owed to the deep friendship which existed between Izaak Walton and Bishop Morley, under whose episcopal roof, either at Worcester or

[1] Izaak Walton, *Life of George Herbert.*

Winchester, the former wrote his Lives of Hooker, Sanderson, and Herbert, revised his earlier biographies of Donne and Sir Henry Wootton, and enlarged *The Compleat Angler* for its fifth and last edition. Bishop Morley, who founded at Winchester a still flourishing "College" for the widows of priests who had served in the diocese, was a man of ascetic life,[1] and the duties of his chaplain are unlikely to have been arduous. But Ken was young and energetic, and to keep him occupied he was given charge of the then derelict parish of St John in the Soke, as that part of the city of Winchester is known. Here he was able to perform the pastoral ministrations always so near to his heart, and the tradition of his connection with this parish is still firmly treasured at St John's, and in Winchester generally.

In December 1666 Ken was elected a Fellow of Winchester College, resigning his Fellowship of New College to which, when his circumstances later permitted, he gave a hundred pounds as a small acknowledgement of the benefits and happiness he had derived from his connection with the college. But once again he was called upon to undertake a pastoral cure. In July 1667 he was instituted to the Rectory of Brightstone, a small village in the Isle of Wight, nestling under the lee of sheltering hills about four miles from Carisbrooke Castle where, twenty years before, the ill-fated Charles I had vainly sought shelter from his foes, finding instead the first of his several places of confinement.

Ken continued to hold his position as chaplain to Bishop Morley, and from time to time he was called upon to accompany the Bishop on his periodic visits to London where he stayed in the newly-purchased Winchester House in Chelsea. Mary, Countess of Warwick and sister to the scientist Robert Boyle, also had a house in Chelsea and records in her diary some of the occasions on which she heard

[1] In Farnham Castle there is a tiny cell of a room known as Bishop Morley's Chamber, in which the good man is said nightly to have slept in his coffin.

Ken preach at Chelsea Old Church. She was a devout woman who had probably suffered much from many preachers, but she appears to have found the young chaplain's sermons not unimpressive.

Easter Day, 7th April, 1667. Went to Church, where I heard Mr Ken preach. . . . I was very attentive at the sermon, and moved by it: when sermon was done, I found my heart exceedingly to long after the blessed Feast. . . .
Sunday, 22nd December, 1667. After I came home in the afternoon from hearing Mr Ken, God was pleased to move my heart to speak to my Lord [i.e., the Earl of Warwick] about things of everlasting concernment; and I was enabled, in an awakened frame of spirit, to persuade him to repentance, and to make his peace with God.
Christmas, 25th December, 1667. In the afternoon Mr Ken preached. His text was, "For this cause was the Son of God manifested in the flesh, that He might destroy the works of the Devil." I was attentive and affected at the Sermon.

After only two years spent in ministering to his tiny flock at Brightstone, Ken was recalled to Winchester where he was installed as a Prebendary on 12 April 1669. In the following month Bishop Morley instituted him to the vacant rectory of East Woodhay, a village a few miles from Newbury and now in Berkshire and in the diocese of Oxford. Despite the custom of the times Ken was no pluralist, and though a prebendal stall which carries with it by way of income nothing more than an honorarium is commonly held by a priest who also has a parochial charge, he resigned his living of Brightstone upon his appointment to Woodhay. He steadfastly refused to accept any preferment the duties of which he was unable to perform, a scruple in which he was commendably in advance of his day. He was succeeded at Brightstone by John Fitzwilliam, a Fellow of Magdalen College, who, years later when Ken had been deprived of his bishopric and was in straitened circumstances, left him the annual interest on an invested sum of £500 which was afterwards to go to Magdalen College.

Ken held the living of Woodhay for some three and a half years, and part of that time at least he would appear to have had his elder brother and his sister-in-law staying or living with him at the rectory, for in the parish register there is an entry recording the baptism of "Rose Ken, daughter of Mr Ion Ken, born 23rd June, 1670". This brother, with the unusual name of Ion, was an official of the East India Company and had married a sister of Sir Thomas Vernon, a merchant in the City of London. He probably died sometime before 1707, for in that year Ken writes of his "poor sister Ken, now in great affliction for the loss of her only son who died at Cyprus", making no mention at all of her husband, his brother.

The parochial part of Ken's career terminated when he resigned the living of Woodhay on 8 November 1672, his successor being his friend of University days, George Hooper, already a Canon of Christ Church, Oxford, and held in high distinction as a philosopher, mathematician, antiquary and linguist. Ken returned to Winchester to be near his friend and patron, the ageing Bishop Morley. From then onwards his vocation was to be followed in the dignified and exalted atmosphere of cathedral closes and episcopal palaces, with interludes spent in the possibly less dignified but even more exalted climate of the Court. Ken the parish priest gave place to Ken the dignitary, but the pastoral care, the humble mind, and sympathizing heart were too much a part of the consecrated man of God ever to be concealed or consumed by the prelate's purple.

Ken's priestly and pastoral ideals are perhaps best summarized in the words of his own lines, in volume two of his collected poems:

> Give me the Priest these graces shall possess—
> Of an ambassador the just address:
> A father's tenderness, a shepherd's care,
> A leader's courage, which the Cross can bear;
> A ruler's awe, a watchman's wakeful eye,
> A Pilot's skill the helm in storms to ply;

A father's patience, and a labourer's toil
A guide's dexterity to disembroil;
A prophet's inspiration from above,
A teacher's knowledge, and a Saviour's love.

Whether as country parson, cathedral prebendary, diocesan bishop, or as one dispossessed for conscience' sake, he here unwittingly portrays for posterity his own character, qualities, and gifts of grace; the epitome of that excellence which won for the Anglican clergy of his day the proud appellation of *stupor mundi*.

Ken returned to Winchester to resume his varied round of duties—as Prebendary of the Cathedral, Fellow of the College, Bishop's chaplain and, once more, as unpaid pastor of the sadly neglected parish of St John. Here he became renowned for the eloquence of his preaching which he undertook with regularity and considerable effect, particularly in weaning many of the weaker souls from their sins and the disaffected from the allurements of schism. We are told that the inhabitants of the Soke crowded to the church to hear the sermons of their acting parish priest, just as in later years, when he had become a bishop, the courtiers at St James's flocked to hear him discourse in the Chapel Royal of the Palace. The Anabaptists were numerous in Winchester at this period and many parishioners of the pastor-less St John's had been deluded into attending their meetings and prophesyings. Not only was Ken, by his eloquence and zeal, instrumental in winning numbers of these wanderers back into the Anglican fold, but his biographer Hawkins records that many of the Anabaptists themselves were converted by the preaching of Ken on the Catholic doctrine of Baptismal Regeneration, and were by him received into the Church of England and baptized.

From the same source we learn also something of the self-discipline practised by Ken at this period of his life. "In the evening," says Hawkins, "when he loved to enjoy the society of his friends, he was so worn down with the exertions and fatigue of the day, that with difficulty he kept his eyes open."

Nevertheless, "that neither his study might be the aggressor on his hours of instruction; or what he judged his duty prevent his improvement; or both interrupt his closest addresses to his God; he strictly accustomed himself to but one sleep, which often obliged him to rise at one or two of the clock in the morning, and sometimes sooner; and this grew so habitual that it continued with him almost till his last illness." This asceticism in the matter of sleep seems to have been not uncommon amongst the Caroline divines who, by their bodily mortifications, offered a silent and salutary reproach to the growing licentiousness of the Court and fashionable society.

Ken's devotion to his *Alma Mater* and his love for its scholars, in whom no doubt he saw the reflection of himself when young, prompted him in 1674 to compile a *Manual of Prayers* for the use of the boys of Winchester College. He could scarcely have devised a legacy of greater worth to the school which had nurtured him and to the souls of those who lived and worked and played, as he had himself, within its ancient walls. It was at once a token of his affection and gratitude towards the school, and of his pastoral zeal and care for its scholars.

The *Manual* was full of affectionate counsel and of the kind of prayers that were then considered suitable for the daily devotions of schoolboys. Compared with our less heroic ideas, a somewhat formidable degree of piety would seem to have been expected from those for whom the *Manual* was composed. There were prayers for use in the morning, at noonday, in the evening, and at midnight; devout ejaculations to be uttered "in their first waking, at going to bed, before and after reading Holy Scripture, between first and second Peal, when they go circum,[1] in temptation, after sin committed, after any blessing or deliverance, at giving alms —before, and in, and after Church". There were "Directions for receiving the Holy Eucharist—the Blessed Sacrament,

[1] I.e., in procession round the College cloisters.

which is the most divine and solemn act of all our religion". These Directions throw a most valuable light on what Ken himself believed and taught concerning the Holy Sacrament of the Altar—even though many of the sentiments expressed in them may strike us as being scarcely of the kind which would come naturally, or with comprehension, to the lips of schoolboys.

"On the Inward Part of Thing signified", for instance, we read:

I know, O my God, that I must look through the outward elements, and fix my faith on that which they signify, and which is the inward and invisible Grace, even Thy own blessed Body and Blood, which is verily and indeed taken and received by the faithful in the Lord's Supper. But tell me, O Thou Whom my soul loveth, how canst Thou give us Thy flesh to eat? Lord, Thou hast told me that Thy words are spirit, and they are life, and are therefore not carnally to be understood; Lord, I believe, help Thou my unbelief.

And again:

I believe Thy Body and Blood to be as really present in the Holy Sacrament as Thy divine power can make it, though the manner of Thy mysterious presence I cannot comprehend. Lord, I believe that the Bread that we break, and the Cup that we drink, are not bare Signs only, but the real communication of Thy Body and Blood, and Pledges to assure me of it; I verily believe, that if with due preparation I come to the Altar, as certainly as I receive the outward signs, so certainly shall I receive the Thing signified, even Thy most blessed Body and Blood; to receive which inestimable blessings, O merciful Lord, do Thou fit and prepare me: Amen, Amen.

These are the authentic tones of Catholic doctrine, of Holy Scripture, of the ancient Fathers of Christendom, of the Church of England, her Prayer Book Liturgy and Catechism; and whatever we may think of their appropriateness on the lips of the young, it cannot have been without effect upon the subsequent history of our Church and nation that so many of those who were to be of influence in both were led in their youth in the paths of primitive piety and truth. It is curious to reflect that in the next century so uncompromising a Calvinist as George Whitefield should have admired the "Directions for Receiving the Holy Sacrament" from Ken's *Manual* so sincerely that he incorporated the greater part of them word for word in his *Communion Morning's Companion* for the use of his followers in the Countess of Huntingdon's Connexion.

The second edition of the *Manual* was issued in 1675, a third appeared in 1680, a fourth in 1681, and a fifth and revised edition in 1687 after Ken had become a bishop. This revision seems to have been undertaken for the purpose of refuting Romanist claims that in the *Manual* its author had implied belief in the doctrine of Invocation of Saints as defined by the Council of Trent. It contains the following "Advertisement" or Preface:

Whereas a late Popish Pamphlet has injuriously affirmed that in a Manual of Prayers for the use of the Scholars of Winchester Colledge [sic], I have taught the Scholars of Winchester to invocate the whole Court of Heaven, citing these words, page 93, "Help me, then, ye blessed Host of Heaven", &c. I think myself obliged to declare that by that apostrophe, I did no more intend the Popish Invocation of Saints and Angels, than the holy Psalmist did, when he calls upon the Sun, Moon, and Stars; Fire, Hail, and Snow, &c., to praise God, Ps. 148; and to prevent all future misinterpretations, I have altered, not the sense, but the words of that paragraph, and I do solemnly profess that I believe the Invocation of Saints and Angels, as it is practised in the Church of Rome, to be *"a fond thing, vainly invented, grounded on no warranty of Scripture, but rather repugnant to the Word of God"*, as the XXII Article of the Church of England styles it, to whose judgment I humbly submit.

Tho. Bath and Wells

If the words in question as they appeared in the editions of 1681 and 1687 respectively are compared, the changes made by Ken in that of 1687 are seen to be of considerable significance. In the earlier edition the "invocation" in question reads:

Help me, then, O blessed Host of Heaven to celebrate that unknown sorrow, that wonderful Love which you yourselves so much admire, help me to praise my crucified Saviour.

In the revised edition of 1687 the passage appears thus:

O ye blessed Host of Heaven, Who rejoice at the conversion of one single sinner, adore and praise my crucified Saviour, who died for the sins of the world; adore and praise that unknown sorrow, that wonderful Love, which you yourselves must needs admire.

The revision, by omitting the ambiguous word "help", makes clear the difference between direct invocation of the saints and angels in appealing for their assistance, for which, indeed, there is no sound theological warrant; and comprecation or apostrophizing of them in the sense of Psalm 148 or the Apocryphal "Song of the Three Children", better known as the *Benedicite*, which is one of the Canticles used in the Prayer Book Office of Mattins. This distinction, involving as it does an important doctrinal issue, remains to this day one of the major outstanding points of dispute between the Anglican and Roman Churches. It may be briefly summarized by saying that whereas the Romanists, taking for granted that the saints can not only hear our prayers but are in a position to comply with them, unhesitatingly ask the blessed ones for specific favours, Anglicans, holding this assumption to be at the very least "not proven", are content to ask God that his saints and angels may give us whatever aid may lie within their powers. In maintaining a reverent agnosticism on a subject concerning which Holy Scripture is silent, the Church of England is surely on the safer ground, and Ken, in revising the prayer in question, brought it into conformity with Anglican belief and expression.

That he had a deep and active veneration for the saints is abundantly clear from the *Manual* as well as from many of

3

the hymns which he wrote, especially in his *Hymns for all the Festivals of the Year*. These emphasize beyond all doubt his sincere belief in the Catholic doctrine of the Communion of Saints, and illustrate his sense of the nearness of that unseen world of the Heavenly Vision in which they have their being. The angels, too, were very real to him and in his hymn for the Feast of St Michael and All Angels he salutes their heavenly perfection, recalls their Scripturally-recorded share in the divine work of Redemption and affirms that in loving obedience to the Father's will they do succour and defend us here on earth.

> To work our bliss, to guard from woe,
> You the expanse pass hourly to and fro.
> You on the heirs of Heaven attend,
> To comfort, counsel, warn, defend,
> You in their infant age
> To tender them engage.
> You quicken Saints who grow remiss,
> And you at death transport their souls to bliss.

It has often been erroneously stated that Ken's *Manual of Prayers* originally contained his famous and familiar morning and evening hymns—"Awake my soul, and with the sun"[1] and "Glory to Thee, my God, this night"[2]—but this is not so. Although these hymns were indeed written for the boys of Winchester College, they do not, in fact, appear in the *Manual* until the seventh edition of 1700, in which the Bishop exhorts the boys to "be sure to sing the Morning and Evening Hymns in their chamber devoutly", by which he doubtless means that he hopes that the hymns will form part of the boys' daily devotions, "sing" being used metaphorically in the sense of "recite". Ken's hymnal legacy to Winchester has become the inheritance of the entire English-speaking Christian world and is known and loved far beyond

[1] *The English Hymnal*, No. 257.
[2] *The English Hymnal*, No. 267.

it, for these hymns have been translated into many more tongues than the good Bishop who wrote them even knew to exist. How immeasurably poorer would have been our English hymnody, rich in morning and evening hymns though it is, without their hallowed household phrases, in spite of the fact that they are nowadays seldom to be found printed in full or precisely as Dr Ken wrote them.[1]

And when we consider how few good English hymns there are with which we may celebrate the festivals of the Mother of Jesus, how ill could we afford to be without that other lovely poem of Ken's (No. 217 in *The English Hymnal*) "Her Virgin eyes saw God incarnate born". In these verses are expressed the deepest love and veneration for her whom John Keble was, nearly two centuries later, to hail as "our human nature's solitary boast". Ken, loyal to Anglican principles and unwilling to accept as of faith devotions or doctrines unsupported by Scriptural or universal authority, does not hesitate to express his firmest faith in Mary's unique position, in heaven as on earth, as *Theotokos,* the "God-bearer", the Mother of the Word made Flesh.

> Heaven with transcendant joys her entrance graced,
> Next to his throne her Son his Mother placed;
> And here below, now she's of Heaven possesst,
> All generations are to call her blest.

The un-Catholic dogma of Mary's bodily assumption into Heaven Ken would undoubtedly have rejected; that she is nearest and dearest to Jesus on his throne of Glory as she was to him in the humble home of Nazareth and that, full of grace, she is blessed among women and worthy of all veneration short of the worship which is due to God alone—to this Ken would equally have rendered his fullest affirmation.

While on the topic of Ken as hymn-writer, a quotation from the works of an eighteenth-century Anglican divine,

[1] The original version of these two hymns will be found printed at the end of this book.

Alexander Knox, may serve to illustrate the high esteem in which Ken was held in this respect by Churchmen of a later generation than his own: "A comparison of the hymns of Doddridge, Watts, Ken and Wesley [Charles] would show that Doddridge rises above Watts from having caught the spirit of Ken: and Wesley is deep and interior, from having added to the Chrysostomian piety of Ken the experimental part of St Augustine. Watts is a pure Calvinist; Ken is as pure a Chrysostomian. Doddridge is induced to blend both, and the effect is valuable and interesting."

This judgement is interesting, too, to modern readers, though how valuable as an assessment of the relative worth of the four hymnographers in question is debatable. To attempt to compare, let us say, "Glory to thee, my God, this night" (Ken); "O God of Bethel, by whose hand" (Doddridge); "When I survey the wondrous Cross" (Watts); and "Rejoice, the Lord is King" (Wesley) would be to embark upon an exercise as unprofitable as it must be indecisive. It is enough to say that each of these four men has made his invaluable contribution to English hymnody, that the compositions of each will continue to be loved and sung as long as English-speaking Christendom endures, and that of the four names under consideration that of Ken is least in length alone.

3

INTERLUDE

IN THE second decade of the restored monarchy the "Roman question", which was ultimately and finally to send the Stuarts upon their travels once more, began to loom large in English domestic politics. The menace of the Papacy, real or imagined, was still painfully present in the minds of most Englishmen. Once associated with the threatening power of Spain, it was now linked with the rapidly rising hegemony of France under Louis XIV. The Inquisition was not yet forgotten; the fires of Smithfield still smouldered in the memories of a people whose fears were inflamed by its prejudices, with the assistance in due course of a skilfully manipulated propaganda.

The Queen of England and the Duke of York were avowed Roman Catholics; the King, while professing allegiance to the Church of England, was a Romanist at heart, though not prepared to forfeit his throne by admitting it publicly—in spite of the secret Treaty of Dover[1] by which, in return for French financial aid, he had undertaken to do so.

The strongly Anglican Cavalier Parliament had insisted upon carrying, contrary to the wishes of the King, a series of enactments aimed at all dissenters—Protestant and Romanist alike; and these two oppressed minorities, each in a sense reaping the whirlwind of its own intolerant behaviour when in power, Charles proceeded skilfully to play off one against the other. With equal adroitness he continued to dodge the

[1] Signed on 22 May 1670.

crucial issue of declaring his Catholicism. His evasiveness in the matter of his Treaty undertakings was masterly, if scarcely creditable. His excuses for failing to fulfil them were varied and ingenious. First he pleaded the fact that the Pope was mortally ill; he could not be expected to submit to a dying pontiff. Then it would be necessary for an Englishman to receive his submission; a theologian of world-wide eminence, by whom Charles could pretend to have been utterly overwhelmed and persuaded. Furthermore, as the King now discovered for the first time the presence of doubts in his own mind arising from recent scientific discoveries, it was essential that the theologian in question should also be learned in chemistry and natural philosophy. It is hardly surprising that such a paragon was not immediately forthcoming, nor that in the minds of his French allies there began to dawn a suspicion that the King's papalistic zeal was of a rather fluctuating variety, ebbing and flowing as his need for funds became progressively more or less acute.

All the same, anti-Romanist feeling grew steadily both in Parliament and in the country, and libellous pamphlets began to appear to testify to its existence. The war with England's principal naval rival, Holland, which broke out in 1672, was viewed with mixed feelings by the populace. War with England's most powerful naval and mercantile rival was popular enough, but war in alliance with a Catholic power (France) against a sturdily Protestant one caused many a doubt to afflict the minds of the British public.

In an attempt to unite the nation and allay Protestant suspicions, Charles issued on 15 March 1672, a Declaration of Indulgence by which the penal laws were suspended against Romanists and Protestants alike. The former were to be free to worship in their own houses, the latter to build and worship in their own conventicles. The Romanists hailed the Declaration with relief; but the Protestant dissenters, in theory ardent devotees of toleration, could not in practice stomach the idea of toleration for any form of religion but their own. Their gratitude was perfunctory, their suspicions of the King's motives merely accentuated. The Declaration enjoyed no general measure of approval, and almost exactly a year later the House of Commons, insisting that Parliament alone had powers to suspend penal statutes, forced Charles to withdraw it. A few days later a Test Act, by which all persons holding public office would be required to receive the Sacrament at an Anglican altar and take an oath against the doctrine of Transubstantiation, was passed by both Houses of Parliament and received the King's reluctant, though outwardly unruffled, assent.

As a result of this illiberal and vindictive piece of legislation the King's brother, the Duke of York, was forced to relinquish his post as Lord High Admiral, and the rough, honest, old Romanist Clifford resigned the office of Lord High Treasurer in favour of a Yorkshire country squire, the Anglican Sir Thomas Osborne.[1]

Meanwhile, the war dragged on. The fleet, in spite of all Mr Secretary Pepys's efforts to make it an efficient fighting force, was starved of men and supplies by a niggardly and suspicious Parliament, and suffered more than one humiliation at the hands of the Dutch Admiral De Ruyter. The French armies overran Holland but the Dutch, rather than surrender, opened the dykes and let in the sea, robbing Louis to the vast delight of the great majority of his English allies of the victory that had been all but within his grasp.

In January 1674, Charles submitted to Parliament terms for an Anglo-Dutch peace treaty. His financial resources were exhausted and there was no money to fit out the fleet. Parliament had refused supplies to prolong a war it detested, and Louis declined further aid to an ally who had proved singularly unhelpful and in whose sincerity with regard to Treaty obligations he could no longer pretend to believe. Peace between England and Holland was signed at the

[1] Later created Earl of Danby.

Hague on 9 February. The Treaty of Dover, to all intents and purposes, was a dead letter.

The last troubled decade of Charles II's reign was a difficult one for the Church of England, for the venomous political strife which marked it, the turbulent disloyalty of the Whigs, the self-seeking manœuvres of the Tories, the shiftiness of the King and the obstinate ineptitude of the Duke of York were largely occasioned by the bitter cross-currents of religious controversy. These lay behind the twists and turns of foreign policy; behind the Parliamentary wrangles about toleration, "exclusion", and "moderation"; and behind the astounding credulity which led men to listen to the perjured testimony of the obscene Titus Oates by which he was enabled to swear away the lives of innocent men. It lay behind the blind, unreasoning "anti-Popery" craze which swept the country, and London in particular, and which gave the malevolent Shaftesbury and his "brisk boys" their opportunity to terrorize the capital, the legislature, the judiciary, and, but for the cool courage of the King, the Court itself. It was an age of cynical self-seeking and utter unscrupulousness on the political plane, in which men of principle in public affairs were few and far, and of small account.

It is with a considerable measure of relief that in reading the history of this period one turns from the activities of the politicians and "statesmen" to contemplate the men at the helm of the Church of England. The later Caroline divines, as they are commonly called—such as Isaac Barrow, William Sancroft, Gilbert Sheldon, Thomas Sherlock, John Pearson, George Morley, John Cosin, and John Tillotson—were almost all men of massive learning and, in many cases, of deep spirituality. Though it is true that there were occasions when their influence was brought to bear upon one side or another in the religio-political controversies of their time, it is also true that in the main they were content to leave such matters to the politicians, devoting their time and energies to spiritual, pastoral, and theological concerns. In an age notorious for every conceivable kind of corruption and venality in high places, they stood out as burning and shining lights, earning for their order a contemporary approbation which a few years later became apparent in the ecstatic general rejoicings over the release of the Seven Bishops from the Tower, and a place of imperishable glory in the annals of the Anglican Church.

Such, then, was the troubled, perilous background against which Thomas Ken grew to maturity and began to play an ever-increasing rôle in the affairs of Church and State; such were the eminent Churchmen with some of whom he was to share so tempestuous and fiercely illuminated a stage.

In 1675 he set out on a tour of Italy, taking with him as companion his nephew, Izaac Walton the younger. So far as is known this was the first time that Ken had been out of England, but it is probable that in the accomplished manner of his times he had some acquaintance with foreign languages. In his will, for instance, he bequeathed to the public library in Bath all his "French, Italian and Spanish books", and as languages other than one's own are more easily acquired in youth than later, these volumes may well represent an important part of his early studies.

The Pope, Clement X, had proclaimed 1675 a Jubilee year and the city of Rome was preparing to accommodate a vast influx of pilgrims and visitors, and to celebrate the year with traditional splendour. This fact may have had some influence with Ken in the planning of his foreign tour, though in the dangerously inflamed state of public opinion in England he no doubt found it politic to avoid undue mention of it before leaving the country. As the Low Countries were at this time in process of being ravaged by Louis XIV's war of aggrandisement, Ken and his young companion journeyed southward through France, most likely by way of Paris, Lyons, Avignon, Marseilles, and along the Riviera coastal road. Unfortunately the travellers left no record or diary of their journeyings, so that details of their mode of transport and the names of the places visited must remain largely a matter for conjecture.

From contemporary accounts it would appear that the Jubilee of 1675 was bigger and better than any of its predecessors; the numbers of pilgrims more prodigious, the ceremonies and public entertainments more lavish, the profits accruing to the papal treasury from the offerings of the faithful more prolific than ever before. Vast crowds daily thronged the churches of Rome, and especially St Peter's; purchased their pardons and certificates of pilgrimage; gazed with credulous awe upon such remarkable "relics" as the handkerchief (somehow miraculously preserved) which bound the head of Christ as he lay in the sepulchre, or the proof-probing finger of doubting Thomas; got what they could in the way of free meals and hospitality, but more often, probably, suffered themselves to be fleeced, if not butchered, to make a Roman holiday.

What effect all this ecclesiastical excitement and worldly glitter had upon the sober Anglican minds of Ken and his youthful companion we can only deduce from a statement made by his earliest biographer, Hawkins. "He [Ken] was often heard to say, that he had great reason to give God thanks for his travels, since (if it were possible) he returned rather more confirmed of the purity of the Protestant religion than he was before." Ken, of course, used the term "Protestant", as did all his contemporaries, not in the sense in which it is so often employed to-day as meaning "anti-Catholic", but in the sense of "anti-Roman" or "anti-papal" —a very different thing. Of Ken's Catholicism, and of his firm belief in the Catholic Faith of undivided Christendom, there was never any doubt at all. To him the Church of England was the true Catholic Church of these islands, and all forms of dissent, whether Romanist or Puritan, from her teaching and communion were clearly and inexcusably schismatic. It is not, therefore, likely that as he continued his journey to Venice, by way of Terni, Spoleto, and Assisi, he found himself any more favourably disposed towards "the meretricious gaudiness of the Church of Rome", as observed by him at its heart and centre, than towards "the squalid sluttery of the fanatick conventicles" to be seen at home in England. Ken was born, and remained, a loyal son of the English Church, even when in later years he felt himself conscientiously impelled to withdraw himself from her active ministry and communion. Never did it occur to him to attach himself to any other Christian body.

There is a further reference to Ken's Italian tour in a doubtful anecdote quoted by another of Ken's biographers, Dr Markland, relating to the time when he had become a bishop. Complimented by James II on certain of his writings which seemed to the King to show Ken's opinions as not so far removed from his own, Ken in reply is said to have told the King that he had once been inclined to his (i.e., the King's) religion, but that the New Testament and his journey to Rome had quite cured him. Whatever truth there may have been behind this alleged comment on the result of his tour, there is no evidence that Ken ever suffered from "Roman fever", nor does it seem very consistent with his respect for the royal office that he should have spoken to its holder in so uncomplimentary a fashion. It is not unknown for even public utterances to become distorted in the course of time, and words spoken in the semi-privacy of a royal court are even more vulnerable to this procedure.

Whatever Ken's opinions, however, they did not preserve him from the suspicion that by his visit to the Eternal City he had become more than tinged with the hues of Popery. In the artificially exacerbated state of religious opinion in England at the time, such a charge is not, perhaps, surprising. If so sturdy an Anglican and so regular a Churchgoer as Mr Secretary Pepys could in all solemnity be arraigned before Parliament and committed to the Tower on a perjured and trumped-up accusation of "Popery", it is not unduly remarkable to find one so devoted to ancient Catholic teaching as Ken incurring a similar suspicion. His aloofness, too, from the noisy disputations of the time may have suggested a secret attachment to Romanism for which there was not the smallest foundation of fact. While always ready to extend towards the adherents of that Faith the same Christian courtesy which he showed to all, and prepared as he was to allow his loyalty to a Roman Catholic King to go far beyond what many men might consider reasonable, Ken's Anglicanism was unqualified and unshakable.

Not that Ken could have believed the Church of England, as it then was, to be perfect or incapable of improvement. The effects of what the Preface to the Prayer Book of 1662 restrainedly, not to say euphemistically, refers to as "the late unhappy confusions"[1] was still only too apparent. Evelyn, in his diary, records, during a prolonged visit to Lord Arlington in Suffolk, that "most of the houses of God in this county resemble rather stables and thatched cottages than temples in which to serve the Most High". This was written in 1677, and there is no reason to suppose that the condition of the village churches in Suffolk was any worse than that prevailing in churches throughout the rest of the country generally. Ken knew only too well the scars and defects which at that time marred the appearance of the English Church. But he also knew what, by God's grace, she could become—a Church without blemish and without spot, expressing the purest and deepest spiritual aspirations of the English people and offering them the venerable faith and practice and sacraments of Catholic Christendom, free from all un-Scriptural and un-historical innovations, Papalist and Puritan alike.

---

[1] A remarkable phrase as applied to a revolution, a civil war, the judicial murder of a King, a Viceroy, and an Archbishop, the imprisonment or exile of a whole Bench of Bishops, the ejection and deprivation of an entire parochial clergy, the abolition of all religious feasts and the proscription of the Church's Book of Common Prayer.

With his loyalty to her tenets, and his belief in her destiny, undisturbed by what he had seen and heard abroad, Ken returned to Winchester to pursue for three more years his dedicated life of pastoral duty, sacred study and spiritual self-discipline. It was the year 1676. Ken was now 39 and advancement in the Church was soon to deprive him of the peaceful, ordered existence so congenial to him, lived beneath the shadow of Winchester's cathedral, with the humble parishioners of St John's to call forth his pastoral enthusiasm, and the boys of the College to be lured and encouraged into the paths of virtue and truth.

It was a period of calm and happiness, such as many men have known and enjoyed who were later summoned to play their part on a wider and less tranquil stage—the sabbath calm of Galilee before the turbulent and sombre days of a Judæan ministry. Ken was able to enjoy to the full the beauty of Winchester's ancient buildings—the Cathedral itself with its fine west front, the massive Norman pillars of its mighty nave, the soaring clerestory and magnificent vaulted roof. Here as prebendary he ministered in choir and at the altar. At the square black font of Tournai marble, which stands in a bay between two of the pillars on the north side of the nave, he baptized the babies of the good burghers of the city.

The fabulous shrine of St Swithun had disappeared nearly a century and a half before—victim to the greed of Henry VIII and his jackal Thomas Cromwell—just as the remaining shrines and chantries, Wykeham's excepted, had fallen before the destructive frenzy of the followers of another Cromwell only thirty years previously. Most of the lovely medieval glass had gone from the windows, too—smashed to fragments to the greater glory of the strange, harsh, beauty-hating deity which these godly men had made in their own image. But Wykeham's shrine had been spared, and so had the medieval choir stalls, with their misericords upon which the old craftsmen had carved so many curious and often humorous figures—monks, wolves, cats, old women, owls, and bishops, and even a family group of a sow and her busily-feeding litter of piglets. These would be as familiar to Ken as they are to those who know the cathedral to-day. So, too, would be the medieval wooden caskets reputedly containing the bones of those Saxon and Danish bishops and monarchs who saw the first beginnings of Winchester's glory: Cynegils, Ethelwulf (father of Alfred the Great), Egbert and Kenulph who built the first cathedral, Edmund (Alfred's eldest son), Canute the Dane and his wife Emma, widow of the unhappy and unready Ethelred.

The great fifteenth-century stone reredos behind the high altar had been left cruelly defaced by the Cromwellians, its niches denuded of the sculptured figures of saints, angels, bishops and kings which had once adorned it. These niches have now been refurnished with modern figures, among them one of Ken himself; but his heart must often have been saddened by the bare and desolate look it bore in his time. Perhaps he could find a measure of consolation in the quaint carvings and engravings in the Lady Chapel, among them one of a choirboy depicted in the act of divesting himself of his surplice. One likes to think that this engaging little sculpture sometimes lured a smile to the lips of the author of the *Manual of Prayers* and the morning and evening hymns, written for the Winchester boys of his own and later generations.

Outside the Cathedral were all that were left of the monastic buildings: the Deanery, the Pilgrim's Hall, Cheyne Court, the Close Wall with its massive entrance gate, and just beyond it the tiny church of St Swithun, spanning the roadway arch of the King's Gate. If he passed through this archway and turned to his left, leaving the wall and build-ings of his well-loved College on the right, Ken could soon have come to Bishop Morley's brand-new palace of Wolvesey —built to the designs of Christopher Wren himself, largely from the stones of the nearby ruined castle—erected by

Bishop Henry of Blois in the twelfth century and demolished by Cromwell in the seventeenth—within the gaunt ramparts of which the Cathedral choristers nowadays play cricket and football.

From Wolvesey it is not far to those pleasant "Meads" where Winchester Collegians still disport themselves beside and upon Izaak Walton's "fishful Itchen", just as they had done when Ken was one of them and as they no doubt still did as he passed by in sober clerical habit on his way to the nearby Hospital of St Cross. Here, in the Norman church of this ancient institution founded and endowed by the same Henry of Blois who built Wolvesey Castle, for thirteen poor men under the care of a Master, Ken may have ministered from time to time. Perhaps, too, he received from the Hospital buttery the traditional "wayfarer's dole"—a token survival of Bishop Henry's bounty in the form of a morsel of bread and a sip of ale, such as can be had by modern visitors to the lovely old Hospital of St Cross, calm, peaceful, self-contained; so near to the noisy, traffic-laden Southampton road, yet in spirit half a dozen centuries away.

Ken's Winchester was a small place compared with the present flourishing city, and little of it lay outside its medieval walls. Just inside the West Gate (which is still standing) were the ruins of Winchester's other castle—likewise reduced by the Roundheads after they had besieged, bombarded and captured the city. The great Hall still stood intact and remains to-day, containing the massive circular table top fancifully ascribed to the semi-mystical King Arthur and his brotherhood of shining knights (for Winchester has been said to be Camelot of the medieval Arthurian legend). Below the Castle ruins they were building in Ken's time a royal residence—never completed for Charles II, who found Winchester so greatly to his liking. The King is reputed to have bought the site from the citizens for five shillings, and no doubt when he commissioned Wren to draw up the plans for it he visualized a palace which might in time have rivalled Versailles or Fontainebleau. But the necessary years were denied him: after his death the unfinished building became a barracks and most of it was destroyed by fire in 1897.

Passing from his contemplation of these royal schemes of grandeur, along Jewry Street (the medieval ghetto) and through the North Gate (long since demolished), Ken would soon come to yet another indication of Winchester's eventful and often tragic past: the ruins of Hyde Abbey, where pious hands once laid the honoured bones of "England's darling", Alfred the Great, and from whence, at the spoliation and destruction of the monasteries, they were dug up by sacrilegious ones and flung away into shameful oblivion. Sombre associations such as these can still sadden the sensitive visitor to the capital of Saxon England, with her ancient glories and ancient wrongs. So, too, one feels, they must have affected the gentle soul of Ken as he took his walks abroad, perhaps with brother-in-law Walton for companion, during those peaceful prebendal years before matters of more worldly importance claimed him, and Winchester for a season saw him in its streets no more.

4

ROYAL CHAPLAIN

IT WAS in the year 1679 that Ken was called from the comparative seclusion of Winchester to move for a time in more exalted circles. Two years earlier King Charles, in a shrewd attempt to allay the still simmering suspicions of his Protestant subjects, had brought about the marriage of his niece Mary (daughter of the Duke of York and his first wife, Anne Hyde) to William, Prince of Orange. The bride and bridegroom were cousins, for the latter's mother, Mary, was a daughter of Charles I. Furthermore, William was something of a popular hero in England on account of his determined defence of the Dutch Netherlands against the embattled might of *Le Grand Monarque*; and as Charles his uncle was without legitimate issue he stood next but one in the succession to the throne of England.

The marriage was consequently received with great enthusiasm by the English Whigs and Puritans, with distasteful, sulky acquiescence by the father of the bride, with admirably counterfeited *bonhomie* by her uncle, and with repugnance by the Princess Mary herself. For William, for all his courage and determination, was a dull dog—sour, taciturn, querulous, undemonstrative, and seldom in the best of health or humours.

The marriage ceremonies and honeymoon lasted just three weeks, at the end of which time William took his 15-year-old bride to her new home, the sparse and cheerless court at the Hague. Mary was permitted to take with her, in addition to

her English ladies-in-waiting, a priest to act as her almoner
and chaplain. It was possibly at the instance of Bishop
Morley, who had been the Princess's confessor ever since she
was 12, that Ken's friend of Oxford days, George Hooper
(who had succeeded him, it may be remembered, at Woodhay), was appointed to the post. He performed his duties to
the complete satisfaction of the Princess for some eighteen
months, but by the end of that time he felt that he had had
as much as he could endure of William's moroseness and in-
civility. Furthermore, all the time that he was in Holland
Hooper received not one penny for his services—a state of
affairs which clearly could not be tolerated indefinitely, and
so, reluctantly and to the sincere sorrow of the Princess Mary,
he felt obliged to tender his resignation. It is true that the
night before Hooper was due to return to England William's
minister Bentinck, afterwards to become Lord Portland, sent
him by the hand of a servant the sum of seventy pounds, a
paltry payment for a year and a half of constant and loyal
service.

No doubt William was relieved to see Hooper depart, for
the High Anglicanism of his wife's chaplain was far removed
from his own dour Calvinistic beliefs. Coming one day to the
Princess's apartments, he noticed among her books Eusebius's
Church History and Hooker's *Ecclesiastical Polity*. "I suppose", he observed bleakly, "that Dr Hooper persuades you
to read these books!" No chapel had been provided for the use
of the Princess, who accordingly was constrained to sacrifice
her private dining-room for the purpose, taking her meals in a
much smaller and gloomier apartment. Hooper was instructed
to fit the dining-room up as a place of Anglican worship and
when he had done so William arrived to inspect it. His
manner was chilly and clearly disapproving, but beyond in-
quiring curtly why there was a step before the Holy Table,
what the chair placed near it for the Princess was for, and
kicking at the latter with his foot, he made no further comment. He would sometimes attend the evening service, but

never came to the celebration of Holy Communion at which his wife was present every Sunday morning.

If William thought that Hooper's departure would result in his wife being exposed to religious influences of a different kind he must have suffered a measure of disappointment for, as Hooper had succeeded Ken at Woodhay, Ken was now nominated by the King to take his friend's place at the Hague. This appointment he, too, may have owed to Bishop Morley, or perhaps to the recommendation of Archbishop Sancroft who already thought highly of him. It was probably towards the end of 1679 that Dr Ken, as he now was (for Oxford had honoured him with a Doctorate in Divinity in June of that year), arrived at the Hague. The English envoy at the Stadtholder's Court was the Honourable Henry Sidney, who recorded in his diary for 14 December: "I was at Church, and heard Mr Ken preach." And on Christmas Day: "There dined with me Mr Ken and Mr Bowyer."

Ken found William of Orange no more sympathetically disposed towards him than had his predecessor, and he quickly observed the deplorable effect that the Prince's sullen boorishness was exercising upon his wife's health and spirits. With characteristic courage he determined to remonstrate with William. Sidney records in his diary for 31 March 1680: "Dr Ken was with me. I find he is horribly unsatisfied with the Prince, and thinks that he is not kind to his wife; he is resolved to speak with him, though he kicks him out of doors." And a few days later, on 11 April, we find the Envoy writing: "Sir Gabriel Sylvius and Dr Ken were with me, and both complain of the Prince, especially of his usage to his wife; they think he is sensible of it, which doth contribute to her illness; they are mightily for her going into England, but think he will never give his consent."

Unfortunately there is no record of how Ken fared in his approach to the Prince on this delicate domestic matter, but, his character being what it was, it is not to be doubted that approach the Prince he did, and as certainly spoke his mind.

His forthrightness can scarcely have endeared him to William, but he was soon to bring upon himself an even deeper measure of the Prince's disapproval. Among the Maids of Honour brought from England by Mary was a certain Jane Wroth, niece to Lord Maynard, Ken's friend and earliest patron. This young woman was of considerable attraction and soon had many admirers among the gentlemen of the Dutch Court. These included one Count Zulestein who courted the lovely Jane, seduced her under a promise of marriage, and then jilted her. When the news of this reached Ken's ears he at once applied himself to the righting of the injured girl's wrongs. William was absent in Amsterdam, but Ken went directly to the Count and upbraided him for his treatment of one to whom, as the Queen's Chaplain and as an old friend of the girl's aunt and uncle, he felt a double responsibility.

Whatever the methods employed by Ken to bring the evasive lover to a sense of his obligations, they were completely and speedily successful. The Count agreed to marry Jane and the wedding took place forthwith. Honour and everyone concerned were satisfied—with the exception of Zulestein's princely master. When, on his return to the Hague, he heard of what had taken place, William flew into a great state of fury and denounced Ken unsparingly for his part in the proceedings, threatening, even, to dismiss him from his post.

It was an unfortunate line to take with one so disinterested as Ken, to whom the anger of princes meant little. He was conscious of having acted perfectly correctly in the matter; he would have been quite content to exchange the dreary atmosphere of the Dutch Court for the quiet and tranquillity of his beloved Winchester, and he accordingly begged leave of the Princess to withdraw from her service. William, however, was of too calculating a disposition to allow his transitory wraths to divert him from the carefully formulated paths of policy, and in view of his expectations of ultimately succeeding to the English throne he had no wish to alienate his possible future subjects by treating too cavalierly one whom they clearly held in such great esteem. It was not long, therefore, before William was appealing to the chaplain to return to his post and Ken, who was anxious to be of service to the obviously unhappy Princess and who, in any case, was not the man to harbour grievances, agreed to do so for a further twelve months.

Nothing could be more indicative than this episode of Ken's outstanding characteristics of courage and chivalry, his passion for justice and utter disregard for his own advantages. These qualities he was to exhibit on many future occasions and never more conspicuously than in his dealings with those of the most exalted rank. Charles II, James, William, and Anne were all to have first-hand experience of one or more of them, and all except James—for whom, ironically enough, Ken was to make the greatest sacrifices—respected the man who possessed such qualities even when he displayed them to their own royal disadvantage. In an age of widespread venality and corruption, when most men in public life had their price and were prepared to exact it, Ken stood out in splendid prominence as an Englishman without fear and without reproach—an Israelite, indeed, in whom there was no guile.

At the end of the period he had agreed to with the Prince, Ken returned to England. While still in the royal service he had been approached by both William Lloyd, a learned Anglican divine who became Bishop successively of St Asaph, Worcester, and Lichfield, and Henry Compton, Bishop of London, on the possibility of persuading some of the more eminent and influential Dutch ministers to embrace Anglicanism. Ken does not appear to have considered the plan very feasible, and in a letter to the Bishop of London dated 19 August 1680 he explains why. The Dutch divines, he points out, have little regard for ecclesiastical tradition and antiquity; it is the Protestant nonconformists whom they regard as their brethren in England and whose writings they read with approval, while Anglicans they look upon as little better than papists. Furthermore, they are most of them of such a disposition that did they consent to join the Church of England and accept her discipline they would each expect nothing less than a deanery by way of reward. But the greatest obstacle of all that Ken foresaw was that if the Dutchmen were approached on the subject of reunion their demands in certain respects would be totally unacceptable. "I foresee that the next thing they will expect from us will be our subscription to the validity of their Orders, and as a further confirmation demand that the Princess may come to their sacrament, which hitherto she has never done, and if ever she does do it, farewell all Common Prayer here for the future."

Ken goes on to hint that he has previously been attacked by the Dutchmen on the question of Orders, and remarks, "the resentment they have at our reordaining them sticks in their stomachs". He makes plain his opinion that nothing could possibly be gained by any attempt to proselytize the Dutch ministers and expresses his reluctance to start anything in the way of religious controversy, particularly as at the time of writing he is enjoying a brief spell of princely favour. In all this he demonstrated both his firm grasp of Catholic principles and his admirable clarity of thought in perceiving that a superficial unity which was not based upon common acceptance of fundamental doctrinal beliefs would be nothing but a sham, and would merely sow seeds of future weakness and dissension within the Anglican Church.

One true conversion to Anglicanism he was concerned with at this time, though of a rather different kind—that of a certain Colonel Fitzpatrick, who was evidently a person of some importance in the English community at the Hague— from the Roman Church to Anglicanism. Henry Sidney writing to Sir Leoline Jenkins on 31 August 1680 says: "Colonel Fitzpatrick having for these six months began to

consider that he was not in the right religion, and having
read many books, and used all the means to be instructed in
the right, is at last convinced that the Protestant religion is
the true religion; and this day in my chamber he made a
declaration of it to Dr Ken, the Princess of Orange's
Chaplain."

Ken himself reported the matter, a fortnight later, to
Sancroft, Archbishop of Canterbury, and to the Bishop of
London under whose jurisdiction all Anglican congregations
abroad at that time came. A few days later, on 17 September
1680, Ken wrote again to the Bishop of London to report
that the Colonel's conversion had been sealed by his recep-
tion of Holy Communion according to the Anglican rite.

My very Good Lord,
   In my last, I gave your Lordship an account of Colonel
Fitzpatrick's resolution to receive the Holy Eucharist in our
Chapel; which last Lord's Day he did, to the great satisfaction
of the Court. The Prince and Princess, His Majesty's Envoy, Mr
Sidney, and Monsieur Bentin [Bentinck], and several persons of
quality, were at the Prayers and Sermon; and I question not but
you will find the Colonel extremely satisfied with his change, for
I hear he goes for England with Mr Sidney within a few days. I
cannot give your Lordship a greater demonstration of the
Colonel's sincerity than to let you know that he has discoursed
with some of his Romish friends so effectually that we are in
hopes of more converts to our Church, and those considerable
ones too. I am but just come to town, and it being post day am
straitened in time, which is the reason I cannot wait on him till
to-morrow; and his Highness, who went yesterday for Germany,
before he left Honnsterdyke, commanded me to pay a visit to a
Lieutenant-Col. who, we hope, will suddenly embrace our communion. I was at her Highness's Chapel with the Colonel, but of
this person I hope to send a more perfect account by Mr Sidney.

My Good Lord,
Your Lordship's most humble
and most obedient servant,
Tho. Ken[1]

[1]Bodleian Library, Rawlinson MSS. c. 985. ol. 7.

Whatever gratification Compton (a somewhat fanatical Protestant) may have felt at this access of martial strength to the Anglican forces, together with the prospect of more to come, he tempered by the chilling observation that the Colonel, before being admitted to Church of England altars, ought to have been required to abjure his former Faith. Ken, in a further letter to the Bishop, explains why this was not done.

I am sensible that when the Colonel was received into our Church, by a statute of Queen Elizabeth, he should have made an abjuration of Popery, but I having not the Statute book here, and not being able anywhere in the Hague to procure it, thought it presumption in me to pen any form of my own, and I could not expect the return of a post, because I did earnestly persuade the Colonel rather to own our profession here than to defer it till his coming to England, for the sake of my master and mistress here.

In October of that same year (1680) Ken arrived back in England and was immediately appointed one of His Majesty's chaplains. Whatever ups and downs he may have had with William of Orange, Ken clearly stood high in the opinion of the King, and no doubt his bearing and behaviour during the time he had served as her chaplain had earned from the Princess Mary a favourable report and recommendation. Even if William was still resentful against Ken and had not endorsed his wife's testimonial, this would not have carried much weight with Charles who had a poor opinion of his nephew and possible successor. The two men had little or nothing in common, and religion least of all. Charles, during his enforced sojourns in Holland, had seen enough of Calvinism to have acquired a hearty distaste for it, and William could probably have done his wife's late chaplain more harm by adding his approbation to hers than by withholding it, or indeed than by writing adversely of him to Charles.

Ken's appointment was speedily followed by a command

to preach before the King. The letter bidding him to do so is signed by the King's Secretary of State, Henry Bennett, Earl of Arlington—a member of the famous "Cabal".

October 21st, 1680.

Sir,

There being five Sundays of this month of October, I have thought proper to appoint you to preach before his Majesty at Whitehall upon the last Sunday in this month; but understanding that it would be more convenient for you to preach upon Sunday next, I have prevailed with the Dean of Chichester, who is in waiting, to preach upon the last Sunday, and that you should preach before his Majesty upon Sunday next at Whitehall, and so perform that duty accordingly.

Thus I rest your loving friend,

Arlington

For Dr Ken,
    at Dr Turner's, Amen Corner.

There is no record of this first sermon preached by Ken before the Court, nor does his name appear in the list of Lent preachers for 1681 and 1682 as published in the *London Gazette*. In the lists of 1683 and 1684, however, his name occurs as being appointed to preach before the King on Ash Wednesday, but on the second occasion other duties claimed him and a substitute had to be found. In the absence of any mention of his presence in London other than on Ash Wednesday 1683, it is reasonable to assume that during most of this period he was once more quietly fulfilling his duties in Winchester.

In the summer of 1682 he was called upon to minister, in what proved to be her last illness, to his friend and penitent of earlier days, Lady Maynard. He had acted as her confessor over a number of years and now, on her deathbed, he administered the last rites of absolution and Holy Communion. At her funeral, on 30 June, he preached the valedictory sermon, taking as his text Proverbs 11.16—"A gracious woman retaineth favour". This long and eloquent panegyric was Ken's last tribute to one who had, by her unassuming piety and probity of life, provided a challenging contrast to the dissoluteness and laxity so common in the higher grades of contemporary society.

For this state of things, of course, the example set by the Court was to no small degree responsible. Charles, wearied and disgusted by the political strife and chicanery, the religious animosities, the real or imaginary Popish or Protestant plots, the humiliating shifts to obtain sufficient funds to which he was perpetually exposed, turned increasingly to the pleasures to which he had been for so long an addict. His mistresses, his race-horses, his raffish friends, his spaniels, and his houses, claimed more and more of his time and attention—in particular the palace in building at Winchester, the foundation stone of which he laid on 23 March 1683. This ill-fated scheme was probably the most ambitious that Charles ever embarked upon. Temperamentally he was disinclined to large-scale enterprises which called for perseverance and sustained interest for their completion, and in any case such undertakings were normally far beyond the resources of his straitened purse. Only timely financial assistance from Louis of France, and his own liking for the city, ensured the continuance of Charles's interest in the Winchester plan right up to the time of his death.

He intended that there should be a splendid new street from the Palace to the Cathedral and considerable lands were purchased for the laying-out of a royal pleasure park. His house at Newmarket had recently been burned down, and he hoped this new residence would supply an alternative centre from which to indulge in the outdoor activities that provided him with so much enjoyment as well as with an outlet for his super-abundant physical energy. He was especially fond of hunting, hawking, horse-racing, and walking and for these, as also for his less innocent recreations, Winchester offered an excellent *milieu*.

Charles and the Duke of York, with their respective entourages, were frequently in the city, inspecting the progress of the building operations and enjoying the bracing airs of the neighbouring downs. Their presence there, of course, attracted a vast number of people of all kinds; sightseers, tradesmen, cheapjacks, mountebanks, suitors for the royal favour, and hangers-on of the Court in general. The capacity of the city, confined within its medieval boundaries, to accommodate all these invaders of its ancestral calm must have been taxed beyond endurance. The King himself used to lodge at the Deanery, and before each visit a Court official known as the Harbinger arrived in the city to arrange for quarters for His Majesty's guests, courtiers, gentlemen-in-waiting, servants, and mistresses. It was to this billeting officer that Ken made his historic refusal to put his house at the disposal of the notorious Nell Gwyn. No doubt the Harbinger, noting the convenient propinquity to the Deanery of the prebendary's residence, thought that the latter would be willing and gratified to serve his King by offering its shelter to the reigning courtesan. But if so, he mistook his man. Ken was no time-serving cleric out to gain preferment by obsequious pliability. Whatever the lady's charms, and however human his Sovereign's failings, Ken knew sin when he saw it and he had a disconcerting habit of calling it by its name. Though she may have been the darling of the King and the London rabble, to Ken Mistress Gwyn was an unrepentant prostitute and as such no suitable occupant for a clergyman's house and that of the King's chaplain to boot. Not for all Charles's kingdom would Ken condone his adultery, and the billeting officer was forced to seek elsewhere for Nell's lodgings. In the end a small apartment was built by Dean Meggot on to one wall of the Deanery to accommodate her, but this was demolished early in the nineteenth century by a dean who perhaps disliked being reminded of his predecessor's complaisance.

To Charles's eternal credit he bore no malice towards Ken for his spirited intransigence. Courageous himself, he respected courage in others; and though circumstances had developed in him a duplicity, at least in public affairs, that had almost become second nature, he fully appreciated straight dealing and single-mindedness when he saw it— which was all too rarely amongst those with whom he had most to do. Ken may well have felt that by his conscientious refusal he was likely to forfeit the royal favour and to imperil his chances of promotion so far as they were dependent upon royal patronage. In the case of a Henry II, a Richard III, a Henry VIII, an Elizabeth, this would most certainly have been so. But the lazy, cynical, good-natured Charles was cast in a more tolerant mould; malice had no place in his make-up, and when next he had occasion to make an ecclesiastical appointment of some importance his thoughts turned without grudge or resentment to "the little fellow who refused poor Nelly a lodging". Before the King could give this demonstration of his fundamental generosity of disposition, however, Ken was called upon to perform yet another piece of public service beyond the borders of his own land.

5

A NAVAL OCCASION

WHEN CHARLES II married the Princess Catherine of Braganza in 1662 his bride brought to him, as part of her marriage dowry, the town and harbour of Tangier on the African side of the Strait of Gibraltar. The Rock itself did not come into British possession until it was stormed and captured by Admiral Rooke in 1704, the year of Blenheim, so that Tangier was at first a welcome acquisition on account of its strategic importance. It provided a useful base for ships-of-war stationed in the Mediterranean for the protection of British shipping, particularly from the depredations of the Algerine Corsairs who terrorized the western end of the inland sea from the Barbary coast.

Tangier, however, proved itself to be a somewhat expensive possession. Vast sums of money had been poured out every year to fortify and maintain the town and its harbour, a good deal of the money spent finding its way, after the manner of the time, into private pockets. Among those whose personal fortunes had been materially assisted by the maintenance of Tangier as a naval base was that of Mr Secretary Pepys of the Admiralty Office, who had had much to do with the affairs of the place over a long period of time. A costly mole had been constructed for the protection of shipping, and houses erected for Government officials and commercial personnel; while on the landward side of the town elaborate defence works were required to protect the inhabitants against the ever-present threat of attack from the hostile Moors who lurked in the fastnesses of the surrounding hills.

By the year 1683 Parliament at last reached the conclusion that this part at least of Queen Catherine's dowry[1] was too expensive a luxury to be maintained any longer. Further grants for the purpose were refused and Charles was reluctantly forced to agree that it should be abandoned. To put this decision into effect a naval expedition was organized under the command of Lord Dartmouth and despatched with secret orders to demolish the harbour and port installations, and to evacuate the English garrison and their possessions. This expedition consisted of twenty-one ships—nine men-of-war and the rest mercantile craft—and among those who sailed aboard Lord Dartmouth's flagship, the *Grafton*, was Pepys himself, who had done so much to establish the fortunes of Tangier and his own at the same time. He had ceased to be Secretary to the Admiralty five years before, when his Whig enemies—foremost among them Shaftesbury—had forced Charles to dismiss him and then had done their best to swear away his life. But now the so recently exultant Whigs were in decline and discredited, their power to harm the King's friends was gone, while Shaftesbury, after disgrace and exile, was dead. Soon the King was to see to it that the efficient, methodical Pepys was back at his old post as administrative head of the Navy, which during his five years of enforced absence had very largely been allowed to revert to the state of chaos, corruption, unpreparedness, and inefficiency from which he had devoted years of laborious and unsparing effort to rescue it. Meanwhile he accompanied the expedition as an observer, with instructions to make careful observations on the proceedings which were toward, and in due course to render a report thereon in person to His Majesty.

Lord Dartmouth was a man of high integrity who had always stood high in the opinion of the King and of the Duke

[1]Another part of it was the island and town of Bombay.

of York, not least perhaps for his father's sake. For he was the son of that gallant Colonel Legge who had proved such a devoted servant to Charles I during his times of adversity, and had helped him to escape from Hampton Court. Shortly before his execution, the King commended this loyal and devoted follower to the Prince of Wales, charging him to "take care of honest Will Legge, for he was the faithfullest servant that ever any Prince had". Colonel Legge survived the Commonwealth to welcome the Restoration, but he refused a peerage and died in 1670. His son George quickly distinguished himself as a naval officer, rising to the rank of Admiral, becoming Master of the Ordnance and a Privy Councillor, and in 1682 he was raised to the peerage as Lord Dartmouth.

Like Samuel Pepys (who, incidentally, was summoned to join the expedition at forty-eight hours' notice), Lord Dartmouth was anxious to tighten up the appallingly lax discipline then prevailing in the Navy and also to improve its general moral condition. To the furtherance of this end he instructed Pepys to secure a senior chaplain for his flagship—one who would be an example, by his sobriety, devotion to duty, and pious habits, to the regular chaplains of His Majesty's Fleet. Pepys at once offered the appointment to Ken, who appears to have accepted it with as little ado as, and at even shorter notice than, Pepys had received his own commission.

It is abundantly clear from contemporary accounts that the general corruption prevalent in the fleet at that time had not left the chaplains untouched, and that a notable example —not to say a more direct influence—was greatly needed to recall them to a sense of the responsibilities of their posts and of the sacredness of their calling. Of one of the chaplains appointed to serve on this expedition Pepys was moved to confide, in the Journal which he now began to keep again: "What a chaplain the Admiralty did send to my Lord Dartmouth in the *Grafton*! A little deaf, crooked fellow, full

of his design of going a-hunting with my Lord." The
Admiralty themselves were largely to blame for the quality
of the chaplains with which the fleet was provided, for little
was done to assist them to perform their by no means easy
duties. They were provided with none of the books and other
necessities for conducting public worship and administering
the sacraments. They were at the complete mercy of their
commanding officers, at a time when His Majesty's ships were
under the orders of as scoundrelly and immoral a set of men
as has ever disgraced the Service. The chaplains had no control over the times, places, or frequency of divine service,
which was held or omitted entirely at the whim or convenience of each particular captain. The chaplains frequently
felt that their ministrations were considered unnecessary,
and this gave them a sense of inferiority and frustration.

Although modern service conditions are vastly superior in
this respect to those of the seventeenth century, yet even
present-day chaplains have at times experienced similar diffi-
culties and discouragements. The modern chaplain, however,
has one material advantage over his predecessor of Stuart
times. He does at least receive the same pay as a junior officer,
whereas the chaplains of King Charles's navy received the
same pay as an ordinary seaman and no doubt received it
just as irregularly. It is indicative of the utter lack of provision for their professional needs that the chaplains of the
fleet should have requested, through Pepys, "that the King
allow a great Bible, a surplice, and several books of Common
Prayer to each ship". It is only fair to add that soon after
its foundation in 1698, the Society for Promoting Christian
Knowledge undertook, as part of its activities, the supply of
Bibles and Prayer Books for use in His Majesty's Fleet and
garrisons; but that this duty should have devolved upon a
voluntary Society reflects no credit upon the Government,
Lords of the Admiralty, or public opinion of the time.

It was because he felt that he could do something to
alleviate the lamentable conditions under which his fellow

priests strove to perform their duties at sea that Ken agreed
to accompany Lord Dartmouth's expedition. The voyage can
have offered little in the way of attractions for him; few men
put to sea in the comfortless, slow-sailing ships of the seventeenth century with any idea of enjoying a pleasure cruise.
Long weeks at sea in cramped, airless quarters, on a diet of
salted pork, weevily biscuits and brackish water (while
supplies held out) can have been anything but luxury travel.
Had he consulted his own inclinations Ken would no doubt
have elected to remain quietly going about his duties in
peaceful Winchester, but here was a clear call to render a
rather unusual kind of service, and his profound sense of
obligation led him to regard it as one to be accepted, however distasteful it might appear.

Pepys, travelling by road from London to Portsmouth, left
the main road at Petersfield and betook himself to Winchester, where he slept on the night of 31 July, dined next
day at the College, and then proceeded upon his way to
Portsmouth which he reached that same night. It seems
reasonable to suppose that Ken accompanied him on this
stage of his journey and that together they reported to Lord
Dartmouth aboard the *Grafton*.

Neither he nor Pepys knew at this stage the purpose for
which the expedition had been fitted out. Writing from
Portsmouth to his friend John Evelyn, the latter remarks:

The King's command (without any account of the reason for it)
required my repair hither at less than eight and forty hours'
warning. What our work is I am not solicitous to learn, nor forward to make guess at, it being handled by our Masters as a
secret. This only I am sure of; that, over and above the satisfaction of being thought fit for some use or other ('tis no matter
what), I shall go in a good ship, with a good fleet, under a very
worthy leader, in a conversation as delightful as companions of
the first form in divinity, law, physic, and the usefullest parts of
mathematics can render it, Dr Ken, Dr Trumbull,[1] Dr Lawrence,[2]

[1] A brilliant young lawyer, appointed as legal adviser to the
expedition.
[2] Lord Dartmouth's personal physician.

5

and Mr Shere,[1] with the additional pleasure of concerts (much above the ordinary) of voices, flutes and violins; and to fill up all, good humour, good cheer, some good books, etc., and a reasonable prospect of being home again in less than two months.

For a full and fascinating account of the voyage to Tangier, the conditions of the port as the party found them on their arrival, the demolitions and evacuation, and the perilous homeward journey, the reader cannot do better than turn to Sir Arthur Bryant's third volume of his Pepysian trilogy— *The Saviour of the Navy*—where the whole enthralling story is told with characteristic charm and distinction. Here we may content ourselves with a few quotations from the journal of the voyage kept by Pepys, with such practised assiduity. Strong, unfavourable winds delayed the sailing of the expedition.

12th August. Sunday. Morning, prayers and sermon by Dr Ken; prayers in the afternoon.

19th. Sunday. Weighed and stood out to sea with the Fleet; all day blowing fresh. No Sermon, but prayers twice by Dr Ken.

2nd September. Sunday. Noon, prayers. The King's declaration about the late (Rye House) plot publicly read. At supper with my Lord. Discourse about Spirits,[2] Dr Ken asserting there were such, and I, with the rest, denying it; referred to another night's discourse.

3rd. Monday. All this morning, till prayers, on deck.[3]

9th. Sunday. Up to read by myself some chapters in the Bible; by and by to prayers. This being the day of Thanksgiving for the King's late deliverance, Dr Ken gave us a very good sermon on the duty of subjects to their Prince.

11th. After supper in my Lord's cabin, Dr Ken and I very hot in dispute about Spirits.

The fleet arrived at Tangier on 14 September after a voyage of five weeks, and Pepys records for that day:

[1] Sir Henry Shere, the engineer who had built the mole at Tangier.
[2] I.e., ghosts!
[3] It would appear from this entry that daily prayers on board were the rule.

Up by break of day (entering the mouth of the Straits of Gibraltar) to see the shore on both sides to my great pleasure. About 10, within the Bay of Tangier.

The expedition found the port in a state of virtual siege, on the landward side, from the Moors whose camps could be plainly seen from the ships. As for the town itself, it provided a pleasing enough prospect with its balmy climate and fertile gardens profuse with every kind of fruit, flower, and vegetable—paradisial conditions matched only by the unbelievable vileness of most of the men and women who inhabited it. The standard in this respect was set by the Governor, Colonel Kirke—a foul-mouthed, drunken, bullying sensualist, who even at official dinner parties would openly boast of his own debaucheries—and the senior naval officer, Admiral Herbert (later first Earl of Torrington), whose bestiality was fully equal to that of the Governor. It is little wonder that, confronted with such a state of affairs, Dartmouth, Pepys, and Ken should have found in Tangier a strong reminder of the cities of the plain and have felt that in hastening its destruction they were in some measure the instruments of God's avenging might.

In the comparatively short space of time that remained to it, there was little that Ken could do by way of recalling the place from its flagrant iniquities, but that little he at least attempted. Pepys records:

30th September. Sunday. To church (in Tangier); a very fine and seasonable, but most unsuccessful, argument from Dr Ken, particularly in reproof of the vices of this town. I was in pain for the Governor, and the officers about us in church; but I perceived they regarded it not.

Pepys himself, as we know from his own revelations of his oat-sowing days, was no Puritan and not over-easily scandalized, but even he on occasions seems to have found the atmosphere of Tangier and the company of its residents more than he could stomach.

26th October. Being a little ill, and troubled at so much loose company at table, my Lord not being there, I dined in my chamber; and Dr Ken, for the same reason, came and dined with me. We had a great deal of good discourse on the viciousness of this place, and its being time for Almighty God to destroy it.

Pepys and Ken, however, were not content to confine their criticisms to their own company and quarters, but at least once followed up one of Ken's pulpit denunciations with a frontal attack on the formidable Kirke in person.

28th October. Sunday. Very high discourse between Dr Ken and me on the one side, and the Governor on the other, about the excessive liberty of swearing we observe here. The Doctor, it seems, had preached on it to-day.

Unfortunately, we are not told which side came off best in these no doubt spirited exchanges.

The fortifications took longer to demolish than had been anticipated, but at length, by the middle of January 1684, the job was finished and the expedition prepared to return to England, carrying with it the evacuated garrison and civilian population of Tangier. There were still many final dispositions to be made before this could come about and it was not until 26 February that the fleet, now increased to nineteen warships and twelve merchantmen, was able to weigh anchor and set sail.

The voyage was anything but a pleasant one, for on the first day out it came on to blow with such fury that ship after ship suffered tremendous damage to masts, sails, and rigging; the fleet was scattered far and wide during the ensuing night, and when in the morning it had with much difficulty been reassembled, Lord Dartmouth considered it advisable to return to the comparative refuge of the Barbary roadsteads, sending some of his smaller ships to seek shelter in Gibraltar Bay. A week later the fleet put to sea once more under slightly more favourable weather conditions, but as they stood out to the open sea and met the full force of the Atlantic swell the gale returned and smote them again with greatly increased velocity. Battered by the mountainous seas, tossed and driven at the mercy of wind and wave, the tiny ships struggled defiantly against the elements, slowly edging their way northward with death and disaster in daily attendance. The conditions under which the brutally-treated, ill-fed, underpaid seamen were compelled to work the ships must have been truly appalling; the lot of the passengers far from agreeable—particularly in the *Grafton,* where Lord Dartmouth, Pepys, and Ken were forced to endure the company of the odious Kirke. At last, after a voyage sailed through one of the most violent gales until then ever recorded, the *Grafton,* and the five other ships which had managed to keep station with her, entered the Channel. The gale abated, the spring sunshine came out to welcome them, and on Easter Day, 30 March, they dropped anchor in Plymouth Sound. After revictualling and taking in water (as well as a detachment of troops who were to be transported to London), they sailed again the following afternoon and two days later reached Spithead.

Here Pepys, with Henry Shere to keep him company, went ashore, setting off by coach for London to lay his diligently-compiled reports before the King and the Duke of York. As for Ken, his difficult and dangerous mission completed—though with a strictly limited measure of success—he, too, was no doubt extremely thankful to exchange the cramped quarters, the noise, and confusion, to say nothing of Kirke's uncongenial companionship, for the quiet loveliness of the Hampshire countryside in spring. Once more he returned to Winchester in search of the spiritual solace which he had never yet failed to find amongst its venerable stones, its leafy arbours, its swift-flowing, silent streams.

Sleep after toyle, port after stormie seas.

6

BISHOP OF BATH AND WELLS

KEN'S RETURN to Winchester was not an occasion of unalloyed happiness, for one familiar and well-loved figure was no longer there to welcome him home. While he was away Izaak Walton, who had been to him brother, father, philosopher, and friend, had been called from the banks of his beloved Itchen to the river which all must eventually cross. Ken would sorely miss his quiet, humorous presence, his sturdy commonsense, his unassuming piety and delight in simple pleasures. Izaak's death meant the severing of the last link with the only boyhood home he could remember, and it must have added to his natural grief at the parting that he himself had not been at hand to administer the last consoling rites as priest and kinsman.

As skilful with his pen as with rod and line, the devout angler-author had gone, but in the simple unaffected prose wherein he declared the glory of God and sang the praise of all his handiwork, Izaak Walton's name lived on and still lives on to-day. They had laid him to rest, some three months before Ken's return to England, in the Cathedral where he had worshipped for so many years and where he had heard so many of his brother-in-law's sermons. A simple stone marks his resting-place in Prior Silkstede's Chapel,[1] the inscription upon which is thought to have been composed by Ken himself:

[1] Now a Vergers' Vestry.

Here Resteth The Body Of
MR IZAAK WALTON
who died the 15th of December
1683.

Alas, he's gone before,
Gone to return no more!
Our panting breaths aspire,
After their aged fire;
Whose well-spent life did last
Full ninety years and past.
But now he hath begun
That which will ne'er be done.
Crowned with eternal bliss,
We wish our souls with his.

VOTIS MODESTIS SIC LIBERI.

In his will Walton bequeathed a number of memorial
rings, suitably inscribed. One of these was left "to my brother
Docr. Ken ... with this motto, 'A Friend's Farewell,—I.W.
obiit 15 Dec. 1683' ". Walton also left him a signet ring
which had belonged to Dr Donne, Dean of St Paul's, one of
Walton's dearest friends. Upon the bloodstone which
adorned this ring was engraven the figure of our Lord
crucified upon an anchor—the symbol of hope. With this
ring Walton sealed his last will and testament, and all Ken's
subsequent letters were likewise to receive its impress, as
was his own will in which he professes adherence to "the
Communion of the Church of England, as it stands
distinguished from all Papal and Puritan innovations, and
as it adheres to the doctrine of the Cross". On Ken's death
the ring passed to Izaak Walton the younger, his protégé and
former travelling companion.

Less than twelve months after the passing of Izaak Walton
Ken was summoned to Farnham Castle, to the deathbed of
another to whom he was bound by ties of friendship and
filial devotion hardly less strong than those which had united
him to his sister's husband. The good Bishop Morley of
Winchester passed to his rest on the feast of St Simon and

St Jude, and Ken was there to minister to him in his dying moments. The Bishop's remains were taken to Winchester for burial in the Cathedral, in accordance with the desire expressed in his will, "without attendance of heralds, or any secular pomp or solemnity . . . at or after evening prayer, with the Office appointed by the Church for the burial of the dead, without any funeral sermon or panegyrical oration, because (besides mine own being unworthy of any such publick commemoration) I have observed that *In hujus-modi multiloquiis aut nunquam aut rare deest peccatum.*"

Morley's benefactions had habitually been on so generous a scale that he could have had little in the way of worldly belongings to bequeath to his friends. To Ken, however, he left a ring, and ten pounds for distribution among his poor people of the Soke in the parish of St John. His altar plate he gave for the use of his successors in perpetuity, and his library to the Dean and Chapter of Winchester "for the use of such Clergymen, Country Parsons, Vicars and Curates of the Diocese, as have not a sufficient stock of books of their own, nor of money to buy them".

Something has already been said of Bishop Morley's austere mode of life. He rose at 5 in the morning, winter and summer, had but one meal throughout the twenty-four hours, and not even in the coldest weather did he have a fire in his room. The King, when appointing him to Winchester, had predicted that he would never be the richer for it, and the royal forecast proved to be correct. No small part of the episcopal revenues were devoted to such objects as the foundation and endowment of the College for the Widows of the Clergy (Morley himself was unmarried) at Winchester, the rebuilding of Wolvesey Palace, the repair and restoration of Farnham Castle,[1] as well as munificent gifts to Christ Church, Oxford, and towards the rebuilding of St Paul's Cathedral after the Great Fire of London.

[1] Then one of the residences of the Bishops of Winchester. Since 1927, when the diocese was divided, it has been the residence of the Bishops of Guildford.

As to his disposition, the Whig Bishop Burnet, in his *History Of My Own Time,* remarks waspishly that Morley "was too soon provoked, and too little master of himself upon occasions". Against this biased and censorious judgement may be set Clarendon's summing-up: "Dr Morley was a gentleman of very eminent parts in all polite learning; of great wit and readiness and subtilty in disputation; and of remarkable temper and prudence in conversation, which rendered him most grateful[1] in all the best company."

In his younger days Morley's humorous observations and retorts had earned him in some quarters a reputation, quite undeserved, for facetiousness, and it is said that for this reason Archbishop Laud, whose sense of humour was not perhaps his outstanding quality, disapproved of him. Those were the days of eternal doctrinal wranglings in the Church of England between Arminians and Predestinarians. Asked by a country gentleman to explain just what the Arminians held, Morley (according to Clarendon) replied that they held "all the best bishoprics and deaneries in England"—a pleasantry quoted to his discredit by his enemies and not altogether appreciated by his friends.

The see of Winchester, widowed by Morley's death, was filled by the translation of Dr Peter Mews, Bishop of Bath and Wells, and to succeed the latter the King turned to Morley's chaplain whose loyalty, Charles knew, was matched only by his outspokenness in denunciation of evil. Ken's refusal to provide accommodation for the King's mistress was in itself a reprobation of the royal mode of life, but Charles's indolent good nature rendered him constitutionally incapable of taking offence, and for all his personal licentiousness he recognized and respected goodness in others.

Ken's preferment inspired yet another of Burnet's back handed testimonials.

Ken succeeded Mews in Bath and Wells—a man of an ascetic course of life, and yet of a very lively temper, but too hot and

[1] I.e., acceptable.

sudden. He had a very edifying way of preaching; but it was more apt to move the passions than to instruct, so that his sermons were rather beautiful than solid; yet his way in them was very taking. The King seemed fond of him; and by him and Turner the Papists hoped that great progress might be made in gaining, or least deluding, the clergy.[1]

Burnet's innuendo, that the Romanists hoped for many clerical converts as a result of the raising of Ken and Turner to the episcopate, was utterly unwarranted, as is plain enough from the former's obviously sincere satisfaction at Colonel Fitzpatrick's conversion from Romanism. It was proved to be completely groundless by Ken's unequivocal opposition, three years later, to James II's Declaration of Indulgence and the penalty he incurred by his attitude.

The congé d'élire having been duly issued, the Dean and Chapter of Wells elected Ken as Bishop on 16 December, 1684. He then took the Oath of Allegiance, a step which was to lead to momentous consequences for him, and on the Feast of St Paul's Conversion, 25 January 1685, he was consecrated in Lambeth Palace Chapel by Archbishop Sancroft. His friend Francis Turner had been consecrated Bishop of Ely two years before and was now amongst the prelates who assisted the Primate in the laying-on of hands, the others being Henry Compton of London, William Lloyd of Peterborough, Nathaniel Crewe of Durham, and Thomas Sprat of Rochester. The sermon was preached by one of Ken's co-Fellows of Winchester, Edward Young, later Canon and subsequently Dean of Salisbury.[2]

Ken was 48 years of age and at the height of his powers. In the light of subsequent events, his elevation to the episcopate could not have been more timely for the Church, or more fraught with difficulty and danger for himself. Troubled times lay ahead for Church and State in England, and the

[1] History Of My Own Time.
[2] He was the father of that Edward Young who was the author of Night Thoughts.

hearts and principles of many were to fail them grievously. But through all the changes and chances of political upheaval the Church of England had cause for pride in the courage and constancy shown by many of her sons, and not least among them, a burning and a shining light, the newly consecrated Bishop of Bath and Wells.

His episcopate was inaugurated by a breach with established custom which was as bold as it was beneficial. It was usual in those days for a newly appointed Bishop to provide, at his own charges, a sumptuous banquet to which were bidden the cream of the nobility and clergy, His Majesty's Judges, Privy Councillors, and the like. Ken decided to dispense with this function and to devote the money it would have cost him to other purposes. In the general list of contributions to the fund for the rebuilding of St Paul's Cathedral appears this entry: "January 26th, 1685, Dr. Thomas Ken, Lord Bishop of Bath and Wells, in lieu of his consecration dinner and gloves————100l."

On this occasion, also, Ken made a donation of thirty pounds towards the cost of building a new schoolroom at Winchester College and a similar sum, together with a number of rare and valuable books, to the College Library. At this time, too, he resigned his Fellowship, the following entry appearing in the College Rolls:

Nos Thomas, permissione Divinae Bathon et Wellen Episcopus, et Collegii Beatae Mariae prope Winton Socius, totum jus quod habemus, vel unquam habuimus, in isto Collegio in manus venerabilis viri Domini Johannis Nicholas S.T.P et ejusdem Collegii Custodis libenter resignamus. In cujus rei testimonium Sigillum nostrum Episcopale apponi fecimus.
Jan. 26, 1685.   Thomas Bathon et Wellen.

These matters attended to, Ken entered upon his episcopate, but he was to have little immediate opportunity of getting to know his peaceful West Country diocese. Within a week of becoming a bishop he was summoned to take part in the last tragic scenes of Charles II's far from tranquil reign.

On that very Sunday, 25 January, upon which Ken was conse-crated, Evelyn records in his diary: "I saw this evening (at Court) such a scene of profuse gaming, and the King in the midst of his three concubines, as I had never seen before—luxurious dallying and profaneness." And writing later, with reference to the same occasion, he adds:

I can never forget the inexpressible luxury, and profaneness, gaming and all dissoluteness, and as it were total forgetfulness of God (it being Sunday evening), which this day se'nnight I was witness of: the King sitting and toying with his concubines Portsmouth, Cleveland and Mazarin, etc., and a French boy singing love-songs in that glorious gallery, whilst about twenty of the great courtiers and other dissolute persons were at Basset round a large table, a bank of at least 2,000l. in gold before them; upon which two gentlemen, who were with me, made reflections with astonishment. Six days after, all was in the dust.

Burnet, in his *History Of My Own Time,* describes the King's fatal attack. "The physician," he says, "was scarce come in, when the King, who seemed all the while to be in great confusion, fell down all of a sudden in a fit, like an apoplexy: he looked black, and his eyes turned in his head."

Ken, described by Burnet who had little love for him as "the most in favour with him [Charles] of all the Bishops", was at once summoned to the bedside of the dying monarch who had so recently nominated him to his see. At Whitehall he found a state of confusion and dismay prevailing. He also found his friend Bishop Turner of Ely and their Lordships of London and Durham, but, as yet, no Archbishop. There exists a letter from Turner to Sancroft which suggests that the latter might have been a trifle dilatory in putting in an appearance.

My Lord,
I am advised by some that love us, and honour your Grace, to write you this short account of the King's condition. His fever is high upon him, and he breathes extreme short. His Physicians are divided; some of them say he is in extreme and immediate

danger: they sadly foretell this night will be a black one. Most of the Bishops are here, and several Lords ask "Where is my Lord Archbishop?" If your Grace thinks fit to come over presently, I shall attend to give you further informations.

Your Grace's most obedient Serv't,

Fran. Elie

Thursday,

between 6 and 7 at night.

Whitehall.

Perhaps Sancroft had some premonition of the unseemly tussle about to ensue between his Anglican colleagues and the Romanist priest Huddlestone, and preferred not to become too closely embroiled. Ken, at any rate, had no such inhibitions and remained assiduous in his attendance at the King's deathbed, urging repentance upon the dying man and offering to communicate him. Evelyn states in his diary that Charles had received the Blessed Sacrament according to the Anglican rite as recently as the previous Easter (March 1684), so that up to within a few months of his death it is clear that he conformed, outwardly at least, to the English Church.

The accounts of the closing hours of the King's life are confused and contradictory, and reflect in their divergences the conflicting influences with which he was surrounded. What does appear beyond doubt, being attested by more than one witness not particularly favourable to Ken or his views, is that the latter was largely instrumental in causing the King to send for the Queen, and to have his French mistress, the Duchess of Portsmouth, excluded from the death-chamber.

Mistress and shut out she might be, but not for one moment did Louise de Keroualle forget her Romanist upbringing, and she in whose arms the King had so often sinned now became belatedly solicitous for his soul's salvation. It was unthinkable to her that Charles, for so long at heart an undeclared son of the Papacy, should die surrounded only by heretic bishops and unfortified by the sacraments of the one true Church. So Barillon, the French Ambassador, was approached and the King's peril made plain. Barillon sought out the Duke of York, of whose Romanism there was no dispute or doubt, and he in turn brought his persuasions to bear upon the scarcely conscious King. Father Huddlestone was sent for secretly and smuggled into the palace in disguise. Then the royal bed-chamber was cleared of all but the Earls of Feversham and Bath, and Huddlestone was brought in. Charles was asked if he was prepared to be received into the Roman obedience and to receive the last ordinances according to papal rites. He replied that such was his desire, expressed his sorrow for so long delaying his submission, made a full and general confession of his sins and was given absolution. He received Holy Communion, struggling to raise himself in his bed and exclaiming, "Let me meet my heavenly Lord in a better posture than in my bed". Huddlestone then administered Extreme Unction and, withdrawing from the bedchamber, returned whence he had come. The doors of the room were again flung open and the gaping courtiers once more admitted to watch the long-drawn dissolution of their King, who—cynical, humorous, courteous to the end—apologized to them for being so unconscionable a time a-dying.

The Queen came again to take her final farewell, his sons—the exiled Monmouth excepted—were brought in to receive his benediction, and then, at the Bishop's request, the dying King blessed the kingdom over which, for a quarter of a century, he had exercised so uncertain and precarious a rule. The Duke of York was implored to make provision for Louise and the royal progeny, and bidden, "Let not poor Nelly starve".

All through the night the King lingered on, and far into the following day. Gradually he sank into unconsciousness until, shortly after noon, he passed into the realm where kingship, with its pomps, its pleasures, and its burdens, must be laid aside for ever. His failings were many and plain for all to see, but if he had lived with little regard for religion or morality, the manner of his dying must have gained for him some measure of remission and mitigation. He had the qualities of his weaknesses, too, for he was kind and generous to a fault, tolerant, humorous, charitable, and entirely devoid of malice. Better men have occupied the throne of England, under far more favourable conditions, and have been less deserving of the affection and gratitude of their subjects. Charles had few illusions about himself; fewer still about his successor. When James, at the time of the Rye House Plot, urged the King to take greater precautions for his own safety, he is said to have received the sardonic rejoinder, "Don't worry, James; they won't kill me to make you King!" Nor had they. It was left to Nature to effect the change which was to bring irrevocable disaster upon the Stuart line and the ruin of all that both men had hoped and planned and striven for.

7

THE NEW REIGN

THE LATE King's fatal illness, coming so soon upon Ken's appointment to Bath and Wells, had prevented the latter from assuming possession of the temporalities of his new see and from embarking upon his episcopate. As soon as the new sovereign's accession was completed, however, he was able to go down to the West Country and take over the administration of his diocese.

It was no easy task to which he was called. Church life generally, if not precisely at a low ebb, could hardly be said to flourish. Then, as now, the personal example of the monarch and court counted for much, and neither Charles's cynical indifference nor James's fanatical Romanism was calculated to inspire Englishmen with loyal enthusiasm for the Church and Faith of their fathers. Many of the parochial clergy were non-resident, ecclesiastical discipline was slack, and nonconformity was beginning to exercise that ever-increasing influence over the humbler sections of the population which it was not to relinquish until the end of the nineteenth century.

From the outset the new King made it abundantly clear that he intended, by every means at his disposal, to advance throughout his realms the cause of Papalism and those who adhered to it, even where necessary at the expense of the religious rights and beliefs of the majority of his subjects. Immediately on the death of his brother, James had called a meeting of the Privy Council at which he faithfully promised to maintain the existing laws of England as they affected both Church and State, and largely on the strength of this declaration his accession was received with considerable popular acclaim. The worth of his protestations, however, was made manifest only too soon, and increasingly so as his brief, tragical reign proceeded to its fatal and inevitable conclusion. The open celebration of the Roman liturgy at Whitehall, the numerous Jesuit priests soon to be seen about the Court and the appointment of Roman Catholics to high positions in Ireland, as well as in the commissioned ranks of the Army and Navy, rapidly brought to the surface the latent Protestantism of the English people. Suspicion and distrust quickly superseded the enthusiasm with which the new King had been welcomed and the first ominous rumblings of disaffection began to proffer their warning to those who had ears to hear.

James himself was not among those who were capable of recognizing any portents of the approaching storm, and blissfully he pursued his course of folly and fanaticism. Misled by his fair words at his accession, or else with some faint hope of tying him down to honour them, those bishops who were in Town, including Ken himself, had at once waited upon the new King with a loyal address in which they thanked him for his affirmation of support for the Church of England, a declaration which, they assured him, they would treasure in their hearts as the greatest foundation of comfort which the world could afford them. How insubstantial the King's assurance was, how unfounded and misplaced their own confidence in them, they were soon to discover to their cost.

Meanwhile the new Bishop of Bath and Wells took up the task which, all unsought, had been laid upon him. The Cathedral with its noble west front, the surrounding build ings cradled in their ancient peace, the moated Palace girt about with ramparts thrown up in less tranquil times, present to this day an appearance little changed from that which met the eyes of Ken. In the great banqueting hall—long since

6

become a ruined shell—Richard Whiting, last Abbot of Glastonbury, was tried and condemned to be hanged at the gates of the Abbey which he steadfastly refused to surrender to the minions of Henry Tudor. The memory of Whiting's courageous though unavailing resistance a century and a half before still clung to the stones of the ancient Palace, and may well have strengthened Ken in his determination to withstand, first the onslaughts of a Romanist King upon the Church of the English people, and secondly the usurpation of the English throne by a foreign Protestant Prince. In his stand for what he conceived to be truth and justice, Ken was prepared to face whatever might be the consequences, as Abbot Whiting had done before him. The fact that he lived in a more civilized age, and under more humane and tolerant sovereigns than the Tudor despot, does not in any way detract from the quality of Ken's self-sacrificing courage. From what we know of his character we may be confident that he would have faced death in defence of his beliefs as firmly and boldly as he went to imprisonment in the Tower (with the possibility of execution hanging over him), and later to deprivation and dispossession.

For the present, however, more peaceful activities occupied Ken's time and attention. Taking up his pen in constructive, uncontroversial defence of the English Church and its principles, he produced a work which, though little known or valued nowadays, was highly esteemed in its time and placed its author in the forefront of contemporary English religious writers. This was his *Exposition of the Church Catechism*, a work which—however archaic its style and outmoded its theological approach—still diffuses something of the deep spirituality which informed its authorship.

Before the work appeared in print Ken was summoned to preach a Lenten sermon before the Court at Whitehall. Amongst his auditors was the Princess Anne who, according to Evelyn, "sat on the left hand of the King's chair in the gallery, the Clerk of the Closet standing on the other side, as if his Majesty had been there". His Majesty, however, was presumably at his devotions elsewhere in the Palace for, only a few days previously, the diligent Evelyn had confided to his diary how he had seen "a new pulpit set up in the Popish oratory at Whitehall for the Lent preaching, mass being publicly said, and the Romanists swarming at Court with greater confidence than had ever been since the Reformation".

The Bishop's sermon, based on the text "A man greatly beloved",[1] was an eloquent exposition of the fearless prophet who withstood the wrath of princes and the ferocity of lions in defence of his religious convictions. Perhaps, had he heard this discourse, James might have found in it matter for serious and not unprofitable meditation; might possibly have discerned the writing upon his own palace wall and have profited from the folly and fate of Belshazzar. But James was not present and the warning note was uttered in vain.

Not long after this—on 23 April, being St George's Day— Ken was again called to London, this time to assist at the King's Coronation. This was an occasion of much searching of hearts and a matter of considerable delicacy. It must have gone greatly against the grain with James to submit to his anointing and crowning at the hands of Anglican bishops, but he was not yet so far gone in folly as to outrage public feeling by refusing to do so, or by attempting to have things otherwise. Special demands, however, he did make, and the unhappy Archbishop Sancroft had considerable difficulty in drafting the details of the ceremony to conform with the requirements of the royal conscience.

From time beyond telling the hallowing of the sovereign has taken place, like the bestowal of the three orders of the sacred ministry, within the framework of the Holy Eucharist, and has culminated in the newly crowned and anointed monarch, all the panoply of regal grandeur laid aside, kneeling before the altar of God humbly to receive the Bread of

[1] Dan. 10.11.

Life. James, however, as a Papist was manifestly unable to communicate at an Anglican altar, and so it was decreed that the whole Eucharistic rite should be omitted. In addition to this drastic curtailment of what James had complained was an inordinately lengthy service, other minor changes and modifications were made to meet the scruples of the King, who at last signified his acceptance of Sancroft's laborious compilation.

To Ken, as Bishop of Bath and Wells, fell the duty of walking beside the King, beneath the canopy of state, from Westminster Hall and of standing beside him during the ceremonies in the Abbey. His old friend of Winchester and Oxford days, Francis Turner, now Bishop of Ely in succession to Peter Gunning, was chosen to preach the Coronation sermon. The atmosphere in which these solemn proceedings took place, in view of the new King's attitude to the Church of England and its clergy, can hardly have been of the best, either from the point of view of devotion or enthusiasm. To James it can only have been a distasteful formality, without spiritual value or significance, performed by prelates whose ecclesiastical authority he repudiated and the validity of whose orders he was unable to recognize.

It is scarcely surprising to learn, on the eye-witness testimony of Simon Patrick[1] that whereas the Queen, Mary of Modena, bore herself throughout the service with serious-ness, humility, and devotion, her husband merely exhibited an attitude of indifference to all that was said and done. This, perhaps, was only to have been expected but to loyal Church-men such as Ken and Turner, whose attachment to the monarchy and to the royal House of Stuart was only exceeded by their zeal for religion and devotion to the Church of England, the occasion must have been one of sadness and humiliation. What prospect of national unity and concord could there ever have been under a ruler who, at the most

[1] Dean of Peterborough 1679–89; Bishop of Chichester 1689; Bishop of Ely 1691.

solemn moment of his inauguration, could muster so small an
amount of interest and enthusiasm in what was taking place;
whose own religious loyalties were so manifestly at variance
with those of the majority of his subjects as to constitute,
ecclesiastically and spiritually, not peace but a sword? It is
surprising to our modern way of thinking that, at a time
when religion meant so much to so many, it could ever have
been supposed that the reign of a Roman Catholic sovereign
over a predominantly non-Romanist people would prove a
prosperous and happy one. But this is merely wisdom after
the event—after the tragic events which were to prove the
arrangement to be unworkable, and were to lead to the
passing of that Act of Succession which ensured that the
situation should not again arise.

In 1685, however, so strongly was the principle of
legitimacy held and adhered to, that even those in Church
and State who felt the liveliest apprehensions were prepared
to do what they could to make the best of things and, to begin with at least, to accept James's assurances at their face
value. When, accordingly, the King opened Parliament soon
after his Coronation and promised again to support and defend the Church of England, the Lords and Commons were
still prepared to rely upon his pledges. By a unanimous vote,
the Commons agreed that he should receive during his lifetime all the revenues enjoyed by his brother, the late King.
Furthermore, in presenting the Bill for the royal assent, the
Speaker expressed the House's satisfaction in His Majesty's
"gracious and sacred word, in his repeated declarations, and
assurance that he would support and defend the religion of
the Church of England, as is by law established"; and humbly
besought His Majesty "to accept this revenue, and along
with it our hearty prayers that God Almighty would bless
you with a long life and happy reign to enjoy it". This
generous if misplaced confidence drew from the King an
expression of his earnest thanks, in the course of which he
declared himself as possessing "a true English heart, as

jealous for the honour of the nation as you can be; and I please myself with the hopes that, by God's blessing, and your assistance, I may carry the reputation of it yet higher in the world than ever it has been in the time of any of my ancestors."

Fair enough words, whose sincerity was so soon to be put to the test by the remorseless progression of public events.

Scarcely had this interchange of civilities between the King and his faithful Commons been completed than news was received in London that the late King's natural son, the Duke of Monmouth, had landed at Lyme Regis in Dorset and raised the standard of revolt. Monmouth had been banished by his own father for plotting with some of the more extreme Whigs to seize the Crown in the name of Protestantism, and recently reports had been reaching the Government, from its agents on the Continent, of the exiled Prince's activities in Holland. It was known in London that Monmouth had purchased two sizable ships, and naval vessels in the Channel were warned to keep a strict look-out for them. To such a numerically low state, however, had the parsimoniousness of Parliament brought the British fleet that Monmouth's ships had little difficulty in eluding the intercepting craft. The news of their arrival at Lyme reached London on 13 June, and Secretary Pepys at the Admiralty at once took characteristically energetic measures to deal with the situation from the naval angle. All available ships were immediately instructed to proceed to Lyme Bay, to seize the rebel vessels and to prevent reinforcements being landed from Holland. By 23 June Pepys was informed that both of these tasks had been accomplished. Monmouth's retreat was cut off; his only possible supply line was destroyed. Henceforth he must fight his way on land—to success or destruction.

To begin with he enjoyed a brief period of popular enthusiasm for his cause. Breaking out of Lyme with his small force of disaffected republican exiles, he quickly captured Taunton and Bridgewater, where the misguided citizens rapturously received him as the Protestant saviour and recruits flocked to him from the Somerset farms and villages. His rapid advance threatened Bristol and Exeter, and the King's army was compelled to undertake forced marches in order to bring the rebels to battle before their numbers increased to more threatening proportions. A Bill of Attainder was passed by Parliament and a reward of £5000 offered to anyone who should apprehend the King's rebellious nephew. To the King himself the Commons voted an emergency grant of £400,000 and then adjourned in order that members might return to their own seats and constituencies, there to rally the local inhabitants to the royal cause and prevent the spread of disaffection.

It is likely that Ken was present in the House of Lords during this brief Parliamentary session but, if so, it was probably his last appearance there for, except for a few days in the following autumn, James never again summoned Parliament. Ken at once returned to his West Country diocese, the main theatre of operations against the rebels, to do what he could to exercise a stabilizing and pacifying influence. The peaceful and pastoral episcopate for which his gifts so eminently qualified him, and which the constantly recurring pressure of political upheaval had so far prevented him from embarking upon, remained remote and unrealized. It is one of the minor tragedies of English history that this man, who seemed under the Providence of God destined to exercise so salutary a spiritual influence over his fellow countrymen, should have been so consistently baulked in his endeavours by secular crises beyond his control.

Now he found his diocese the centre of a senseless rebellion, raised on behalf of a man whose pretensions were as ill-founded as his character was weak and his supporting forces inexperienced and ill-equipped. So foolhardy and reprehensible an enterprise could have had only one possible result. James had not yet succeeded in completely alienating the loyalty of his army, and amid the swamps and ditches of

Sedgemoor his trained, disciplined, well-armed troops under the command of the Earl of Feversham had little difficulty in defeating and utterly routing "King Monmouth's" rabble of raw ploughboys, for the most part weaponless save for their pathetic pitchforks, scythes, and mattocks.

In the action and subsequent pursuit over 1300 of Monmouth's misguided followers were killed, and an almost equal number of prisoners taken, to be treated with inhuman savagery. Harried through the meadows and lanes of Somerset by the dragoons of the infamous Kirke, late of Tangier, shamefully bullied and browbeaten by the sadistic Jeffreys, these unhappy wretches were executed by the hundred, their mangled bodies exposed and left to rot by the Wessex roadsides. That this savage and revolting revenge was perpetrated on the direct orders of the King there can be little doubt, nor was it at all doubted at the time. Few even of the moderate Whigs had supported Monmouth's mad enterprise or wished it to succeed. In taking prompt measures to defeat it the King had had the approval of all reasonable men. By the callous inhumanity with which he avenged himself upon his nephew's dupes, and by his choice of two such repellent monsters as Kirke and Jeffreys to be the instruments of his vindictiveness, James forfeited, as it were overnight, most of the loyal support which had rallied to him, and by the general abhorrence felt for the activities of Kirke's "Lambs" and the "Bloody Assize" he kindled the first sparks of popular rage and revulsion which were to drive him from his throne and country.

Stricken with grief and horror at the savageries inflicted upon the captured rebels, Ken promptly and fearlessly wrote to James in protest, at the same time busying himself in personal intervention, often successfully, on behalf of as many as he could of those condemned to death or transportation. A large number of prisoners were immured in one of the churches in Ken's cathedral city of Wells and these he was assiduous in visiting, doing all he could to alleviate the material and spiritual misery of their condition and freely forgiving them the sacrilege they had previously committed in using the cathedral as billets and stables.

Meanwhile the cause of all this wretchedness and brutality, the vain, worthless Monmouth, had been discovered by some of Feversham's troopers cowering in a ditch, dressed in a shepherd's clothes and partially covered with reeds and ferns. For one who had aspired to kingship, he now exhibited a lamentable lack of royal spirit. Without any apparent remorse for all the slaughter and suffering of which he had been the cause, without any appeal for clemency for the deluded men who had followed and fought for him so blindly, he wrote to the King—whom he had denounced in his proclamations as a usurper, murderer, and enemy of religion —an abject letter, laying all the blame for the rising on others—"horrid people whom it was my misfortune to meet with"—and begging the King to receive him. His request was granted, but it did him no good. The cold-hearted King was impervious to the tearful appeals of the terrified youth grovelling at his feet. The fact that this was his brother's son left him unmoved. Implacable for revenge, he ordered Monmouth to return to the Tower, where he was soon informed that he had but one day in which to prepare for his end.

Further passionate letters of appeal proved as unavailing as the interview, and so did the intervention of various influential persons about the Court. Monmouth must pay the penalty of his treason, and Ken was sent for to attend him during his last hours. Associated with him yet again in this sad office was Francis Turner, Bishop of Ely, as well as Dr Tenison, later Archbishop of Canterbury. Ken and Turner spent the night of 15 July in the Tower with Monmouth, endeavouring to move the condemned man to contrition for his sinful life and so to prepare him for eternity. At first they found him utterly unrepentant, protesting that he had wronged no man, and that he died with a clear conscience. Reminded, however, of all the innocent blood his ambitions and plottings had caused to flow, he at length expressed sorrow for invading the country, for causing the deaths of so many and the sufferings of so many more. At last he was induced to acknowledge himself repentant for all his sins, "known and unknown, confessed or not confessed". The Bishops pronounced a general absolution and "then all went to solemn commendatory prayers, which continued for a good space; the Duke of Monmouth and the company kneeling, and joining in them with great fervency".

The next day Ken stood on the scaffold, a silent participant in the last sad scene of this sordid story—one of the most tragic in our history—of intrigue, envy, ambition, bloodshed, cruelty, and despair. By his courageous bearing at the end Monmouth partly atoned for his earlier cowardice, and his handsome appearance won for him the sympathy of many who would never have desired to have him as their King. Whoever profited by the course of these unhappy events, it was not King James, nor the opinions he held with such fanatical tenacity. Ken must have returned to his recently ravaged diocese more deeply disillusioned, more disturbed and bereft of hope than ever for the future of Crown and Church and Realm. As he visited the jails of Taunton, Bridgewater, and Wells, ministering as best he could to the hapless wretches who thronged them—victims alike of Monmouth's insane ambitions and James's merciless inhumanity —he cannot but have realized that the King, like a second Rehoboam, was riding to his own destruction; and that the activities of his minions, Kirke and Jeffreys, had done more in a fortnight to discredit and damage the Stuart cause than all the Whig intrigues of the previous twenty-five years.

8

THE BISHOP AND HIS DIOCESE

IT MUST have been with the utmost relief that Ken found himself at last free to turn from affairs of State and political strife to the pastoral care of his diocese and its people. He was pre-eminently a shepherd of souls, and though fate so consistently cast him for a prominent part on the stage of public events he was no ecclesiastical statesman, no seeker after high position or lover of churchly prominence. The rural diocese, to the care of which he had been summoned and from which he was so untimely to be torn away, provided him with an ideal sphere for the exercise of those gifts of personal care and contact with which he had been so remarkably endowed.

Among the problems which claimed his early attention was that of religious education. The political and ecclesiastical upheavals of the previous century, whatever may be reckoned their long-term advantages, undoubtedly had the immediate effect of producing widespread ignorance of primary religious truths. The steps which Ken took to combat this ignorance were threefold: the setting up of parochial schools in which children were to be taught to read, write, and learn their Catechism; the recalling of his clergymen to their responsibilities as leaders and teachers of the Church's Faith; and lastly, by the writing of works of instruction which could be read and assimilated by such of his flock as were sufficiently literate.

The first step taken in this latter direction was the publication, in August 1685, of Ken's *The Practice of Divine*

Love, being an Exposition of the Church Catechism. This book seems to have been begun as soon as Ken entered upon his episcopate, and it provides not only a mark of the love which its author felt towards the souls committed to his care, but also an illuminating revelation of his doctrinal standpoint. The dedication reads as follows: "To the inhabitants within the diocese of Bath and Wells, Thomas, their unworthy Bishop, wisheth the knowledge and the love of God." It begins with the Rubric at the end of the Prayer Book Catechism and goes on to lament the gross ignorance and irreligion which, the Bishop says, "our woeful experience shows us abound where catechising is neglected". It is to remedy these defects that the work has been undertaken, and he passionately beseeches all the adult members of his flock to do everything within their power to ensure that the young are encouraged and persuaded to come forward for instruction and Confirmation. Were Bishop Ken living at this hour he would undoubtedly approve wholeheartedly of the efforts now being made in various rural areas to promote Confirmation schools, and so to counteract the secularizing effects of the passing of the control of primary and secondary schools from the Church to the State.

Ken's treatment of the Catechism is primarily devotional and only incidentally expository. He declines to be lured to the baser levels of controversy and conventional moralizing so congenial to the more rabid partisanship of his age. His theme throughout is the redeeming love of the Father, revealed in Jesus Christ and sealed through the Holy Spirit; his method is reminiscent of St Ignatius in his *Epistle to the Romans.*

Nowhere is Ken's convinced Catholicism, firmly Anglican and non-Roman, more clearly revealed than in the pages of this work. Nothing, in a biographical portrait such as the present one, can be more wearisome than the introduction of lengthy and indigestible portions of the subject's prose works, and yet to omit quotation of any kind is to leave the

reader unjustifiably uninformed. Here we must content ourselves with the briefest of extracts from this, the most
important of Ken's literary works.

The Holy Catholic Church

I believe, Lord, this Church to be Catholic or universal, made
up of the collection of all particular Churches; I believe it to be
catholic in respect of time, comprehending all ages to the world's
end, to which it is to endure; catholic in respect of all places, out
of which believers are to be gathered; catholic in respect of all
saving faith, of which this creed contains the substance, which
shall in it always be taught; catholic in respect of all graces,
which shall in it be practised; and catholic in respect of that
catholic war it is to wage against all its ghostly enemies for which
it is called militant. O preserve me always a true member of thy
Catholic Church, that I may always inseparably adhere to thee,
that I may always devoutly praise and love thee.

Glory be to thee, O Lord my God, who hast made me a
member of the particular Church of England, whose faith and
government and worship are holy and Catholic and Apostolic,
and free from the extremes of irreverence and superstition; and
which I firmly believe to be a sound part of thy Church universal,
and which teaches me charity to those who dissent from me; and
therefore all love, all glory, be to thee.

The Communion of Saints

I believe, O most holy Jesus, that thy saints here below have
communion with thy saints above, they praying for us in heaven,
we here on earth celebrating their memorials, rejoicing at their
bliss, giving thee thanks for their labours of love, and imitating
their examples; for which all love, all glory, be to thee.

Baptism

Glory be to thee, O most indulgent Love, who in our baptism
dost give us the holy Spirit of love to be the principle of new life
and of love in us, to infuse into our souls a super-natural,
habitual grace and ability to obey and love thee; for which all
love, all glory, be to thee.

The Eucharist

O God incarnate, how the bread and the wine, unchanged in
their substance, become thy body and thy blood; after what
extraordinary manner thou, who art in Heaven, art present

throughout the whole sacramental action, to every devout receiver; how thou canst give us thy flesh to eat, and thy blood to drink; how thy flesh is meat indeed, and thy blood is drink indeed; how he that eateth thy flesh, and drinketh thy blood, dwelleth in thee and thou in him; how he shall live by thee, and be raised up by thee to life eternal; I can by no means comprehend; but I firmly believe all thou hast said, and I firmly rely on thy omnipotent love; to make good thy word; for which all love, all glory, be to thee.

These excerpts, brief though they are, should suffice to illustrate the traditional orthodoxy of Ken's theology, and at the same time absolve him completely from those charges of Romanism which were so indiscriminately hurled at him by some of the less charitable of his contemporaries. It was, in fact, to remove the grounds of misunderstanding and to meet the criticisms of his theological opponents, that Ken altered certain expressions in the passage upon the Eucharist quoted above. As it originally stood, it was capable of being twisted by unscrupulous controversialists to make it appear that he held and taught a belief in the papalist doctrine of transubstantiation. By inserting the words "unchanged in their substance" Ken effectively drew the teeth from this unwarranted accusation.

The Practice of Divine Love was followed by another work of a less ambitious nature—*Directions for Prayer in the Diocese of Bath and Wells.* The contacts he had been able to make with the unlettered Somerset country folk, and more particularly his ministrations to the prisoners taken at Sedgemoor and afterwards, were sufficient to convince the Bishop that the practice of prayer was almost non-existent amongst them. Either through ignorance, carelessness, or guilt, the instinct lay dormant or atrophied. Their want of all contact with the spiritual world merely accentuated the dull, brutish misery of their lives, leaving them little higher than the beasts of wood and field.

It was in a determined effort to end this state of affairs that Ken issued his little book of *Directions.* He knew that lengthy and ornate devotions would be worse than useless to people who had forgotten, or never known, the very rudiments of prayer. They must be treated as beginners; in his own words, "as children in understanding though not in age". Consequently many of the prayers he provides and recommends to their use are little more than brief ejaculations, easily learned, remembered, and understood.

Parents are exhorted to teach these short prayers to their children, together with some of the simpler psalms; while for family use he urges upon the more literate members of his flock the recitation of the familiar and authorized devotions of the Prayer Book. In particular he commends the saying of the first of the two prayers for the Sovereign in the Communion Office. "This", he says, "I exhort you never to omit, because you know that the country wherein you live [i.e., Somerset] was the only seat of the late rebellion, and the tares of sedition have been industriously sown among you, and you have the greater reason to pray that you may be firm in your allegiance."

One more devotional work came from the Bishop's pen, probably in this same year of 1685. The city of Bath, from which part of his episcopal style derived, had not at this date entered upon the fashionable era which owed so much to the peculiar genius of John Nash and Ralph Allen, but its medicinal waters were frequented by wealthy sufferers from sundry ailments, as they had been, to greater or lesser degree, from Roman times. The great days of Bath were still to come; its noble buildings, streets, terraces, crescents, and circus as yet unthought of; its seasonal round of routs, balls, banquets, and assemblies reserved for the polite society of a later age. But rank and fashion were from time to time to be seen negotiating its narrow, medieval, and no doubt insanitary streets, *en route* for the saline waters where men and women bathed together in cheerful, and sometimes boisterous, promiscuity.

To Bath, in September 1687, came James's Queen, Mary

of Modena, attended by a retinue of papist chaplains, to seek through the lustrations of *Aquae Sulis* the gift of a son and heir to her husband's throne and the consequent settlement of the Stuart succession. This royal patronage no doubt increased considerably the influx of visitors to the city, and Ken's active pastoral conscience was soon occupied with the problem of provision for their spiritual and moral welfare. The good shepherd, concerned for these sheep not of his fold yet temporarily within it, addressed himself to the task of their instruction and exhortation.

In a short manual of devotion, characteristically entitled *All Glory be to God*, he makes his appeal from "Thomas, unworthy Bishop of Bath and Wells, to all Persons who come to the Baths for cures". He "wisheth for them from God the Blessings of this Life and the Next". He urges them, in the pursuit of relief from their own sufferings, to bear in mind the lifelong burdens of the poor and needy, especially those stricken with similar complaints whose poverty prevented them from seeking remedial treatment at the Baths. It is typical of Ken that, in a work addressed primarily to those in affluent circumstances, he should lay such stress upon the need for true Christian charity. Again and again he returns to the theme that it is more blessed to give than to receive, a scriptural admonition not at that time rendered otiose by the all-embracing activities of the Welfare State.

There was further scope for Ken's charitable instincts and exhortations when, on 18 October 1685, Louis XIV revoked the Edict of Nantes, issued nearly ninety years earlier to secure for the Protestants of France unhampered freedom of worship and full civil rights and liberties. Under this liberal and statesmanlike measure (the outcome of Henry IV's enlightened attitude towards his former co-religionists) the Huguenots had flourished and increased numerically. Particularly were they successful in the fields of commerce and manufacture; by their business acumen, industry, and craftsmanship materially adding to their country's wealth and prosperity. Their ministers were prominent for zeal and learning, many of them corresponding on terms of the highest cordiality with some of the most eminent of contemporary Anglican divines; notably with John Cosin, the High Church Bishop of Durham, who had lived in Paris throughout most of the Commonwealth period, ministering to the exiled Anglican community and maintaining the proscribed liturgical services of the English Church.

Ken, too, on his travels through France, had no doubt had contact with Huguenot leaders and though his doctrinal position was in many respects so dissimilar from theirs, he, who had known what it was to belong to an outlawed persecuted Church, was not wanting in sympathy when the Grand Monarch's sudden access of papalist zeal (inspired, it is believed, in part by Madame de Maintenon) once more brought suffering upon a loyal and inoffensive minority. As a fresh reign of religious terror broke out in France and refugees in their thousands began to arrive from across the Channel, Ken was moved to immediate action on their behalf. A pastoral letter was sent to the clergy of his diocese enjoining that collections of money be made in every parish for the relief of the refugees, many of whom had been forced to leave behind everything they possessed and to arrive on these shores beggared and penniless. The clergy were to stir up all under their care "to contribute freely and cheerfully to the relief of these distressed Christians, and to do it with as well-timed an expedition as you can"—the latter phrase a variant on the theme of *Bis dat qui cito dat*.[1]

This pastoral letter was issued with the backing of Royal Letters Patent, support reluctantly conceded by the King only after considerable pressure from Sancroft, Ken, Turner, and other Anglican bishops. James was in something of a quandary in this matter. On the one hand, to advance the cause of the religious minority to which he himself belonged, he was committed to a policy of religious toleration—at least

[1]"He gives twice who gives quickly."

7

until his ends were accomplished; on the other hand Louis XIV was his friend, ally, and co-religionist, and to harbour and support the French King's outlawed and proscribed subjects must clearly have been a distasteful proceeding. Consequently he wavered and procrastinated, alternately sanctioning and then forbidding, through Jeffreys his Lord Chancellor, the launching of the appeals. The French ambassador not unnaturally did all he could to influence the King against helping the exiles, and it was not until March 1686 that the royal permission was finally forthcoming and the Brief authorizing the taking of collections read in the churches of the City of London. Even then the clergy were directed by the King to content themselves with reading the Brief, and to refrain from sermonizings and other public references to the sufferings of the persecuted Huguenots.

This was a royal injunction which Ken at least did not feel called upon to obey, and preaching at Whitehall, on 14 March, what Evelyn describes as "a most excellent and pathetic discourse", he urged his hearers to give liberally in aid of the unhappy victims of the French monarch's cruel measures. The courage of Ken's utterance is all the more marked in that it was made in the royal chapel and was bound to be brought at once to the King's notice. Furthermore, only the previous Sunday Frampton, Bishop of Gloucester, had angered James by the boldness of his defence of the Anglican Church, and poor Archbishop Sancroft had been favoured with a royal complaint about his suffragan's temerity.

Ken, however, seems to have called forth no royal rebuke on this occasion and, on the other hand, Evelyn makes it clear that his passionate advocacy, coming from one whose Catholicism had been so consistently misunderstood and misrepresented as popery, made a very favourable impression upon the more Protestant-minded of his contemporaries. "This sermon", notes the diarist, "was the more acceptable, as it was unexpected from a bishop who had undergone the censure of being inclined to popery, the contrary whereof no man could show more."

By example as well as by precept did Ken seek to stir up the generosity of his compatriots. A large sum of money, £4000, had recently accrued to his episcopal treasury from legal dues on the renewal of certain leases. The whole of this sum he made over to the refugee relief fund, probably the largest contribution made by any one donor.[1] In considering this benefaction it should be borne in mind that Ken was a poor man who, when he was appointed to his bishopric, was obliged to borrow the money for his legal fees and other expenses from the nephew of his friend and mentor Bishop Morley. As for his episcopal income, Bath and Wells had one of the smallest in the country.

A striking and most valuable light is thrown upon conditions of Church life at this period by the *Articles of Visitation and Enquiry* which Ken addressed to the incumbents, churchwardens, and sidesmen of each parish in the first year of his episcopate. From these it emerges that in certain churches in his diocese there was no proper altar in the chancel, no surplice, Prayer Book, Authorized Version of the Bible, or even chalice and paten for use at the Communion. Some churches were clearly in a state of extreme disrepair, and there were cases where part of the fabric had actually been demolished and the materials sold or pilfered. Churchyards and parsonages, it appears, were frequently neglected, church registers not kept up, infants baptized without sponsors to answer for them, banns of marriage unpublished, and marriages celebrated in private houses, as well as outside the statutory hours. Many incumbents failed to reside in their parishes, to preach on Sundays, to wear a surplice when conducting divine service or administering the sacraments, and generally omitted to observe the rubrics of the Book of Common Prayer.

[1] The King gave £1500; others of wealth and rank sums varying from £1000 downwards.

The moral state of the countryside in general would seem to have left much to be desired; sexual laxity, blaspheming and swearing, quarrelling and brawling, were lamentably commonplace. All this must have been grievous to one of Ken's orderly, disciplined nature, and he addressed himself with determination to the task of reformation.

It was about this time that prominent Churchmen, clerical and lay, who were distressed at the prevailing ignorance and degradation of the poorer classes of the population, sought to provide a remedy by the setting up of so-called charity schools. Foremost amongst these men were Archbishop Tenison (then Vicar of St Martin-in-the-Fields) and Ken's lay friends, Robert Nelson and Lord Weymouth. These schools were for the free education of the poor, based upon the religious teaching of the Church of England, and were dependent upon endowments made possible by the generous benefactions of a few wealthy enthusiasts and the voluntary contributions of the faithful. By 1712 there were over 100 such schools in London and some 500 altogether throughout England and Wales. They were the precursors of the parochial schools set up by the Society for Promoting Christian Knowledge (founded by Dr Bray and others in March 1698/9), and, but for the century of Hanoverian sloth which was to follow the death of Queen Anne, they might have anticipated, by a hundred years, the work of the National Society[1] in laying the foundation of a national system of free elementary education.

Ken, as might be expected, was not backward in playing his part in so admirable a project, and we have it on the authority of his great-nephew and first biographer, William Hawkins, that he set up schools "in all the great towns [sic] of his diocese for poor children to be taught to read and say their catechism . . . and the ministers of the parishes were by him furnished with a stock of necessary books for the use of the children".[2]

[1] An off-shoot of the S.P.C.K., founded in 1811.

[2] Hawkins's short life of Ken prefixed to the Bishop's collected sermons.

It is to Hawkins, too, that we owe the further glimpses we are vouchsafed of Ken's pastoral and diocesan activities. In the summer—for the state of the Somerset roads ruled out winter travel in rural districts—he visited as many parishes as he was able, preaching, confirming, catechizing; the eloquent preacher before fashionable congregations in metropolitan churches and chapels royal discoursing as happily and as earnestly to the simple-minded peasants who gathered to hear him in the little village shrines of remote West Country parishes.

Nearer home, in his own see city of Wells, Ken was distressed by the conditions in which the poorer people were compelled to live. His social conscience was generally in advance of those of most of his contemporaries and derived directly from his doctrinal beliefs. If one held firmly to the dogma of the Fatherhood of God with its corollary of the Brotherhood of Man, the question "Am I my brother's keeper?" was one no Christian had need to ask. There was considerable unemployment in Wells and much consequent distress. As a measure of relief Ken advocated the setting up of workhouses—not the repellent, prison-like, residential institutions of the nineteenth century, but co-operative undertakings, where men who were standing idle for want of someone to hire them might find labour suited to their various skills and abilities and a fair day's wages for a fair day's work. This projected scheme, which in more recent depressions has been put into operation with greater or lesser degrees of success, was altogether too revolutionary for Stuart England, and since it could not be launched without considerable financial backing it came to nothing for want of the necessary local support.

The Bishop was accordingly forced to confine his efforts at amelioration to what he was able himself to achieve in the way of private charity. "When he was at home on Sundays," Hawkins tells us, "he would have twelve poor men or women to dine with him in his hall, always endeavouring while he fed their bodies to comfort their spirits by some cheerful discourse, generally mixt with some useful instruction. And when they had dined, the remainder was divided among them to carry home to their families." Let not the pale pink intellectuals of a State-pampered age mock Ken's simple hospitality, which was at least inspired by a genuine, God-given love of his fellow men rather than by political contentiousness and class hostility. It was no doubt what we, with our modern superior notions, would dismiss contemptuously as "ambulance work", but it is at least arguable that to entertain the poor at one's own table indicates a charity as true and admirable as that which finds its expression in filling in forms and sticking stamps on cards. There is no argument as to which is the easier way of manifesting it.

Yet another of Ken's pastoral letters should be mentioned here, that which he addressed to the clergy of his diocese before Lent in the ill-omened year of 1688. The sombre tone which prevails throughout this document almost suggests that the Bishop may have had some sort of premonition of the sore trials and dark days which lay ahead. It is almost Pauline in its call to prayer, penitence, mortification, and charity towards all; in its strong encouragement to stand firm under all discouragements, to strengthen the weak-hearted and, as "God's remembrancers", to put all men in mind of the need to bring forth fruits worthy of repentance. It is St Paul writing to Timothy from the Mamertine prison; it is St Cyprian in exile penning words of encouragement to the persecuted Church of Carthage; it is Archbishop Innitzer of Munich urging courage and firmness upon his flock in the face of Nazi hatred and aggression. The very words of the Pastoral sound at once an alarm and a call to action.

I thought it most agreeable to that character which, unworthy as I am, I sustain, to call you and all my brethren of the clergy to mourning; to mourning for your own sins, and to mourning for the sins of the nation.

... your greatest zeal must be spent for the public prayers, in the constant and devout use of which, the publick safety, both of Church and State, is highly concerned; be sure, then, to offer up to God every day the Morning and Evening Prayer ... and say over the Litany every morning during the whole of Lent.

Be not discouraged if but few come to the "solemn assemblies", but go to the House of Prayer where God is well known for a sure refuge; go, though you go alone, or with but one besides yourself. ...

I exhort you to endeavour all you can to reconcile differences, to reduce those that go astray, to promote universal charity towards all that dissent from you ... to read over daily your ordination vows, to examine yourself how you observe them. ... Teach publicly, and from house to house, and warn everyone night and day ... to repent, to fast and to pray, and to give alms ... warn them to continue steadfast in that "faith once delivered to the saints", in which they were baptized ... warn them against the sins and errors of the age ... to deprecate publick judgments and to mourn for public provocations ... to pray that we may know in this our day the things that belong to our peace, lest they be hid from our eyes.

After these solemn, stimulating words of warning and admonishment comes the closing valedictory utterance characteristic of one so ready, when the occasion called, to witness a good confession.

"Now the God of all grace, who hath called you unto his eternal glory by Christ Jesus, make you perfect, stablish, strengthen, settle you", in the true Catholick and Apostolick Faith professed in the Church of England, and enable you to adorn that apostolick faith with an apostolick example and zeal, and give all our whole Church that timely repentance, those broken and contrite hearts, that both priests and people may all plentifully sow in tears, and in God's good time may all plentifully reap in joy.

Your affectionate friend and Brother,
Tho. Bath and Wells

From the Palace in Wells,
   Feb. 17th, 1687[1]

[1] 1688 by our reckoning. In Ken's time each new legal year began on 25 March, Lady Day.

9

GATHERING TEMPEST

IT IS difficult for us, at this distance of time, fairly and
adequately to assess the merits or demerits of the issue
which was to bring Bishop Ken into open conflict with
his sovereign, and which was to prove such an important
contributory factor in James's ultimate abdication and flight.
It is, however, vital that some effort should be made to
appreciate the points of view and motives which animated
its protagonists if we are to approach an understanding of the
conflict.

We shall do well, first of all, to dismiss from our minds the
biased and unfair delineation of James's character by which
Macaulay and the Whig historians sought, not without success, to blacken him beyond redemption in the eyes of nineteenth-century Englishmen. Many of our school textbooks,
which invariably tend to lag far behind current historical
trends, still reflect their unbalanced and vindictive judgements. To the Whigs James was pure villain, for whom
nothing good was to be said and no abuse too violent. Modern
assessments of his peculiarly complex personality lean towards a juster and more charitable viewpoint, though few
historians of the present day are prepared to follow Hilaire
Belloc all the way in his efforts to whitewash a much
maligned and bespattered monarch. The truth, as so often,
probably lies somewhere midway between these two extreme
positions.

What is reasonably plain is that James was his own worst

enemy. The favourite charge of his detractors is that he was a religious bigot; in other words, that he held religious views of which they disapproved and held them, moreover, with a tenacity which bordered on fanaticism. This is not, necessarily, a serious defect of character, though it can be extremely trying to those who have to live and work with a possessor of it. It is, however, a complaint so rare to-day, in England at any rate, as to constitute little or no menace to our ease of mind; the trend is all the other way, with the majority of those who profess some form or other of Christianity sitting so lightly to its tenets and obligations, or appearing to do so, that the enemies of the Lord, though given abundance of occasion, scarcely find it necessary or worthwhile to blaspheme. It ill becomes any who live in this Laodicean age to condemn the fanaticism of those of other times who put their religion foremost in their lives and believed it well worth living and, if need be, dying for.

One may disagree profoundly with many of the dogmas which have distinguished the teaching of the Roman Church since the Council of Trent in the sixteenth century, just as one may reasonably deplore James's maladroit, unconstitutional, and ill-advised attempts to fasten his religious attachments and convictions upon the English people. Yet at least he did it openly and above-board, which is more than can be said for his brother, the far more popular Charles II, with his secret undertakings to Louis of France to introduce Catholicism into England, at a propitious moment, in return for considerable financial subsidies. It is no defence of Charles to say that he knew perfectly well that never in his own lifetime were circumstances likely to be "propitious", and that therefore he had no intention of keeping his side of the bargain. If this is so, then is his perfidy that much the greater; and, in any case, as we have already seen from the suspiciously smooth progress of his "deathbed conversion", Charles's Anglicanism was never more than skin deep, a veneer which with varying degrees of success was intended to conceal his inborn preference for Catholicism of the papal kind. Paris was worth a Mass to Henry of Navarre, and the Thirty-nine Articles were a small price to pay for the flesh-pots of Whitehall to a King who had eaten the bread of adversity and exile and was accordingly determined to go on his travels no more.

The success of Charles's subtlety—some might prefer to style it deception—was lost on James. The Whig historians, who would allow him no virtues, said that he was too stupid to profit by it. Might it not be that he was too honest? It is curious that we should be invited to applaud Charles for so consistently, if not always convincingly, concealing his Romanist sympathies and to blackguard James for openly proclaiming his.

Humourless, unbending, unimaginative, James may have been—so have a great many highly successful monarchs, statesmen, military leaders, and big business barons who have been favoured with the flattery of their contemporaries and the plaudits of posterity. Honest and sincere he most certainly was, and, as his active service with the navy as Lord High Admiral abundantly testifies, he was courageous too; though in the ultimate fatal climax it was a failure of nerve which finally settled his fate and made certain his downfall.

But James's outstanding and most tragic shortcoming was his utter want of political sense. If politics is the art of the possible, he can never have had more than an outside chance of achieving success in circumstances which called for political sagacity and adroitness far beyond the ordinary run. Surrounded as he was by political adventurers whose capacity for intrigue and manœuvre was only matched by their utter lack of principle, his one hope of riding out the storm was to do as his brother had done—to play the politicians at their own game, and by working off one group against another to keep the opposition divided and generally powerless to do him harm.

For this sort of thing, however, James had neither the

aptitude nor the inclination. For him, at any given moment, there could be only one desirable goal, only one possible line of action, in pursuit of which all other considerations must be ruled out, all competing claims and interests ignored or swept aside. Had his goals broadly coincided with the pre-dilections and prejudices of the bulk of his subjects he might have successfully achieved them by virtue of overwhelming popular support. But they did not so coincide, and his aims, pursued as they were, violently, obstinately, and without finesse, were doomed from the outset to frustration and defeat.

James has been condemned as cold and cruel, and because of his harsh, unforgiving treatment of his nephew Monmouth in particular he has been held up to execration by successive generations of Whig-inspired historians. Here, too, he may well have been unjustly maligned. It is all very well for critics, sitting comfortably in their studies at this remote distance of time, to condemn a King who declined to reprieve an active rebel simply because that rebel happened to be his nephew. They should at least remember that rebellion is an ugly thing, and men who indulge in it are playing with life and death—their own lives, as well as those of the un-fortunate people whom they may persuade to follow them. Monmouth knew perfectly well what was at stake when he first raised his banner in the West—a throne, if success attended him; a scaffold, if he were to fail. His ambitions had already led to the deaths of hundreds of innocent men; his rising was a gesture of defiance to a lawfully acceded and consecrated sovereign; he himself was the natural rallying point for all the disaffected elements in the kingdom, and his continued existence could have endangered not only James's crown but the nation's peace and security as well. Perhaps Monmouth should have been pardoned (though, apart from his relationship to the King, it is hard to see just why), but we in our day have seen too much of ruthless power politics and summary execution to pontificate too freely upon the rights and wrongs of the decision taken. Did Elizabeth spare the helpless and hapless Mary of Scotland? When Cromwell killed King James's father he called it "cruel necessity", and the Whigs have always purred their approval; when James refused to reprieve the worthless Monmouth the Whigs inveighed against the cruelty and ignored the necessity. Let this at least be said for James, that the harshness with which the rebel prisoners after Sedgemoor were treated was far more due to the brutality of Kirke, Feversham, and Jeffreys, and that when Ken appealed to the King against these cruelties the royal influence was at once used to bring about their amelioration.

A final paradox in James's complex character must here be noted—the existence of a deep and fervid piety side by side with a depressing and habitual sensuality. With the honourable exceptions of Queen Anne and George III, it was almost a convention for the occupants of the British throne from the Restoration to the accession of Victoria to live unchastely and in disregard of marital fidelity; yet it is undoubtedly startling to find so sincerely religious a man as James dividing his devotion between his mistresses and the Mass. It is all the more inexplicable, in so far as his paramours would appear to have been, without exception, so plain that the ribald Charles advanced the opinion they must have been given James by his confessor—as a penance.

Whatever may be thought of the taste of this remark, it at least indicates that James's irregular sexual attachments must have been inspired by something more than merely lustful pursuit of a pretty face and alluring figure. What did inspire them it is difficult to say; perhaps the unhappy, unintegrated, lonely man found in them a sympathy and a feeling of security from which his own personal angularities and the unpopularity of his opinions and policies otherwise excluded him. At least it may be claimed for James that so far as personal conduct is concerned he was no cynical amoralist after the pattern of his brother; that if he sporadically pur-

sued what was worse, he at least recognized what was good
and approved it. Faint praise, maybe, but far from completely condemnatory.

There seems to be little doubt that up to this point the
King held Ken in highest regard, and Ken, while deploring
James's adulteries, held his sovereign in loyal esteem. Evelyn
records a discussion between the two men at Winchester, in
September 1685, on the subject of miracles, which seems to
indicate a considerable sympathy of outlook between them,
despite their divergent ecclesiastical allegiances.

It was not long, however, before James embarked upon
further measures designed to encourage his co-religionists,
and consequently and correspondingly to alienate the remainder of his subjects. The Papal Nuncio, Count Ferdinand
d'Adda, was consecrated as Archbishop of Amasia (in Asia
Minor) in St James's Chapel, and was subsequently received
in state at Windsor on 3 July 1687. Nothing could have been
more calculated to rouse public indignation than this studied
insult to the Church of the English people and its episcopate.
It was followed by the dismissal from the Army of 300 officers
and 5000 soldiers, and their replacement by Roman
Catholics. Romanist priests were appointed as Army chaplains, while under a Declaration of Indulgence many
thousands of Papists and Quakers were released from prison
—a just and merciful act, but highly impolitic in the existing
state of public opinion.

Next was created a Court of Ecclesiastical Commission,
with vague, undefined powers and Judge Jeffreys at its head.
Archbishop Sancroft was invited to serve on it, but when he
declined, pleading the infirmities of age, it was intimated to
him that his attendance at Court in future would be unacceptable to the King. Two Anglican bishops, Crewe of
Durham and Sprat of Rochester, proved sufficiently subservient to sit on the Commission, which proceeded to act
with autocratic illegality. Compton, Bishop of London, was
summoned before it in August 1686, less than a month after

its creation by royal edict, and censured and suspended for failing to discipline the rector of St Giles-in-the-Fields, who had offended the King by preaching a controversial sermon in defiance of a proclamation forbidding all such outspokenness. This Court, which had no constitutional authority whatever, quickly earned for itself the not inappropriate description of the London branch of the Roman College *de Propaganda Fide*. Its other members were the Earls of Sunderland and Rochester, and Herbert, Chief Justice of the Common Pleas.

Meanwhile James, growing daily more and more reckless and infatuated, had confronted the officers of the Royal Household with the blunt choice between accepting his ecclesiastical policy or their own dismissal. Among those who refused to be browbeaten and resigned his office was Ken's old friend Lord Maynard, till now Comptroller of the Household, who forty years before had been impeached by Parliament for his loyal adherence to James's father.

On Passion Sunday 1687 it was again Ken's turn to preach before the Court at Whitehall. The King, of course, was not present, but his daughter, the Princess Anne, was there; and, according to Evelyn, amongst the packed congregation, "at least thirty of the greatest nobility". The Bishop's text was taken from the eighth chapter of St John's Gospel, verse 46, being part of the Gospel for the day—"Which of you convinceth me of sin? And if I say the truth, why do ye not believe me?" In his sermon, to quote Evelyn, Ken described graphically

the blasphemies, perfidy, wresting of Scripture, preference of tradition before it, spirit of persecution, superstition, legends and fables of the Scribes and Pharisees, so that all the auditory understood his meaning of a parallel between them and the Romish priests and their new Trent Religion. He exhorted his audience to adhere to the written Word, and to persevere in the Faith taught in the Church of England, whose doctrine for Catholic and soundness [sic] he preferred to all the communities and Churches of Christians in the world, concluding with a kind

GATHERING TEMPEST 103

of prophecy, that whatever it suffered, it should after a short trial emerge to the confusion of her adversaries and the glory of God.

To be compelled by the perils of the time to preach thus forcefully, to sound the note of alarm and approaching conflict, cannot have been other than deeply distressing to Ken's loyal and sensitive nature. He was no lover of controversy, and it must have grieved him sorely to be forced into open opposition to the policies of the Prince for whom he felt affection as a man and reverence as the Lord's anointed. A week later, on Palm Sunday, Evelyn records a further sermon by Ken, this time at St Martin-in-the-Fields and, out of regard no doubt for the solemnity of the day, with the note of strife and anxiety absent.

March 20th—The Bishop of Bath and Wells (Dr Ken) preached at St Martin's to a crowd of people not to be expressed, nor the wonderful eloquence of this admirable preacher; the text was 26 Matt. 36 to verse 40, describing the bitterness of our Bl. Saviour's agony, the ardour of his love, the infinite obligations we have to imitate his patience and resignation: the means by watching against temptation, and over ourselves, with fervent prayer to attaine it, and the exceeding reward in the end. Upon all which he made most patheticall discourses. The Communion followed, at which I was participant. I afterwards dined at Dr Tenison's[1] with the Bishop and that young, most learned, pious and excellent preacher, Mr Wake.[2]

It is not clear whether Ken and Evelyn were already known to one another, though, in view of the ecclesiastical circles frequented by the diarist and the mutual friends and acquaintances they possessed, it is more than likely that they were. It is abundantly plain, at least, that the Bishop stood high as prelate, preacher, and man of God in the discriminating estimation of the layman. So did he in that of a more exalted personage There exists a letter, undated but most probably written about this time, from the Princess

[1] Thomas Tenison, Vicar of St Martin's; subsequently Bishop of Lincoln (1692–95) and Archbishop of Canterbury (1695–1715).
[2] William Wake, Dean of Exeter (1703), Bishop of Lincoln (1705), Archbishop of Canterbury (1716–37).

Anne to Ken's old friend and school-fellow, Francis Turner, Bishop of Ely.

> I hear the Bishop of Bath and Wells expounds this afternoon at your Chapel [i.e., in Ely House], and I have a great mind to hear him; therefore I desire you would do me the favour to let some place be kept for me, where I may hear well, and be the least taken notice of: for I will bring but one body with me, and desire I may not be known. I should not have given you the trouble, but that I was afraid if I sent any body, they might have made some mistake. Pray let me know what time it begins.

It is obvious from these extracts that Ken's reputation as a preacher ranked high in the general esteem of those best qualified to judge, and this, combined with the known sanctity of his personal life, singled him out as the natural spokesman and leader of those who watched with increasing alarm the successive blows aimed at the rights and privileges of the English Church and the advancement of a Faith which they abhorred as redolent of superstition, tyranny, and foreign domination. The Archbishop, Sancroft, was old and infirm; Compton, Bishop of London, was unjustly and uncanonically under suspension by order of the Court of Ecclesiastical Commission; men looked increasingly to Ken as the one leader who could speak for England and the rights of Englishmen. The political opportunists and careerists would soon be busy behind the scenes; but, playing for their own hands only, they inspired neither respect nor confidence in the minds of their contemporaries. As in the troubled times of Magna Carta, it was to an English bishop that men looked for leadership in the face of what they conceived to be threats to their personal liberties and to the liberty of their Church.

The hour of crisis was now very near at hand. On 4 April 1687, James issued his famous, and fatal, Declaration of Indulgence. This celebrated State Paper, by means of which the King proposed to overthrow the historic position of the English Church and indeed of the whole Reformation settlement, was skilfully drafted with the object of masking its

"MANNERS
MAKYTH MAN"

Keystone Press Agency

WINCHESTER
COLLEGE,
CLOISTERS

Keystone Press Agency

WINCHESTER CATHEDRAL, WEST FRONT

true intentions. The notes of tolerance, breadth of outlook, and of sweet reasonableness pervade it throughout. That many Englishmen were led to accept it at its face value is obvious from the addresses of thanks which at once poured in to Whitehall from many different parts of the country. Quakers, Independents, Anabaptists, and other Nonconforming bodies competed with each other in showering thanks upon the King for his benevolence. The dissenters resident within Ken's diocese were not behind in doing so, addresses expressive of their gratification being received from such groups in Taunton, Bath, and other Somersetshire market towns.

The dissenters had every reason for demonstrating their gratitude. The Declaration aimed at relieving them from most of the disabilities under which they and their co-religionists had for so long suffered. No longer would they be required, under penalty of fine or imprisonment, to attend the, to them, obnoxious worship of the Church of England. No longer would it be an indictable offence for them to pray and preach and prophesy in chapels and conventicles of their own providing. No more would the Bunyans and Penns amongst them be flung into noisome gaols for presuming to do so. No more would they be called upon to subscribe to the sundry Oaths and Test Acts which so outraged their susceptibilities, nor be precluded from practising the learned professions or serving the State because of their refusal to do so. Furthermore, all Nonconformist recusants under sentence for breaches of the penal laws were to be granted forthwith the royal pardon and full indemnity.

To modern ways of thought, wherein one religion is as good as another and possibly better, all this may present itself as the epitome of enlightenment and common justice. Why then did it not so commend itself to the bulk of King James's subjects? Why did some of the most influential of those who stood to gain by it, the leading dissenters of London for example, find in the Declaration no positive

8

grounds for exultation? Why did Ken and his colleagues, none of whom was wanting in charity or a sense of equity, find themselves conscientiously bound to oppose it?

The answer is surely to be sought for in the circumstances in which the Declaration was promulgated, and the hidden motives which its opponents professed to detect behind it. The various penal laws which the Declaration purported to render null and void, unfair and deplorable though they may have been, had been passed by Parliament in full accordance with the processes of English constitutional practice, and in due course had received the assent of the reigning sovereign of the day. They were, in fact, for good or ill, the legislative acts of the representatives of the English people elected according to the prevailing method of franchise. It was, and is, an axiom of English law that what Parliament has done only Parliament can undo; what Parliament has enacted, only Parliament can set aside.

But here was a sovereign to all intents and purposes seeking to override Parliament and parliamentary processes, and by his own *ipse dixit* repealing and setting aside laws without reference to the elected assembly which had made them. This was the action, not of a constitutional monarch, but of a despot. The Declaration was in effect a restatement of the doctrine of Divine Right, a claim that the King was above and beyond the laws of the land; that he could, in fact, exercise a royal veto to dispense from laws of which he disapproved. It was a challenge to the supremacy of Parliament which, if it succeeded, would take away from the people of England and those who represented them the right to a voice in the making of whatever laws they might be called upon to obey, the right so hardly won over so many centuries.

James, it seemed, had learnt nothing and forgotten nothing from his father's ill-fated experiment in autocracy. Without a tithe of his father's personal charm or backing, he was setting out on the same road which had brought Charles to the scaffold and England to civil war and military dictatorship. Had he had behind him a powerful Royalist party and the support, or even the acquiescence, of the leaders of the Church of England, James might have succeeded in getting the Declaration accepted by Parliament in spite of the un-constitutional manner of its promulgation. To attempt to enforce it without Parliamentary approval was to invite re-bellion. For James had no party beyond his co-religionists, a still small minority, behind him. The Royalists were alienated by his religious policy, and of the bishops only a time-serving few—Cartwright of Chester, Crewe of Durham, Wood of Lichfield (who two years previously had been sus-pended for scandalous living), Barlow of Lincoln (a notorious trimmer), and Watson of St David's (subsequently deposed for simony)—proved themselves sufficiently compliant to underwrite the King's Declaration.

Perhaps even more objectionable to the English bishops than James's unconstitutional behaviour was the hidden motive which they were confident lay behind the King's apparent broad-mindedness. To them the Declaration was no measure of general enlightenment, but the thin end of the wedge whereby papalism might be re-established in the land which had so firmly repudiated it. Everything of course depended upon the succession. The next in line was James's elder daughter, the Princess Mary, herself an Anglican married to a Protestant. But James's Roman Catholic Queen was not past the age of child-bearing, and the birth of an heir, who would undoubtedly be brought up in the Romanist persuasion, could by no means be excluded. In such an event, could it be doubted that the Declaration must in-evitably open the door to the ultimate triumph of Roman Catholicism in England, the very thing which lay nearest to the heart of the King?[1] These were the considerations which provoked opposition to a measure of toleration and relief, in itself just and even inevitable, but wrong in the method of

[1] A desire to which the words of the Declaration of Indulgence bear their unambiguous witness.

its launching, ill-timed, and suspect as to its ultimate purpose. It were better, in the opinion of those who opposed themselves, that the victims of the penal laws should suffer their disabilities for a further few years, rather than that the barriers should go down before the irresistible floodtide of continental catholicism.

Soon after the issue of the Declaration of Indulgence the Queen, still hoping for the heir which would aid so materially her husband's ambitions, journeyed to Bath to drink the waters. With her went her step-daughter, the Princess Anne, together with a considerable entourage of ladies and gentlemen-in-waiting, court officials, and popish priests. On Ascension Day, 5 May, Ken preached in the Abbey Church a sermon which shortly afterwards drew forth a pamphlet by way of reply, written over the initials F.I.R. by one describing himself as "a most loyal Irish subject, of the Company of Jesus". This anonymous Jesuit was probably one of the chaplains attached to the Queen's household, and he wrote in a tone of supercilious patronage. He had long wished to hear one whom he had heard spoken of as a great orator, which he thought Ken might have been had he had the good sense to be brought up in the bosom of the true Church. He professes to be shocked because the Bishop did not begin by making the sign of the cross. The sermon, which was, he tells us, of an hour and a half's duration, he describes as "a fling at the Pope's Supremacy". Further, this disingenuous Jesuit professes to discover a discrepancy between the Eucharist doctrine propounded by Ken in *The Practice of Divine Love* and certain statements on the same subject made in the course of the sermon. This, he suggests, is due to a desire on the Bishop's part to allay suspicions of Romanist inclinations, suspicions, he says, which rest upon Ken's celibacy and irreproachable manner of life, in itself "enough for the Rabble to say you are Popishly affected".

If this publication was a piece of coat trailing on the part of its author, an attempt to lure the Bishop into controversial and possibly treasonable indiscretions, it quite failed of its purpose. Ken had no taste for theological disputation at any time, and at a moment of such tremendous national and religious tension he had no intention of being dragged into this kind of argument. The pamphlet was left without a reply.

Meanwhile, the King had dissolved Parliament in the hope that fresh and carefully managed elections might produce a House of Commons which could be relied upon to toe the line and endorse the royal policies. This done, James set out on a royal progress through the western counties, accompanied by an entourage even greater than that which travelled with the Queen and including in its ranks an oddly assorted pair—Father Petre and the Quaker William Penn. Eventually the royal party arrived at Bath, where the Queen was still staying. Determined at all costs to make an impression upon his West Country subjects so recently in rebellion against him, James decided to hold a public ceremony wherein he could touch those suffering from the "King's evil" —scrofula. It was still widely believed that the touch from the hand of an anointed King or Queen was efficacious for the curing of this distressing complaint, and as such "touching" was invariably accompanied by the presentation to the sufferer of a golden "angel" there was seldom a shortage of candidates for the royal ministration. Some of the more enterprising even found it necessary for the completion of their cure to receive a second application of the treatment.

It was unfortunate, however, that the King should have selected the Abbey Church as the appropriate setting for this doubtful procedure. Unfortunate, too, that Father Huddlestone, who appears to have acted as master of ceremonies, should have seized the opportunity of making a proselytizing speech to the crowds attending it, urging them to transfer their spiritual allegiance to Rome. It was more unfortunate still, and entirely inexcusable, that Ken, Bishop of the diocese, should have received no notice of a ceremony arranged to take place in a church under his jurisdiction; one moreover, in which stood one of his two episcopal thrones —the other, of course, being in the Cathedral Church of Wells.

Ken, in reporting this discourtesy and irregularity to Archbishop Sancroft, explains that he had had insufficient warning of what was intended to enable him to intervene, and that even had it been possible to do so it would merely have led to open conflict on an issue not of the first importance. Furthermore, in view of the fact that no other building in Bath could have accommodated the crowds who wished to attend the healing, charitable inclinations alone would have led him to let the matter rest.

From Bath the King continued his progress northwards, visiting in turn Gloucester, Worcester, and Chester. In the latter city, in order to popularize his Declaration of Indulgence, James went to hear a sermon by Penn in a Quaker conventicle. It would be interesting to discover what these two men, holding such widely opposed beliefs, can possibly have held in common—beyond an antipathy towards the Church of England. From Chester the party returned southwards, calling at Oxford, the faithful city which had suffered so much for its loyalty to the Stuarts, where James proceeded to create fresh enemies for himself by dismissing the President and Fellows of Magdalen College and filling their places with Romanists. He seemed determined to prove the truth of the adage: *Quos Deus vult perdere, prius dementat.*

This, then, was the ill-omened note upon which the year 1687 drew to its close. The Bishop of London, Compton, continued under the sentence of suspension passed upon him by the Court of Ecclesiastical Commission. Lord-Lieutenants of counties who would not lend themselves to the business of returning a "packed" House of Commons were relieved of their posts. Civic officials who were members of the Church of England were, in many different parts of the country, summarily dismissed from office under new charters, specially drafted for the purpose, and their places filled with Papists, or with dissenters who had subscribed to addresses of thanks to the King for the Declaration of Indulgence.

Beneath these darkening skies, Englishmen awaited with apprehension whatever the coming year might hold in store for their distracted country.

10

THE SEVEN BISHOPS

THE YEAR 1688 opened with the stage of public affairs in England apparently set for the denouement of the drama which had been progressively unfolding. Many felt that this would be a year of crisis and decision when, for good or ill, the mounting conflict would be resolved and the future fate of the nation made manifest. In this they were not mistaken, though few, if any, can have had any conception of the precise course which events were, in fact, to follow. Were any writer of Ruritanian romance to weave his story around happenings such as those which marked this year of destiny, he might well be charged with having fabricated a plot too far beyond the bounds of likelihood. Here is the very stuff of drama, of high tragedy which, but for its bloodlessness, is almost Greek in its sharp intensity and sheer sense of inevitability. The very gods seem to hold their breath as the clash of human wills approaches and the pattern of events takes shape.

To the troubled minds of Churchmen and political leaders alike, "the future all unknown" must have loomed forebodingly ahead. None could pretend to forecast the turn that matters were likely to take. Few can have felt any real confidence that the outcome would be a happy and peaceful one; only those, indeed, who were fortified either by an abundant faith or an invincible fanaticism.

For Ken, this year held in store his life's climacteric, the turning-point in a career already remarkable for the extent to which it had been concerned with, and involved in, the public affairs of the day. In the short space of a few tempestuous months he was to experience in turn imprisonment and trial for conscience' sake, delirious acclaim as a public hero, deep and genuine grief at the fall of a ruined sovereign, and finally deprivation and homelessness as the reward of constancy to that same unhappy King.

But these things lay hidden from his eyes, beyond the dark horizon and distant rumblings, when Ken was summoned to preach at Whitehall on Passion Sunday, 1 April 1688. The deep solemnity of the season combined with the general tension prevailing in and around the capital to invest the occasion with an intense air of excitement and expectation.

Stillingfleet preached in the morning, but his was not the voice that London was agog to hear. Even before the Liturgy was ended crowds started to fill the chapel for the afternoon sermon so that, as Evelyn records, "the holy office could hardly be heard, or the sacred elements be distributed without great trouble". When Ken entered at the beginning of Evensong he found the building filled to capacity with a congregation keyed up and expectant. Once more the Princess Anne was present in the royal pew.

The Bishop preached without benefit of manuscript, though he may well have previously written out his sermon and committed it to memory. It was certainly published after Ken's death, but whether from his own manuscript or from a contemporary verbatim report is not known. The sermon was undoubtedly a long one, occupying thirty octavo pages and probably taking well over an hour to preach. It should be remembered, of course, that sermons in those days were commonly of far greater length than those we are accustomed to to-day, and a congregation of Ken's time would have felt defrauded had they been fobbed off with one of our familiar twenty-minute affairs, and positively outraged at the five- or ten-minute "talks" which so frequently nowadays have to serve as sermons. In any case this particular allocution was of the nature of a manifesto—a spiritual proclamation, outlining the issues at stake and the attitude which ought to be adopted by those who sought guidance for their troubled consciences. No brief and facile statement could do justice to such a situation or satisfy so deep a need.

It is difficult adequately to summarize an utterance of the length and importance of this sermon of Ken's, or, without interlarding the narrative with lengthy quotations, to convey more than a suggestion of its subject-matter and eloquence. Taking his text from Micah 7.8, 9, the Bishop proceeded to underline the prophetic compulsion to proclaim the truth at all times and irrespective of persons.

"It was a bold undertaking (for the prophets of old) to denounce God's judgements to the King and Court . . . but true prophets, in the delivery of their messages, fear none but God, and dare say anything that God commands them. And there are times when prophets cannot, must not, keep silence." Like Amos, for example, they must be ready to speak even "in the King's Chapel and in the King's Court", even though they suffer, as Amos did, royal displeasure and banishment as the consequence of their outspokenness.

Ken goes on to compare with the abuse which Amos brought upon himself, the happier result of Micah's preaching. "Happy was it for the King that he so devoutly attended to the prophet; happy for the prophet that he had the opportunity of preaching to the King himself." This was obviously a respectful reproach levelled at James for his refusal to attend service in his own royal chapel—the service of the nation's established Church. To modern ways of thinking it may appear unreasonable to expect a monarch to frequent the offices of a Church from which he dissents, but such a thought would be alien to late seventeenth-century minds. Nonconformity was still so novel an attitude as to savour of something anti-social, if not actually disloyal. More than once throughout his sermon Ken alludes, directly or indirectly, to the King's abstention, the more wounding to Anglican susceptibilities in that he had apparently felt no scruples about being present at the Quaker Penn's preaching when it suited his purpose. Furthermore, Ken draws a parallel between those who wilfully misrepresented the Hebrew prophets of old, and those enemies of his Church who would twist Ken's words in reporting them to the absent King.

The sermon consisted mainly of parallels between the present distracted state of England on the one hand, and that of ancient Israel and Judah on the other, imperilled as they were by actual internal dissension and potential aggression from without. With its wealth of allusion to Babylon, Edom, Cyrus of Persia, and the Anti-Christ of the Apocalypse, it assumed on the part of its hearers an extensive acquaintance with Holy Scripture which to-day it would be wildly optimistic to look for in such an audience. There can be little doubt, however, that Ken's hearers took his points and correctly applied his veiled allusions. Judah (or Israel) was England; the danger that threatened from Babylon was the Roman peril (as much political as religious); Edom represented those who had apostatized from England's Church; the peril of exchanging one evil for another by looking for deliverance from Cyrus of Persia might be interpreted by men of sufficient perspicuity as a warning to those who were already in secret and treasonable correspondence with William of Orange.

The King's spies lost no time in favouring their master with an account, possibly highly elaborated, of what had been done and said. Nor did James lose much time in sending for Ken and upbraiding him for the sharply controversial tone of his preaching. The Bishop replied with spirit that if the King had not neglected his duty of being present in the royal chapel, he would have been able to judge for himself whether the sermon was lacking in deference or loyalty, in default of which His Majesty must rely upon the reports of those who were bitterly hostile to the Church. After this brief exchange Ken was dismissed from the royal presence and returned forthwith to his diocese.

If, however, he hoped for a period of tranquillity in which he might minister to his perforce neglected people and in which the general tension might be allowed to lessen, he was soon to be disillusioned. James was determined upon his Gadarene procedure. On 25 April he issued his Second Declaration of Indulgence. It was almost word for word the same as the first, published a year earlier, but its preamble had been re-written and exhibited an altogether sharper and less persuasive tone.

"Our conduct", says the King, "has been such at all times as ought to have persuaded the world that we are firm and constant in our resolutions; yet that easy people may not be alarmed by the malice of crafty, wicked men, we think fit to declare that our intentions are not changed since the 4th of April, 1687, when we issued our Declaration for Liberty of Conscience."

Then follows a reiteration of the Declaration, with a lengthy concluding paragraph in which the King purports to justify his actions of the past twelve months or so, defending, for example, the dismissals of Anglicans from civil and military positions of importance and the filling of them, "without the burden and constraint of oaths and tests", by "good Christians", on the grounds that the safety and honour of the nation required it. The King's subjects are invited to reflect upon their "present ease and happiness", and upon the reassuring fact that their prince had not turned out to be the monster they had been warned against, his chief aim having been "not to be the oppressor, but the father" of his people. Accordingly they are admonished to "lay aside all private animosities, as well as groundless jealousies, and to choose such members of parliament as may do their part to finish what we have begun, for the advantage of the monarchy over which Almighty God hath placed us, being resolved to call a parliament that shall meet in November next at farthest".

There is something almost disarming about the artlessness

and apparent sincerity of these statements, and one cannot easily avoid the conclusion that James was the victim of self-delusion on a quite unparalleled scale. It is difficult to believe that any man of normal perception could honestly believe that the motives and results of his policies were what James claimed them to be, or that failing so to persuade himself he could hope to persuade others. Certainly, while neither he nor anyone else in the Kingdom can have foreseen what the state of affairs would actually be by that November in which Parliament was to be summoned, few indeed can have shared the sanguine outlook of the King as indicated by the phrasing of that ill-fated Declaration.

It may, of course, be argued that James did in fact whole-heartedly believe in the principle of religious toleration for all; that he was simply a nineteenth-century Liberal born out of due time. His tenure of the throne was too brief for the sincerity of his professions adequately to be tested. It can only be suggested that in his dealings with the Church of England generally, and with the University of Oxford in particular, the spirit of tolerance seems to have been sur-prisingly inconspicuous. But perhaps he recognized that the Church of England alone could and did claim to be the authentic and rightful Catholic Church of the country, the real rival and threat to the pretensions of his own com-munion, and therefore a Church to which no concessions could be made.

The First Declaration of Indulgence had been published in the *London Gazette* but, in the absence of a compliant parliamentary majority, no further effort had been made to put it into operation. James had, so to speak, left it to simmer in the minds of his subjects, hoping that time and perhaps a more favourably disposed Commons might remove the obstacles which hindered its application. Had he been con-tent to do likewise in the case of the Second Declaration he might eventually have achieved his object. Much would have depended, of course, upon his success in "managing" the forthcoming elections. Given a subservient Parliament, he could probably have carried through his religious changes in Tudor fashion, in the teeth of an unwilling Church and people. It only needed patience, tact, and political acumen.

But these were precisely the attributes that James lacked. With supreme folly, he proceeded to manœuvre himself into a series of positions from which he inevitably found it impossible to withdraw without loss of dignity and ultimate disaster. The Declaration was published on 25 April. On 4 May the King issued an Order in Council requiring the bishops to have the Declaration read in all churches and chapels in their respective dioceses—in London and within a radius of ten miles on 20 and 27 May, and elsewhere throughout the kingdom on 3 and 10 June.

This was the most serious blow so far struck by James at the Established Church of the country. The command to read a royal declaration in church was not, of course, illegal in itself; the rubric which follows the Nicene Creed in the Order of Holy Communion specifically makes provision for "briefs and citations" and other official announcements to be read at this point before the sermon. In days before newspapers and broadcasting, when worshipping the Lord on the Lord's day was a general rule rather than a mild and comparatively rare eccentricity, such announcements were a quick, inexpensive, and effective means of communicating the King's business to the King's subjects throughout his realm. Used constitutionally and with reasonable restraint, it was a device to which no exception could be taken, and one which had been employed without objection being made on various previous occasions. Furthermore a majority of the bishops held a high doctrine of kingship and of passive obedience to royal demands, even when they proved most unpalatable. It was upon this episcopal habit of thought that James was relying in issuing his Order in Council, even though that Order was directed against the interests of the

Church of which the bishops were the leaders. As he was soon to discover, his confidence was misplaced.

Bishop Morley, on his deathbed, had sent a message to James, by the hand of Lord Dartmouth, warning him that if ever he depended upon the doctrine of non-resistance he would find himself deceived. The clergy might indeed refrain from open denial of the doctrine, but he (Morley) was very sure that they would deny it in practice. James dismissed the warning, with his usual want of judgement, as the well-meant but mistaken advice of a good old man grown confused and fearful. It would have saved James much tribulation, and perhaps his throne, had he paid more attention to Morley's admonition.

Found among Sancroft's papers after his death, and now in the Bodleian Library, is a memorandum setting forth the Archbishop's appreciation of the situation which had now arisen and his own immediate reactions. This document, there can be little doubt, formed the basis for his subsequent deliberations with his episcopal colleagues. In it he makes the two distinct points:

(1) that he is not opposed to liberty of conscience for Dissenters, with whom at all times he is willing to seek a fair settlement through constitutional means, i.e., Parliament and Convocation;

(2) that the Declaration, based as it is on a dispensing power which purports to set aside at will all laws, civil and ecclesiastical, is illegal and that he cannot conscientiously make himself a party to it by ordering it to be read in church.

Meanwhile time was short and events moved swiftly. At a meeting of the clergy held in London, and attended by such prominent clerics as Tillotson, Stillingfleet, Sherlock, Patrick, and Fowler, a resolution was passed and signed by all present refusing to read the Declaration. In this they had the support of some of the more far-seeing of the dissenting ministers, who implored them to stand firm.

On 12 May Sancroft convened a meeting at Lambeth to

discuss the next step. This was attended by four bishops besides the Primate—Compton (London), White (Peterborough), Turner (Ely), and Cartwright (Chester). The latter, an ardent royalist and devoted to King James, appears to have come uninvited. He was known to be whole-heartedly in favour of the Declaration and not until he departed, no doubt to report on the meeting to the King, did the others discuss openly what they proposed should be done. They then decided that other bishops of the Province of Canterbury (the northern dioceses were too remote and the matter brooked no delay) should be summoned for consultation. Six days later a further conference was held at Lambeth, attended this time by Ken, who had set off at once on receiving an urgent, if somewhat cryptic, letter from Sancroft. Doubtless the latter felt far from confident that his correspondence would not be intercepted and read by the King's agents.

My Lord,

This is only in my own name, and in the name of some of our Brethren, now here upon the place, earnestly to desire you, immediately upon the receipt of this letter, to come hither with what convenient speed you can, not taking notice[1] to any that you are sent for. Wishing you a prosperous journey, and us all a happy meeting, I remain

Your very loving Brother,
William Cantuar

This letter, like those sent to the other bishops, was carried for safety by special messenger, and it brought Ken back to London without an instant's unnecessary delay. He probably lodged on arrival with his friend Hooper, who was Rector of Lambeth. At the meeting held next day, 18 May, in the Archbishop's library, those present at the previous gathering (Cartwright excepted) were reinforced by Ken, Lloyd of St Asaph, Trelawney of Bristol, and Lake of Chichester. Peter Mews, Bishop of Winchester, was detained by illness, Frampton of Gloucester arrived a day or two later, and Lloyd

[1] I.e., informing.

WELLS, GATEWAY OF BISHOP'S PALACE

WELLS, RUINS OF THE GREAT HALL

LONGLEAT,
STAIRCASE

A. F. Kersting

National Building Record

LONGLEAT, SOUTH FRONT

of Norwich, by some mischance, had not received in time the summons addressed to him.

Taking Sancroft's brief memorandum as the basis of their discussions, they proceeded to draft a petition to the King, stating their conscientious scruples against reading the Declaration and praying His Majesty not to insist upon their doing so. This petition[1] was signed by Sancroft, Ken, Lloyd, White, Turner, Trelawney, and Lake. On the draft of the petition, other than the copy presented to the King, appear the signatures, added later, of Compton, Bishop of London,[2] Lloyd of Norwich, Frampton of Gloucester, Ward of Salisbury, Mews of Winchester, and Lamplugh of Exeter.

It was decided that the six bishops should carry the petition to the King forthwith. Sancroft, still *persona non grata* at Court, remained at Lambeth. They went, of course, by water and landed at Whitehall Stairs. Leaving his five companions at Lord Dartmouth's house close by, Lloyd, as senior prelate, at once sought out Lord Sunderland, the principal Secretary of State, and besought him to arrange for the bishops to see the King so that they might present their petition. Sunderland obligingly went to the King who, equally obligingly, agreed to receive the petitioners without delay. Probably James had been prepared by Cartwright for some such deputation. It seems equally clear from what followed that he was quite taken aback by the nature of their request. Possibly he had anticipated some application for a little longer time to consider the matter, some minor modification here and there in the phrasing of the Declaration.

He was soon to be disillusioned. The six bishops knelt before him and Lloyd handed him the petition. As James took it he recognized the writing and remarked, "This is my Lord of Canterbury's hand". He then proceeded to read and as he did so his face darkened with rage.

[1] See Appendix.
[2] As he was under suspension he was not asked to sign the copy handed to James.

9

"This", he rasped, "is a standard of rebellion." He went on to tell them, in heated terms, that he was the King and he intended to be obeyed. "Is this your Church of England loyalty?" he demanded—somewhat unreasonably in the circumstances. "I did not expect this from your Church, especially from some of you." He looked pointedly at Trelawney as he spoke, and then repeated harshly that it was nothing more or less than rebellion.

This was too much for the quick-tempered Trelawney. He came from a very ancient Cornish family who had long proved their loyalty to the house of Stuart. The Bishop himself had done much to help in suppressing the recent rising in the West.

"I presume your Majesty was not of that opinion when you sent me into the West", he flashed out. "If some of my family had proved rebellious to the Crown, I should not have much stood in need of your favour or protection."

James was not mollified, however, and stubbornly insisted that the petition was open rebellion. Trelawney stuck to his guns. "Sir, with submission I speak it, you know to the contrary." The King, recounting the incident at a later date, remembered with resentment that of the six appellants the Bishop of Bristol had been "the most saucy".

The others now tried to calm the infuriated James. Lake, who had been Bishop of Bristol at the time, reminded the King in more temperate terms than Trelawney's, how he and his colleagues had striven to put down the Monmouth rebellion. Turner declared that the bishops were ready to die for the King if necessary. Ken, with greater restraint, hoped that His Majesty would grant to the bishops that liberty of conscience which he was ready to grant to the rest of his subjects.

But James was not to be pacified. He reiterated the charge of rebellion and his determination to be obeyed.

Ken tried once more to make the King see their point of view. "We have two duties to perform", he pointed out; "our duty to God and our duty to your Majesty. We honour you; but we fear God."

His Majesty, however, was far too angry to be amenable to reason. He professed himself hurt and bitterly disappointed at their treatment of him—he who had been such a friend to their Church! As he contemplated the affront to his royal feelings, James's wrath reached a fever pitch. They were nothing but "trumpeters of sedition". Let them return to their dioceses and see that he was obeyed. He would keep their petition and would not part with it. Furthermore, he added ominously, he would remember those whose signatures it bore.

"God's will be done", said Ken, and Lake echoed his words. James, however, was more concerned at the moment with his own will, and repeated that as God had given him the dispensing power he meant to maintain it. Finally, with the cryptic comment that there were still seven thousand in the Church of England who had not bowed the knee to Baal, he dismissed the bishops, who returned to Lambeth as they had come, by water; no doubt puzzling over the King's parting remark and debating anxiously what the outcome of their protest might be.

Now we are faced with one of the most peculiar aspects of the whole unhappy affair. Within an hour or two of the bishops' departure from Whitehall copies of their petition to the King were not only in print, but were being hawked through the streets of London and discussed in every coffee house in town. Who was responsible for the leakage? It remains one of the unsolved mysteries of history.

The King is not likely to have caused to be published a document which he had denounced as flagrantly seditious. Sunderland was quite capable of revealing its contents, but there is no evidence that he was ever allowed so much as a glimpse of what was in it. Sancroft consistently declared that he had done everything in his power to prevent the petition from falling into unauthorized hands, and we have no reason to doubt either his veracity or his discretion. So far as he knew there were only two copies of the petition: the copy the bishops presented to the King, and the original rough draft which he himself retained and which was discovered at his death amongst his papers.

One of Ken's biographers, Dean Plumptre, believed that Compton was the culprit. He was present at the discussions and could easily have taken a rough copy of what was decided upon. Furthermore, he was deeply implicated in the negotiations which were, even then, being carried on with William of Orange. He was in constant touch with Henry Sidney, one of the moving spirits in these negotiations, and together they could have arranged for the petition to be printed as a broadsheet and distributed throughout London immediately Compton left Lambeth and while the signatories to it were on their way to Whitehall.

The next day a letter was sent by post and private messenger to every parish priest in the country, urging in the very strongest terms that the Declaration should not be read. Plumptre thinks that Compton may also have had a hand in the drafting and disseminating of this letter. Whoever was responsible for these two astute and timely manœuvres, they succeeded admirably of their object. The following Sunday was 20 May, the first of the days on which the Declaration was to be read in the churches of London and within a radius of ten miles. It was, in fact, read in four churches only of the entire area.

On the orders of the Lord Chamberlain it was read in the Chapel Royal at Whitehall, but not, for some unexplained reason, in that of St James's. When Dean Sprat, who was also Bishop of Rochester, began to read it in Westminster Abbey the entire congregation walked out, leaving only the choristers and Westminster Scholars to hear the royal pronouncement.

During the week that followed the tempo of public excitement rose steadily, and what the King might do next was the main subject of general discussion. There were those who believed that the judges were in favour of prosecuting the bishops separately, and that they had advised His Majesty accordingly. Ultimately it became known that a decision had been taken, on the advice of the Lord Chancellor (Jeffreys), to arraign the seven bishops collectively on a charge of publishing a seditious libel. The presentation of the petition to the King was to constitute the "publication", little confidence being felt, apparently, in the success of any attempt to prove the bishops' complicity in the issue of the printed copies.

Sancroft and his six colleagues received official notice, on 27 May, that they must appear before the King in Council on 8 June. Meanwhile the Order to read the Declaration was proving as great a fiasco in the country as it had been in London and at Westminster. Reports were coming in steadily, indicating that there had been an almost universal ignoring of the Order by the parochial clergy. These tidings, presumably, did nothing towards soothing James's outraged feelings, and any thoughts he may have had of withdrawing the proceedings against the bishops were but briefly entertained.

When the defendants duly appeared before the Council, Sancroft took his place with them. The King presided in person, with Jeffreys to take charge of the legal part of the business. Among the twenty-one Privy Councillors present was the Romanist priest, Father Petre; a curious person, one would have thought, to sit in judgement on the Primate and prelates of a Church to which the vast majority of Englishmen belonged but of which he himself was not a member. The bishops conducted their own case, though doubtless they had already been in consultation with the lawyers who were subsequently to defend them. They had clearly been advised to admit nothing and to leave the onus of proof on the shoulders of the prosecution.

Jeffreys began by flourishing the petition which had been

presented to the King, and demanded to be told whether the writing it bore was Sancroft's. The Archbishop declined to answer, pointing out that an accused person was not bound to answer questions which might amount to accusing himself. This attitude greatly incensed the King, who demanded to know if they were going to deny the work of their own hands. Sancroft repeated that he was not bound to accuse himself, but if the King positively commanded him to speak he would do so, in perfect confidence that a just and generous prince would not permit what he said under obedience to be brought in evidence against him. Jeffreys roughly interposed, saying that the Archbishop must not bargain with his sovereign. James refused to give any such command, observing frigidly that if the bishops chose to deny their own hands he had nothing more to say to them.

As the King could not be summoned as a witness, Jeffreys found himself frustrated for the time being and the defendants were ordered to withdraw to an ante-chamber. Three times this was done, and each time they returned a similar altercation took place. At last the King, losing patience, positively commanded the bishops to admit that the petition was their work. Perhaps they, also, were wearying of this futile insistence upon a technicality; perhaps they thought James would respect the implied condition mentioned by Sancroft. At all events, they dropped what must have been a most uncongenial attitude, and freely acknowledged their respective signatures.

The prosecution now asked whether any others had been present when the petition was drawn up, and also whether the defendants knew anything of the letter which had been circulated throughout the country, advising the clergy not to read the Declaration. But in acknowledging their own share in the matter the bishops felt that they had gone quite far enough in obedience to the King's commandment; they were under no obligation to implicate others.

"It is our great infelicity", protested Sancroft, "that we

are here as criminals. Your Majesty is so just and generous that you will not require me to accuse either ourselves [i.e., on matters other than the question of the petition] or others."

Jeffreys was not hampered by any such scruples of justice or generosity as those which Sancroft imputed to his Sovereign, and he now proceeded to rant and bluster in the well-known Jeffreys manner. The men before him might have been Monmouth's unhappy dupes, instead of being the spiritual leaders of the nation's Church. But he merely wasted his time and breath. The bishops had admitted all that there was to admit and declined to say more. This being so, they were then told that they would be prosecuted for a misdemeanour in the Court of King's Bench and must enter into recognizances to appear when summoned before that tribunal. But here again, and acting upon advice, they were obdurate. They stood upon their privilege as peers, who were not bound to enter into recognizances. They would give their word of honour to appear and that was all. If the King and his advisers had been wise they would have let such an under-taking suffice. But they seemed set upon making martyrs of the bishops and of further inflaming the country against the Crown.

The Council was evidently not prepared for such an attitude on the part of the accused prelates. Jeffreys perhaps had expected them to be easy game, and was infuriated to find that they were not. He now completely lost his head, and shouted that unless the bishops would recant and withdraw the petition he would commit them at once to the Tower. Their reply to this threat was that they were ready to go wherever the King might send them; that they put their trust in the King of Kings to protect and defend them; that they had nothing to fear from having acted according to the law and their own consciences, and that no punishment would shake their resolution.

They were then again ordered to withdraw, and when at last they were brought back into the Council Chamber they saw that the King had departed, leaving Jeffreys to conduct the remainder of the proceedings, which he did in his own inimitable way. After a further vain attempt, by the Earl of Berkeley, to persuade them to yield over the question of recognizances, the Sergeant-at-Arms was sent for to conduct the bishops as prisoners to the Tower. The warrant for committal was signed by fourteen members of the Council, and another, bearing nineteen signatures, was sent to the Lieutenant of the Tower ordering him to keep them in safe custody. To minimize the danger of public demonstrations in their favour, one of the royal barges was provided to convey them from Whitehall by water. It was a wise precaution but ineffective. The news quickly spread and there were large crowds, both at Whitehall Stairs and at Traitors' Gate, to see the Seven Bishops taken to their captivity, to shout encouragements, and to beseech their blessing. On arriving at the Tower they went to the Chapel (so aptly dedicated to St Peter ad Vincula) for Evensong. The second Lesson for the day was from 2 Corinthians 6, and included the words: "We, then, as workers together with him, beseech you . . . that . . . in all things approving ourselves as the ministers of God; in much patience, in afflictions, in necessities, in distresses, in stripes, in imprisonments, in tumults, in labours, in watchings, in fastings . . . by glory and dishonour, by evil report and good report; as deceivers and yet true; as unknown and yet well-known; as dying, and behold, we live; as chastened, and not killed; as sorrowful, yet alway rejoicing; as poor, yet making many rich; as having nothing, and yet possessing all things."

11

"AND SHALL TRELAWNEY DIE?"

IT IS popularly but erroneously believed that the Seven Bishops were sent to the Tower because they refused to read the Declaration of Indulgence. This was not so. They were sent to the Tower because they took their stand on a purely technical point, pleading their privilege as peers and refusing to enter into recognizances. Whatever may have been the motives of those who advised them, it is scarcely credible that, holding the theories of kingship which they did, they adopted this attitude in order to manœuvre their sovereign into a false and invidious position.

Nevertheless, so far as James and the general public was concerned, this is precisely what they succeeded in doing. Unversed in legal technicalities or the niceties of Parliamentary privilege, the people of England were merely aware of two simple and undeniable facts which appeared to them to be related as cause and effect: (*a*) that the Seven Bishops had refused to read the King's Declaration; and (*b*) that they were now imprisoned in London Tower. *Post hoc ergo propter hoc*, they somewhat fallaciously reasoned.

To the King's enemies, the number of which grew daily, this was a highly satisfactory state of mind for the public to be in; to the King himself it seemed yet one more example of the malignity of the fate by which he was pursued, and he was later to complain bitterly of the way in which his hand had been forced and popular opinion inflamed against him. It is painfully obvious that perhaps a major part of James's troubles were of his own making, yet one cannot withhold a

meed of pity from a man so patently sincere in his convictions, so maladroit in his handling of each new situation,
so relentlessly dogged by every possible misfortune. Surely
he must be considered not the least unlucky of all his hapless
royal house.

Meanwhile the bishops in the Tower were the heroes of
the nation. Even their imprisonment was a minor triumph
in itself. They were permitted to walk in the precincts of the
grim fortress which had seen the last tragic days of so many
men and women even then famous in English history.
Crowds of persons of all ranks of society pressed into the
Tower to assure the prisoners of their sympathy, and to ask
their blessings before they would leave. Among these callers
were ten prominent dissenters, as well as Lord Clarendon
and John Evelyn, the latter of whom on the following day
dined with Jeffreys. Unfortunately the famous diary merely
records this engagement and contains no account of the conversation which took place. It is unlikely that the case of the
bishops was not mentioned at all, and one cannot help feeling
slightly aggrieved that Evelyn should fail to enlighten us on
what must have been a highly interesting colloquy.

The tension of this memorable week was still further
heightened by an event which was to prove of the greatest
political significance, and which was destined materially to
affect the futures of the seven prelates in the Tower. On the
morning of Sunday 10 June, in St James's Palace, the Queen
gave birth to an heir to the throne. This meant that on the
King's death the crown of England would pass to a prince
who would undoubtedly be brought up as a Roman Catholic.
Dismay was widespread throughout the country, and while
the gullible and ignorant were being persuaded to believe
that the new-born prince was some commoner's offspring
smuggled into the Palace in a warming-pan, those of the
King's enemies who knew the true facts urgently increased
their contacts with the Prince of Orange. Revolution had
been brought yet an appreciable step nearer.

Within a week of their committal to the Tower, on 15
June, the bishops were brought before the Court of King's
Bench to answer to the charge of misdemeanour against the
King's authority. Again both banks of the river, as well as
their route from Westminster Steps to Westminster Hall,
were lined with cheering, sympathetic crowds. The proceedings on this occasion were brief. The charge was read to
each of them severally and each entered a plea of "Not
Guilty". Bail was not insisted upon, and as the bishops,
having previously pleaded their privilege as peers, were this
time ready to enter into recognizances, they were allowed to
go free on those terms. Had bail been demanded, Compton
and Halifax had arranged for three peers to stand as surety
for each of the bishops. The Earls of Clare, Shrewsbury, and
Dorset had undertaken to answer for Ken, but Macaulay says
that a dissenter prominent in the City of London had begged
that he might have the honour of acting as surety for the
Bishop of Bath and Wells. As the seven men left the Court
they were again given a tremendous ovation by the excited
crowds who thronged the streets, and it was only with considerable difficulty that Sancroft and Ken were able to make
their way to Lambeth; the Archbishop, of course, going to
the Palace and Ken to the Rectory of his friend Hooper.

The trial of the Seven Bishops was fixed for 29 June, and
they spent the intervening fortnight in consultation with
their lawyers and in preparing their case. Letters of sympathy
reached them from all parts of the country, and even from
Presbyterian Scotland came a message of support and admiration. In Cornwall they had revived an old ballad re-
ferring to an earlier Trelawney who was imprisoned in the
Tower for his part in Perkin Warbeck's rebellion, but not
inappropriate to the present condition of the Bishop of
Bristol:

> And have they fixed the where and when?
> And shall Trelawney die?
> Here's thirty thousand Cornishmen
> Will know the reason why.

This was, broadly speaking, the temper of public opinion throughout the country when, on the feast of the martyred Apostle St Peter, who had been so timely delivered by heavenly intervention from the destruction planned by a despotic King, the bishops were brought to trial in Westminster Hall. The court was crowded with anxious, excited spectators who quickly made it clear where their sympathies lay. Undeterred by threats that the Court would be cleared, they greeted with cheers and shouts of laughter every point scored by the counsel for the defence; with cries of derision every failure of the prosecution to consolidate its case.

After much tedious and inconclusive argument between the contending lawyers as to whether or not the presentation of the petition to the King constituted "publication" within the meaning of the Act, during which many witnesses, including Samuel Pepys, were examined, the Court passed to consideration of the King's dispensing power and the right of a subject to petition his Sovereign. Then came Somers' speech for the defence in which he contended, with forceful eloquence, that the petition was not false, for every fact stated in it would be proved beyond question; that it was not malicious, for the bishops had taken no action until forced to choose between obedience to the King or to their own consciences; that it was not seditious, for the bishops had handed it directly to the King and had had no part in its publication abroad; neither was it a libel, for it contained no word which went beyond the limits of respectful pleading.

The law officers of the crown then replied for the prosecution, the Solicitor-General claiming that the bishops had no right of petition except in Parliament, after which the judges proceeded to their summing-up. The Lord Chief Justice (Sir Robert Wright) was generally unfavourable towards the defendants in his findings, and so was the Romanist Allibone; Holloway was less hostile, holding that the petition was such as an aggrieved subject might lawfully and reasonably present; while Powell, with great temerity, gave it as his opinion that the dispensing power, if acquiesced in, would speedily make an end of parliamentary government. "That issue, gentlemen," he said, turning to the jury, "I leave to God and your consciences."

It was now late in the evening. The defendants were permitted to go to their places of residence, again mobbed by cheering crowds as they did so, while the jury were locked in for the night to consider their verdict. They were heard about midnight in heated disagreement, and again about three o'clock in the morning. Whether they were aware of it or not, upon their decision rested the constitutional future of England. Meanwhile the country waited in tense expectancy. It was one of the great decisive moments in British history. Between the hammer and the anvil of these dramatic happenings, the Constitution was undergoing one of its periodic and fateful reforgings.

At ten o'clock on the morning of 30 June the Court reassembled and the bishops were brought in to hear the jury's verdict. The latter were asked if they were agreed. They were. Who would speak for them? Their foreman, Sir Roger Langley; who was now asked, "Do you find the Defendants, or any of them, Guilty of the misdemeanour whereof they are impeached, or Not Guilty?" There was a moment of almost unbearable tension, and then Sir Roger's voice made its historic, decisive answer, "Not Guilty!"

The second word was barely audible, for no sooner was the first out of his mouth than such a mighty shout went up from the assembled spectators as, in Macaulay's vivid description of the scene, "made the old oaken roof crack". Lord Halifax was standing up, wildly waving his hat. The Lord Chief Justice did his best to stem the applause, saying sternly, "I am as glad as you can be that my Lords the Bishops are acquitted; but your manner of rejoicing here in court is indecent; you might rejoice in your chamber, or elsewhere, but not here."

He might as well have attempted to stop the Thames in

its inexorable progress seawards. The cheering inside the Hall was taken up by the crowds outside, whose shout of acclamation could be heard at Temple Bar. The barges on the river took up the mighty roar; guns on the ships were fired—no doubt without authorization; the bells of London's churches set their steeples rocking with frenzied pealing.

"As the news spread," says Macaulay,[1]
streets and squares, market places and coffee houses, broke forth into acclamations. Yet were the acclamations less strange than the weeping. For the feelings of men had been wound up to such a point, that at length the stern English nature, so little used to outward signs of emotion, gave way, and thousands sobbed aloud for very joy. Meanwhile, from the outskirts of the multitude, horsemen were spurring off to bear along all the great roads intelligence of the victory of our Church and nation.

It was not long before these bearers of the most tremendous tidings since the defeat of the Armada just a hundred years before arrived at Hounslow Heath where the King was inspecting his army. He was actually at dinner in his tent when a mighty shout from the soldiers broke upon his ears. The Earl of Feversham was sent out to discover what it meant. He was soon back. "It was nothing", he reported, "but the soldiers shouting for the news of the Bishops being acquitted." "And do you call that nothing?" demanded James bitterly. *"Mais tant pis pour eux"*, he added, falling into French in his deep chagrin.

So much the worse for them—but meanwhile they were being *fêted* like conquering heroes. As they left Westminster Hall the delirious crowds surged rapturously about them, only to be exhorted to "fear God and honour the King". The bishops had made their stand for what they looked upon as a matter of vital principle. Their purpose was not defiance of the Lord's anointed, but defence of the laws of England. They had come through victorious, at the cost of immeasurable grief and heaviness of heart at finding themselves opposed to the wishes of their Sovereign. The clash of loyalties was not

[1] *History of England*, Vol. II, pp. 381–2.

of their making; it had left its mark of sadness and disappointment deep upon them. But wrong-headed though they conceived James to have been, with two possible exceptions they were loyalists, and had no intention of exploiting the favourable verdict of the Court either to embarrass their unhappy King or to bask in the unpredictable sunshine of popular adulation.

Ken and Sancroft left the hall together in the Archbishop's coach. Their route lay through the Strand, along Fleet Street, up Ludgate Hill, by way of Cheapside to London Bridge, and so through Southwark and the Borough to Lambeth. The journey was one long triumphal procession. Everywhere were cheering Londoners, and every now and again the coach was brought to a standstill as the crowds pressed upon it, demanding a blessing from its occupants. These were bestowed again and again, with the added solemn admonition, "Keep your religion." Both men must have known deep down in their hearts that what had been won was merely the first round in the fight for liberty and law.

The rejoicings in London continued for many days. Medals were struck in commemoration of the bishops' acquittal, and throughout the country, as well as in the capital, church bells rang and bonfires blazed nightly, while portraits of the seven prelates were prominently displayed in shops and dwellings, and sold by the thousand. Meanwhile the fateful message which was to end the Stuart tenure of the English throne had been despatched on behalf of several prominent politicians and soldiers, inviting William of Orange to come over to help in the struggle against royal autocracy and Romanist religion. The invitation was signed by only one Bishop of the English Church, Compton of London, who had all along been deeply involved in the secret negotiations.

In the course of the month that followed the acquittal, the Archbishop issued a set of *Instructions* to the bishops for transmission to the clergy of their respective dioceses. As Ken was still in London, and was ever in Sancroft's inner counsels, it is highly probable that the document owed much in its drafting to his pastoral experience and practised pen. The *Instructions* are lengthy and it must suffice here to summarize them. They make clear the attitude of the Archbishop and most of his suffragans; loyalty and obedience to the King in all things lawful, but loyalty and obedience first and foremost to the claims of God and to the Faith of the English Church.

First and foremost the clergy must set an example of holy living and conversation; they are to live in their parishes; to catechize the young with diligence; to say the Offices of Mattins and Evensong daily in their churches; to urge their people to receive Communion more frequently. Never had the prestige of the English episcopate stood higher than it stood at that particular time, as a consequence of the faithful witness of the Seven. It was sound policy to take advantage of this state of affairs and to urge upon clergy and laity alike deeper devotion and greater fidelity to religious obligations. That the admonitions were not unavailing would appear to be implied by the undoubted revival of Church life generally throughout the next two decades or so, in spite of the political upheavals which marked the opening years of the period. Nor were these political confusions entirely ignored in the *Instructions* of 1688. In them the clergy are commanded, "four times a year at the least", to preach against all usurped and foreign jurisdiction (that of the Papacy, of course, being chiefly in mind), while at the same time they are to persuade the people to loyalty and obedience to the King's Majesty in all things lawful, and to promote, as far as in them lies, the public peace and quiet of the world. Finally all are to continue steadfast in the Church's Faith, to beware of all seducers and especially of Popish emissaries, and to pray for a union of all reformed Churches, both at home and abroad: "that all who do confess the holy Name of our dear Lord, and do agree in the truth of His holy word, may also meet in one holy communion, and live in perfect unity and godly love." It is an eloquent reminder of just how powerful was the anti-papal feeling in England, that bishops so convincedly catholic in their outlook could contemplate with equanimity the uniting of the Church of England with bodies which repudiated not only episcopacy but a great many other tenets taught and cherished within the Anglican fold. There can be little doubt, however, that no small part of their purpose in stressing this aspect of the denominational issue was to refute, beyond all argument, the charges of Romanistic sympathies frequently levelled at them by their detractors.

If Sancroft and his colleagues hoped in this way to placate their Protestant critics, they can have entertained small hope of mollifying the King by a document which contained such scarcely veiled references to Rome as "the Old Serpent", "Evening wolves", and "the common enemy"; and, but for the fact that James already had other and more serious matters to occupy him, things might once more have gone hard with the authors of the *Instructions*. It was towards the end of September that he received a warning from Louis XIV, based on a report sent by the French Ambassador to the Hague, confirming reports from James's own agents in Holland, that William of Orange had been invited to England by some of the most influential of James's subjects and was now busily engaged in preparing an expedition to that end. At a levee held on 24 September the King made known the warnings he had received.

"Now", he said, "we shall see what the Church of England men will do!" It was Clarendon who replied. "Your Majesty will see that they will act as honest men, though they have been somewhat ill-used of late."

In spite of all that had passed, James evidently, in his inmost heart, shared this view, for in his distress of mind he now turned to the very men whom only a few weeks before he had sent to the Tower. The Bishops of London, Winchester, Bath and Wells, Ely, Peterborough, Bristol, and

10

Rochester each received a letter from Sunderland informing them that His Majesty wished to speak with them, and fixing, as the date and time of their attendance, 28 September at ten o'clock in the morning.

Ken appears to have received his summons through the agency of Lord Dartmouth to whom his reply, dated 23 September is addressed.

My very good Lord,

The expresse your Lordshippe sent I just now received, and in obedience to His Majesty's pleasure by whose command I presume you wrott, I will make what haste I can to towne, though I am the more unfitt for a journey because I came a tedious one yesterday. I did allwayes thinke that His Majesty could never believe our Church would be disloyall, having given so many undeniable instances to the contrary, and I shall be allwayes ready to serve my Sovereign to the utmost of my power, as far as can be consistent with my superiour duty to God and to that Holy Religion I professe. The declaration you mention is not yett set downe, which I should have been glad to have seen before I leave this place, which I intend to doe, God willing, earelye to-morrowe that I may reach London on Wednesday night if possible, time enough I hope to see you before you goe. My humble service to my good Lady. God, of His Infinite goodnesse, multiply his blessings on you both, and on your children and keepe you all stedfast in our most Holy Faith.

Tho: Bath and Wells

The declaration referred to by Ken in this letter was one issued by James on 21 September, in which he avowed that it was his intention to maintain the Church of England—an announcement to which few men by this time were prepared to attach any great importance. They had heard the same kind of thing before and while, no doubt, James could claim that he had always kept to the letter of such ambiguous promises, the way in which he observed the spirit of them left all too much to be desired. The remark about Lord Dartmouth's departure probably refers to that nobleman's appointment as commander-in-chief of the fleet sent to oppose the passage of the Dutch expedition if it attempted to approach English coastal waters.

James no longer entertained any doubts as to his son-in-law's intentions. Sycophantic courtiers might suggest that when it came to the point the Prince of Orange would hesitate to commit himself to a course of active hostility, but the King knew better. "I know my son-in-law's character so well," he said, "that if he undertakes any design, he will go through with it; he will never be diverted and may hardly be defeated."

James's personal courage, as we have said, was beyond dispute. In his youth he had served with distinction under the great Turenne, who esteemed him highly for his military qualities. In the battles at sea against the Dutch he had behaved with coolness and intrepidity under fire, frequently exposing himself in positions of the greatest danger. So now he prepared with fortitude and spirit to resist invasion from without and rebellion from within. It was not until he found himself betrayed by the officers he had most trusted, and forsaken by the nation at large, that his spirits faltered and his presence of mind deserted him. Meanwhile, with Dartmouth's fleet under orders to assemble at the Nore and the army, 30,000 strong, encamped upon Hounslow Heath, James gave audience to the Anglican bishops.

Six of them presented themselves at Whitehall on the morning of 28 September—Ken, and his brethren of Winchester, Chichester, Peterborough, Rochester and Ely. Sancroft was unwell at the time and Compton not yet restored to his see. If James had been prepared to take the bishops into his confidence, to allay their fears about his intentions towards the English Church and to appeal frankly for their active support, some tangible good might have resulted from this interview. Instead, they found him in one of his most maddening moods of obstinacy and vacillation. He appeared to have no fixed purpose in sending for them, he invited no counsel or expression of opinion, and after stating vaguely his goodwill towards the Church of England, proceeded to lecture them on their duty of loyalty to his person. Ken and his colleagues had obeyed the King's summons without regard to personal convenience. Some of them, like himself, had come a considerable distance at their own charges, leaving their proper pastoral concerns in order to do so. And all, apparently, to no purpose. There is an excusable note of acerbity in Ken's reproach as spokesman of the party. His Majesty's inclinations towards the Church, and their duty to him, were sufficiently understood before, and would have been equally so if they had not stirred one foot out of their dioceses. James curtly replied that he had no leisure to enter into details and forthwith dismissed them.

On hearing from Ken and his companions the barren results of this meeting, Sancroft, two days later, sought and obtained the promise of an audience with the King, to take place on 2 October. It was in fact the 3rd when Sancroft, accompanied by Ken and four of the other five bishops, waited once more upon their sovereign.

The Archbishop began by expressing the regret that the meeting five days previously should have been so unproductive and that his brethren should have been brought so far to accomplish so little, repeating Ken's own words that as much might have been done had they not stirred one foot out of their respective dioceses. He then produced a Memorial, drawn up by himself in consultation with his colleagues for the King's "princely consideration". It consisted of ten propositions, and if only James had been ready to accept and give effect to them he might yet, even at this late hour, have saved a situation which was rapidly passing beyond his power to control.

The propositions were that the King should:

(1) put the administration of government in the several counties in the hands of such of the nobility and gentry as were legally qualified for it;

(2) annul the Ecclesiastical Commission;

(3) withdraw, and in future withhold, all dispensations, under which persons not lawfully qualified had been, or might be, put into offices of trust and preferment in Church or State, or in the Universities, especially such as have the cure of souls annexed to them, and particularly to restore the President and Fellows of Magdalen College;

(4) withdraw all licences for Roman Catholics to teach in public schools;

(5) desist from the dispensing power, until that point had been freely and calmly debated, and settled, in Parliament;

(6) prohibit the four foreign bishops, who styled themselves Vicars-Apostolical, from further invading the ecclesiastical jurisdiction which is by law vested in the bishops of the English Church;

(7) fill the vacant bishoprics, and other ecclesiastical promotions in England and Ireland, and in particular the Archiepiscopal chair of York, which had been so long vacant, and on which a whole Province depended;

(8) restore the ancient Charters of the Corporations, which had been forfeited;

(9) issue writs with all convenient speed, calling a free and regular Parliament, for the purpose of securing the uniformity of the Church of England, due liberty of conscience, and the liberties and properties of the subject, and for establishing, between himself and all his people, a mutual confidence and good understanding;

(10) permit the bishops to offer to His Majesty such motives and arguments as might, by God's grace, be effectual to persuade him to return to the Communion of the Church of England, into whose most Holy Catholic Faith he had been baptized and educated, to which it was then their earnest prayer to God that he might be reunited.

"These, Sir," concluded the Memorial, "are the humble advices which, out of conscience of the duty we owe to God, to your Majesty, and our country, we think fit at this time to offer to your Majesty, as suitable to the present state of your affairs and most conducive to your service. . . ."

James thanked the bishops for their advice—which can have been as little to his liking as the Great Charter was to King John's—and promised to consider their suggestions. On 8 October Sancroft and the other prelates were summoned to Whitehall and were directed by the King to appoint a day of fasting and to prepare forms of prayer to be used in the event of an attempted invasion. He had considered their petition, he said, and was not at all pleased with it. They can hardly have hoped that he would be.

Two days later they again stood before James and presented the prayers they had compiled. There were three of them; one for Repentance, entirely general in its reference; one for the King which, avoiding any suggestion of approval of his past actions, desired that God would inspire him with wisdom; and one for Peace and Unity which asked for the prevention of "the effusion of Christian blood" and the reconciliation of all dissensions. The most remarkable feature of these devotions is their masterly ambiguity. There was nothing in them to which the King could reasonably take exception, they could be used by any of His Majesty's subjects without doing despite to their convictions, and they neither implied nor committed anyone to any particular line of policy. Finding nothing to object to, James indicated general approval of the prayers and commanded that they should be used in churches throughout the country.

This was the last occasion on which Ken set eyes on the sovereign with whose fate his own was so closely bound. Having fulfilled the duty for which he had been summoned to London, and no doubt feeling that little purpose was to be served by lingering in the capital, he returned to Wells to resume his interrupted episcopal duties and to await whatever might prove to be the outcome of events. As it turned out, he had not long to wait.

James made indeed a half-hearted and reluctant effort to

comply with some of the less offensive of the bishops' proposals, but as always it was a case of too little and too late. He restored to the City of London and certain other corporations their lost charters; the Court of Ecclesiastical Commission was abolished; the Bishop of Winchester, as Visitor, was ordered to restore the extruded President and Fellows of Magdalen College, Oxford. But these belated and hopeless attempts to recover ground irrevocably lost passed virtually unnoticed in the face of more portentous tidings from the Hague.

On the evening of 26 October Mr Secretary Pepys was informed that a Dutch fleet, consisting of 500 transports and 52 men-of-war, was at sea in spite of contrary winds which, a few days before, reaching gale force, had all but driven them back to destruction on the shores of Holland. Dartmouth, had he possessed even a modicum of that initiative which characterized a Nelson, a Hawke, or a Duncan, might have seized the advantage thus briefly and providentially offered to paralyse the expedition from the outset. But, more concerned to preserve his ships intact than to pluck the nettle danger, he remained irresolute aboard his flagship *Resolution* and left it to the elements to do his business for him. In this they soon proved regrettably uncooperative. Having provided this unaccepted opportunity, the "papist wind" from the west now veered and became the "protestant wind" from the east; and while King James's fleet lay helpless at its moorings and unable to put to sea, William's armada, with the wind behind it, drove down the Channel westwards and unmolested.

They were seen by watchers on 3 November passing the white cliffs of Dover; on 4 November it was erroneously reported that they had entered Portsmouth Harbour; on 6 November it was known for certain in London that twenty-four hours previously the invaders had dropped anchor in Torbay and were busily engaged in landing arms and men. The invasion was on.

12

THE REVOLUTION

WHILE THESE portentous happenings were toward Ken was at Wells, subject no doubt to highly conflicting emotions. It is a reasonable supposition that he was able to keep himself informed of the rapidly developing situation, from which he can have derived little satisfaction or peace of mind. The West of England, including his own diocese, had scarcely had time to recover from the disastrous consequences of Monmouth's rebellion and now once more, it seemed, a sanguinary civil war threatened to destroy its scarce-won peace.

The Prince of Orange, he would learn, had passed through Newton Abbot with his heterogeneous invading force, some 17,000 strong, of whom three-quarters were foreigners and, ironically, more than a quarter Roman Catholics.[1] Here, in the market place and before a handful of gaping yokels, the Prince's Declaration was read, announcing that he had come to England, on the invitation of those whom he believed represented the wishes of the English people, to maintain the Protestant religion (whatever he meant by that, for he had certainly little sympathy with the Anglican Faith) and the laws and liberties of the country.

On 8 November he entered Exeter, the capital of the West. As an earnest of his religious zeal, this disinterested champion of the rights of Englishmen repaired to the Cathedral to

[1] For purely political reasons, the Pope, the Emperor, and the King of Spain were all hoping for the success of William's invasion.

render thanks for his safe arrival in his father-in-law's kingdom and to listen to a fulsome address of welcome from that notorious busybody, Gilbert Burnet, who had accompanied him from Holland and who was soon to be rewarded for his political activities with the bishopric of Salisbury.

Meanwhile the King, torn with indecision, lingered in London. On 18 November the two archbishops,[1] five other bishops, and a few of the peers who had remained in town, presented a last despairing petition to the King, imploring him to summon a free Parliament while still there was time. Their appeal was made in vain. Perhaps, in the circumstances, this was inevitable.

"My Lords," replied the King, "what you ask of me I most passionately desire; and I promise you upon the faith of a King, that I will have a Parliament, and such a one as you ask for, as soon as ever the Prince of Orange has quitted this realm. For how is it possible a Parliament should be free in all its circumstances, as you petition for, whilst an enemy is in the kingdom, and can make a return of near a hundred voices?"

It was now almost a fortnight since the invaders had landed and that same evening James belatedly set out from London to join his army at Salisbury, having first arranged for the infant Prince of Wales to be taken to Portsmouth in readiness, if need be, for his speedy removal to safety across the Channel. He was in Salisbury on the 19th and news at once began to come in that the enemy forces were moving eastwards from Exeter. Advanced patrols of the two armies met in a brief skirmish at Wincanton a day or two later, and it seemed likely that a decisive battle would be fought out on Salisbury Plain

But the stars in their courses were proving themselves consistently contrary to James's interests. Tormented with doubts, confused by conflicting counsel, sickened by the

[1] Lamplugh, formerly of Exeter, had recently been appointed Archbishop of York.

steady stream of defections, he now succumbed to a violent attack of nose bleeding and for several days was prostrated and incapable of active command. On the 24th, deferring to the advice of his most trusted intimates, he decided to return to London and to take up defensive positions on the line of the Thames.

This was the final ineptitude which made certain his fate and that of the country. No sooner had his decision to fall back on the capital been made known than his two most important generals, his nephew the Duke of Grafton and John Churchill, both of whom had for long been in secret correspondence with the Prince of Orange, made their way to the enemy lines. That same night the Princess Anne fled from the Palace of Whitehall with Churchill's wife and, accompanied by Bishop Compton, was soon on her way north to join her father's enemies. As the King, sick in mind and body, slowly made his way back to his sullenly apprehensive capital, news of more and yet more desertions came in to batter him even further into wretchedness and despair. Anne's husband, the Prince of Denmark, Ormonde, Devonshire, Danby, Mordaunt, Rochester—the rats were falling over each other in their determination not to founder with the doomed barque of their sovereign's fortunes.

All this and more must Ken have heard with a heavy heart at Wells, and soon he found himself more nearly involved in the swiftly developing situation. On the 24th we find him writing to Sancroft.

May it please your Grace,

Before I could return any answer to the letter with which your Grace was pleased to favour me, I received intelligence that the Dutch were just coming to Wells, upon which I immediately lefft the town, and, in obedience to his Majesty's generall commands, took all my coach horses with me, and as many of my saddle horses as I well could, and took shelter in a private village in Wiltshire,[1] intending, if his Ma: had come into my country, to

[1] Possibly Poulshot, near Devizes, where his nephew, Izaak Walton, was Rector.

have waited on him, and to have paid him my duty. But this morning wee are told his Ma: is gone back to London, so that I onely wait till the Dutch have passed my diocesse, and then resolve to returne thither againe, that being my proper station. I would not have lefft the diocesse in this juncture, but that the Dutch had seas'd horses within ten miles of Wells before I went, and your Grace knowes that I, having been a servant to the Princess, and well acquainted with many of the Dutch, I could not have staid without giving some occasions of suspicion, which I thought it most advisable to avoid; resolving by God's grace to continue in a firm loyalty to the King, whome God direct and preserve in this time of danger: and I beseech your Grace to lay my most humble duty at His Majesty's feet, and to acquaint him with the reason of my retiring, that I may not be misunderstood. God of His infinite mercy deliver us from the calamitys which now threaten us, and from the sinnes which have occasioned them.

My very good Lord,
Your Grace's very affct: Servant
and Br.,
Tho. Bath and Wells

This letter is sufficient indication of Ken's indefectible loyalty to the King who had given him so little positive cause for it; a refreshing and wholesome contrast to the spate of treachery, desertion, and double-dealing which otherwise distinguished the progress of this remarkably inglorious revolution. Merely by remaining in Wells or near at hand, Ken could so easily have used the favour in which he was held by the Princess of Orange to ingratiate himself with what, even at this stage, must have looked reasonably likely to be the winning side. Yet no such thought seems ever to have entered his head. Ken, like his superior Sancroft, was cast in a very different mould from the Comptons and the Burnets of his day. It was not in his nature to betray the King whose salt he had eaten, however much the salt might have lost its savour.

On his return to London James had at last, too late, listened to the advice of those who had for so long been urging him to summon a Parliament. The writs were issued and even now, had they been allowed to take effect, something might have been done to preserve the succession. But James, lured once more into even more incredible folly by the fanatical counsel of Father Petre and his friends, countermanded the writs and on 11 December fled by night from Whitehall, casting the Great Seal of England into the Thames as he went.

Two days previously, he had succeeded in dispatching the Queen and the infant Prince of Wales to France under the protection of Lord Powis and the Chevalier de Lauzun, and now he intended to join them there and to throw himself on the mercy of King Louis who would, he confidently believed, assist him to recover his kingdom and expel the usurper.

As soon as the King's flight was discovered, Archbishops Sancroft and Lamplugh, five other bishops (Ken was not one of them), and twenty-two peers met at Guildhall and formed a kind of provisional government to prevent the affairs of the country from lapsing into utter chaos. This was undoubtedly wise, but more questionably they now sent an urgent message to the Prince of Orange, requesting him to come to London with all haste to take over the direction and administration of affairs. But while they awaited his coming news reached them that James's malignant ill-fortune had pursued him even in flight. At Faversham he had been recognized by some Kentish hooligans, roughly handled, robbed of his valuables, and then kept prisoner in some wretched ale house. As soon as they heard of their King's predicament, the provisional Government, to their credit, acted with the utmost despatch. Lord Ailesbury and three other peers, accompanied by a troop of the Household Cavalry, set off at once through a night of violent storm. They reached Faversham by noon of the following day and found James, frightened and angry by turns, but otherwise unharmed.

By tactful and earnest pleading Ailesbury persuaded the King to return with them to London, and by doing so almost altered the entire course of English history. For, with the customary fickleness of mobs, the citizens of the capital who, a day or two before, had been indulging in an insane orgy of anti-papal rioting, murder, and destruction, now received their reluctantly returning sovereign with wild enthusiasm and heart-warming cheers. Those who so recently had been screaming "Crucify", now hailed him with their unaccountable Hosannas. This was a gratifying experience for the sorely distracted James but not, in reality, a salutary one. Bemused and misled by this unexpected demonstration of loyalty into believing that he had the bulk of the people of England behind him, James soon showed that he had learned nothing at all from his recent humiliations. The next day all was as before. Loyal ministers and servants were being angrily scolded for their dealings with the Guildhall committee of public safety; the corridors and ante-rooms of Whitehall once more thronged with Papist priests and agents. No Bourbon was ever more set in refusal to learn and forget, none more firmly determined upon his own destruction.

Events now moved rapidly to the inevitable denouement. On 17th December, as the short winter's afternoon drew to its sombre close and dusk fell upon the now silent capital, William's mercenaries closed in upon it, and before the stroke of midnight the King was a prisoner in his own palace of Whitehall. Soon after, emissaries from his son-in-law arrived to tell him that early next day he must leave London. On Tuesday the 18th, in pouring rain, he came down Whitehall steps for the last time and entered a waiting barge. There were no demonstrations or counter-demonstrations as the crushed and dejected King left his capital; only a chilling silence and the pitiless, drenching rain. With an escort of Dutch soldiers "to protect him from insult", though none was offered by his bewildered humbler subjects, James came by barge and coach to Rochester. Here he found a ship bound for France and on Christmas Day, no man hindering him by gracious order of his son-in-law, the last Stuart King of England sailed away for ever from the realm he had proved himself so sadly unfit to rule.

Back in London the crowds who a few days before had cheered James now turned out to shout for his Dutch supplanter, though rather less heartily, as Clarendon noted in his diary, than they had done for the King. Father Petre and his confrères, who had contributed so materially to their master's downfall, were in hiding or had escaped to France. Lord Chancellor Jeffreys, having narrowly escaped lynching at the hands of an infuriated mob, was now safe, inside the Tower; from whence was now released a far fouler and more repulsive creature, the venomous perjurer Titus Oates, to flaunt once more his abominable presence in public, and eventually to be rewarded for his villainies with a State pension.

Meanwhile the cold, calculating William was consolidating, with every outward semblance of constitutional propriety, the position to which his own good fortune and his father-in-law's folly had brought him. Without a shot being fired, a kingdom had fallen into his grasp like an overripe plum and he had not the slightest intention of letting go. With characteristic intensity of purpose he proceeded to feel his way forward to the vacant throne. Taciturn and aloof, he kept for the most part his own counsel, consulting only with Bentinck and a few other of his Dutch intimates, or with such English toadies and hangers-on as Russell, Harbord, and the foul-mouthed Herbert, who had sailed with him from Holland and compared with whom Father Petre and his colleagues were statesmen of purest probity and wisdom.

William had landed in England ostensibly, not as one bent on conquest or the pursuit of a crown, but as a liberator whose sole motive was to rescue the country from despotic rule and an alien Faith. He could claim, as some measure of justification, that he had been invited to do so by representatives of the country's ruling class. Liberators, however, are frequently more ready to liberate than to depart when they have performed the task for which they were invited. Furthermore, in a monarchy, an empty throne and an unworn crown represent a political vacuum of the kind which nature and the principles of political economy abhor.

Of this William was fully aware, and, playing his cards with exemplary skill and patience, he allowed the course of events to proceed to their foreseeable conclusion. When the House of Lords besought him to assume the temporary management of affairs he showed a prudent and altogether becoming hesitation, insisting that without a similar request from the Commons of England he did not feel at liberty to accept. Consequently, all who had served in any of Charles II's Parliaments, together with the Lord Mayor, Aldermen, and Common Council of the City of London, were invited to wait upon the Prince and to reinforce the petition of the peers. This being done, His Highness graciously consented to issue a summons for the election of a National Assembly to meet at Westminster on 22 January.

Sancroft had absented himself from the meeting of the peers at which the petition to the Prince had been drafted, and on the same day he himself sent a circular letter to all the bishops, once more summoning them to London to confer with him on the situation as it then stood. Ken, in his letter acknowledging receipt of the summons, apologizes for his inability to come to London before Christmas. There is an Ordination to be held in his Cathedral on the Sunday before the Feast, but he promises to set out as soon as the weather permits. He was as good as his word, and by 10 January we find him once more at Lambeth.

It would appear that there was uncertainty amongst the Bishops as to the immediate action which they ought to take —understandably so, as the Prince's own intentions could still only be guessed at. Ken and Turner of Ely seem to have pondered over things together, the result of their conference being a draft memorial drawn up by Ken and an accompanying letter to the Archbishop from Turner. The memorial was intended for the guidance of the bishops in their deliberations, rather than for publication or submission to the Prince. It contained, as a basis of future policy, three "Propositions".

These were:

First—against deposing the King.
Secondly—against electing any other King.
Thirdly—against breaking any one link in the royall chaine; i.e. any way intercepting the right succession to the Imperial crown.

These Propositions should, in my judgment, bee drawne and taken from the very words either of our 39 *Articles*, or our *Liturgy*, or our *Rubricks*, or our *Canons*, or our *Homilys*, or our *Acts of Parliament* and *fundamental laws* of the land, or from our *Oaths and Tests* (which indeed are part of our law).

And this paper of Propositions, with a short Preface before it, or something after it, declaring our obligations to maintain these doctrines, need be directed to no body, though intended, as for our own vindication, so for everybody's satisfaction one day, and for the Prince's presently, and most particularly. This paper should be delivered by one of us to Monsieur Benting,[1] or some chief Minister, to be handed by him to His Highness with as little noise and notice as may bee, and if such a representation dos not putt a stopp (as 'tis to be feared it will not), then it will be time enough, *and high time it will bee, for the Lords Spirituall, and those Temporall that will act conjoyntly* with us, to oppose the common wealth-men openly at the Convention.[2]

Evelyn, who about this time visited the Archbishop, with whom he found the Bishops of Bath and Wells and Ely, tells us that most of the Bench were in favour of a Regency, though it must have been clear to the more far-seeing of them that such an arrangement was bound to create fresh problems of not inconsiderable proportions. The setting up of a Regency would have involved the legal fiction that the King was incapacitated from ruling from physical or mental

[1] I.e., Bentinck. [2] Tanner MSS.

disability. It would also have led to the anomaly of a more
or less perpetuated Regency, governing in the name of a
succession of exiled kings who would be excluded from
reigning on account of their unacceptable religious attachments. An alternative solution, of course, was a republic, and
there were some who advocated it, with William as President
or Stadholder on the Dutch pattern. But there were still too
many with memories of England's only experiment in this
particular political field, and few who were anxious to see a
repetition of it. The rule of the saints and the major-generals
had very successfully inoculated Englishmen against the
fever of republicanism.

Meanwhile the Prince maintained his impenetrable reserve, and left it to such spokesmen as Bentinck and Burnet
to give repeated assurances that it was a wicked insinuation
to say that he aspired to the Crown and that he would on no
account take the title of King even if it were offered him.

On 22 January 1689, the Lords and Commons met in
Convention at Westminster to settle the question of the
future government of the country. It was a momentous
gathering, when once more the destinies of the nation were
committed to the melting pot. Sancroft declined to be
present, perhaps on the score of advancing age and infirmity,
but more likely to avoid taking part in deliberations the
legality of which he doubted and the outcome of which he
feared. In spite of the pleadings of Turner, Ken, and Lord
Clarendon, he steadfastly persisted in his refusal to attend
any further meetings of the House of Lords, whether held
separately or conjointly with the Commons. One can respect
the firmness and consistency of his attitude, but at the same
time it is difficult to avoid the conclusion that had he felt
able to attend the Convention, with his prestige and influence still at their height, the decision taken might have
been different from what in fact it was.

On 28 January the Commons passed their memorable
resolution, based upon a wholly unwarranted assumption

11

and no known principle in English law, that the King "having withdrawn himself out of the Kingdom, had abdicated the government, and that the throne had thereby become vacant". On the day following, the Lords debated the question of whether William should be Regent or King. Ken voted for a Regency, but when the count was taken he found himself in a minority of 51 to 54. When, on the 31st, the Lords debated the Commons' resolution declaring the alleged vacancy of the throne, Ken voted, as one would expect, against it, this time in a majority of 55 to 41.

While all these discussions were going on William was emerging from his strategic silence. He had let it be known, to a gathering of peers addressed by Bentinck, that he had no desire to be in the position of his wife's "gentleman usher"; and Mary herself, in a letter to Danby, affirmed that she would wish to surrender any powers that might be hers into her husband's hands. Then the Prince summoned Danby, Shrewsbury, Halifax, and other prominent politicians, and bluntly informed them that he had no intention whatever of being Regent, or even King Consort. The Convention could take what course they liked; he was free to take his.

This forthright ultimatum had the effect of resolving the minds of all but a minority of the Convention. They now saw clearly that it was a question of accepting William on his own terms, i.e., as King, or doing without him altogether. As no one was ready with any other alternative policy or proposal, it was felt that the pill, however unpalatable, must perforce be taken with as good a grace as might be.

Yet the minority was still by no means negligible and the debates continued to be protracted. At a joint session of the two Houses the motion declaring that the throne was vacant was only carried by a majority of 15—62 for, 47 against. Ken was amongst the dissentients. The resolution that William and Mary should be declared King and Queen was carried without a division, but a protest was entered against it signed by thirty-seven peers, twelve of them bishops, of whom Ken was one. On the days which followed he continued to vote steadily against each measure designed to effect a transfer of authority and allegiance from the absent James to his son-in-law and daughter. The Convention completed its work on 12 February, and on that day Ken quitted the House of Lords, never to enter it again.

The Revolution, for all practical purposes, was now complete. Only the formalities remained to be attended to. On the day after the Convention ended its business of King-making, both Houses waited upon William and Mary in the Banqueting Room at Whitehall and there, in the name of the people of England whose wishes no one had troubled to ascertain, the Crown was solemnly conferred upon the Dutch Prince and his long-suffering spouse. Neither Ken nor Sancroft, of course, was present on this, as it would have seemed to them, melancholy occasion.

In an inevitable reaction from the immoderate rhapso-dizings of Protestant Whig historians who were able to see nothing but the workings of a benevolent Providence in this strange and complex chapter in the story of England, there is perhaps a tendency to blame William of Orange over much for his share in the proceedings. It is not an attractive or likeable personality who looks out at us from the pages of history. Dr Johnson's description of him is probably a fair one: "He [William] was arbitrary, insolent, gloomy, rapacious and brutal; he was at all times disposed to play the tyrant; he had, neither in great things nor in small, the manners of a gentleman; he was capable of gaining money by mean artifices, and he only regarded his promise when it was in his interest to keep it."[1]

Until the success of his invasion was assured, he professed a deep respect for the father-in-law whom he purposed to supplant; but once in secure occupation of the capital, with his mercenary troops at hand to enforce his wishes, he wasted neither time nor ceremony in ordering the King to be gone.

[1] *Works*, Vol. VI, p. 6.

In the public Declaration by which he sought to justify his invasion of England, he appeared, by references to the suppositious birth of a Prince of Wales, to encourage belief in a canard which he must have known to be utterly and basely untrue. If he really believed the ridiculous and malicious "warming-pan" calumny, it is scarcely creditable to his judgement; if, as is almost certain, he disbelieved it, his behaviour in apparently accepting it in order to inflame public opinion against the King is beneath all contempt.

His own personal life, as we have seen, was far from irreproachable, for all his Calvinistic sanctimoniousness. His cold and callous harshness towards his wife, his sordid and joyless adulteries, his calculated political manœuvrings and duplicities, preclude any attempt to present William of Orange as a pure-souled, high-minded, disinterested lover of liberty and true religion.

Yet few men are altogether bad and William had his good points, little calculated though they may have been to inspire affection. Even that stern critic of his character, Dr Johnson, whose views on the Prince are quoted above, was ready to admit that "none ever denied him the resplendent qualities of steady resolution and personal courage".[1] These, indeed, were the very qualities—in combination with his political acumen, lack of scruple, and shrewd judgement of men—which had won for him the glittering prize now firmly in his grasp. They were the qualities most needed now that he found himself the *de facto* ruler of a nation, of which a majority regarded him merely as the lesser of two evils and a considerable minority as an unwanted usurper.

Even with the powerful support of the influential faction which had brought him to England, William soon discovered that his new subjects were no more minded to submit to arbitrary rule on the part of a Dutch Presbyterian Prince than they had been to that of a Papist one. The Convention, in conferring the Crown upon William, had thoughtfully

[1] *Life of Prior.*

linked the offer with the passing of a Bill of Rights, by which the Royal prerogatives were very effectively limited. It began with a detailed recital of James's arbitrary measures, by way of a gentle hint that the day of royal autocracy was over and the era of parliamentary supremacy begun. The religion of the Sovereign was specified, the alleged "dispensing power" of the Crown declared illegal, prerogative Courts outlawed, a freely elected Parliament, to which freedom of speech was assured, was to have complete control over finance and taxation, while in time of peace there was to be no standing army.

The Convention, or a majority of them, were well content to have William as King, but only as a constitutional King prepared to govern according to law and subject to parliamentary control. It is no small tribute to William's political sagacity that he accepted without challenge or complaint the conditions upon which the Crown was offered him, and was so far successful in sublimating the imperious side of his nature that, while the English people never had cause to hold him in any deep affection, neither had they reason to regard him with feelings of rebelliousness or hate. The men who made the revolution of '88 were neither saints nor heroes. Most of them were not even men of honour. Yet because they built on sound foundations, and chose as their King a man who understood that politics is the art of the possible, their structure survived and, with modifications to meet the needs of a world vastly different from theirs, in all its essentials still survives to-day. If the end can ever be said to justify the means, then surely does the British Constitution justify the sometimes equivocal progress of the British Revolution.

13

THE OATH OF ALLEGIANCE

IT WOULD not be strictly accurate to say that with the assumption of power by the Prince of Orange there arose a King "which knew not Joseph". Nevertheless, with the usurpation of the throne the days of Ken's career of active usefulness were clearly numbered. Although he had been a bishop for only a comparatively brief period, he had occupied for many years now a prominent place in public affairs and had become, not only the adviser and confidant of rulers and leaders in Church and State, but a man deeply revered for his personal integrity and selfless attachment to duty. There can have been at that time few men who stood higher in common repute. No breath of scandal had sullied his reputation; his fearless resistance to James's wrongful requirements had gained him the respectful admiration of the majority of his fellow countrymen. They had, incidentally, served to disperse most, if not all, of the quite unwarranted suspicions of Romanist leanings which had from time to time been levelled against him. He had walked with crowds and kept his virtue; talked with kings nor lost the common touch.

Now his affairs were to be decisively moulded by the demands of an inflexible conscience, his future plotted by a categorical imperative which neither crowds nor kings could control or comprehend.

This is not to imply that the decision which Ken felt called upon to make was an easy one. It is not to imply that there were no pros and cons to be considered. Life seldom presents its problems in sharply pointed contrasts of black and white, and that which now confronted him was no exception. So complex was it, indeed, that many of those with whom Ken had most in common were able to reach a solution precisely opposite to his own and yet retain his friendship and respect.

When James had succeeded to the throne, Ken and all his fellow bishops and priests had solemnly sworn allegiance to the new King and his lawful heirs and successors. This oath they were required to take by Act of Parliament, but by its very nature it was a *religious oath*, a solemn promise and vow made, as it were, in the presence and name of God. Parliament could compel them to take it, but Parliament could not dispense them from keeping it. It was too much to ask the very men who had risked their lives resisting a King's claim to dispense from the laws of England to agree that a Parliament, and a Parliament of doubtful authority at that, could dispense from promises made with one's hand between the hands of the Lord's anointed.

Yet that is precisely what Parliament now demanded they should agree to. All holders of civil or ecclesiastical office were required to swear fealty to the new ruler. It is greatly to William's credit that he tried hard to persuade Parliament to include in the Act for settling the new oaths a clause excepting the bishops from its application. He at once found himself, however, up against a legislature far less liberal and tolerant in its outlook than himself, and the Act was passed without exceptions. William had proposed that the bishops should not be required to take the oaths unless specially tendered to them by the King in Council—a weapon of restraint which he thought to hold in reserve and only to apply it, at any time, the security of his throne and of the State required it.

The proposal was defeated, however, because the Tories would not agree to the repeal of the Test Act which debarred dissenters from holding offices of trust under the Crown; so by way of retaliation the Whigs opposed the projected clause in favour of the bishops. Not for the last time was party faction and spite thus permitted to triumph at the expense of equity and commonsense. All that William was able to obtain, by way of relieving the situation which he seems to have foreseen, was a clause authorizing the Crown to grant to any members of the clergy who might be deprived under the Act an allowance out of their benefices not exceeding one-third of the value thereof. There is no evidence, so far as I am aware, that any clergyman deprived under the Act benefited from this clause.

The Act was finally passed on 23 February; the clergy were required to take the oaths by 1 August at the latest. Those who failed to do so were to be suspended from their benefices; and if, by 1 February 1690, they remained obdurate in their refusal, they were to suffer absolute and permanent deprivation.

When the news of the passing of this Measure reached him Ken was once more back in his diocese, exercising the pastoral functions and episcopal oversight so dear to his heart. It is unlikely that he allowed this latest development to deflect him in the slightest degree from the steady performance of his duty. As one of his earlier biographers put it, "he considered the day of death, and the day of judgment, to be as certain as the 1st of August and the 1st of February, and acted accordingly". He can have been in no doubt what refusal to take the oaths would mean, nor is it likely that at this stage he had any serious doubt what his own course of action would be. The civil power might indeed take from him the temporalities of his see, and prevent him from continuing to rule his diocese. His spiritual office and authority the State had power neither to bestow nor take away. "Once a bishop, always a bishop"; and secure in this knowledge he continued, calm and unshaken, to tend his flock, leaving the morrow to take care of itself.

It was not long, however, before he was brought up against

the Act in operation. One of the functions of a diocesan bishop is to collate and institute duly appointed clergymen to vacant benefices, and an essential part of his function when doing so is to administer oaths, not only of canonical obedience to himself, but also of allegiance to the reigning sovereign. As Ken was unwilling himself to take such an oath of allegiance to William, he could not, he felt, conscientiously administer it to others. In order that those who felt differently from himself on this matter should suffer neither loss nor inconvenience, Ken commissioned his diocesan Chancellor to institute to benefices in his stead. Sancroft and other of the bishops made a similar arrangement, a fact which brought forth accusations of inconsistency from the waspish Burnet, in spite of the fact that he owed his own consecration to this device. Burnet, a dweller in glass houses if ever there was one, would have done better to commend the thoughtfulness of others which it implied, rather than to have engaged in the dangerous and un-rewarding occupation of stone throwing.

It is indicative of the way in which Ken would neither presume to judge others whose consciences led them to act differently from himself, nor to allow such differences to influence his appointments, that to the four benefices in his gift which fell vacant after the passing of the Act he presented four priests, each one of whom had either already taken the oath or did so readily at their institution by the diocesan Chancellor. Even to those with whom he found himself in deepest disagreement, he was always ready to give the fullest credit for acting according to the dictates of conscience, a breadth and charity of outlook not invariably to be detected on the part of some of his later critics.

Two of Ken's colleagues, men of the same loyalty of outlook, high courage, and fearless principles as himself, were called to their rest before the inevitable storm could break and engulf them. William Thomas, Bishop of Worcester, had

for long been in failing health, and on 23 June he wrote thus
to Dr Hickes, Dean of Worcester:

Mr Dean,

I was glad when I heard you was come home, for I longed to
speak with you before I dyed; for I perceive that I have but a
short time to live. I bless God that I have twice suffered in the
same righteous cause,[1] and it is time for me now to dye, who have
outlived the honour of my religion and the liberties of my
country. It hath been a great comfort to me in this general
apostacy of my Clergy, whom I have endeavoured to keep up-
right and steady to their principles, that you have not forsaken
me, but keep constant with me to the same principles. I have
read all the books written for taking the oath; in which I find
the authors more Jesuit than the Jesuits themselves: and if my
heart deceive me not, and the grace of God fail me not, I think
I could burn at a stake before I took this new oath. I pray God
bless you, and reward your constancy. I desire your daily prayers.

The other was John Lake, Bishop of Chichester—a man
of indomitable courage and fortitude, whose devotion to the
House of Stuart had been amply proved in the darkest and
most perilous times. Before his ordination, he had served
with distinction as a soldier in the Royalist army during the
Civil War. He was captured by the Roundheads and imprisoned at Cambridge, but contrived to escape and to rejoin
the King at Oxford. He endured two successive sieges—first,
as one of the valorous defenders of Basing House, and later
with the garrison of Wallingford Castle. His ultimate reward
for these services to Charles's cause was to be sent to the
Tower, as one of the Seven Bishops, by Charles's son. His
return to his diocese after the trial and acquittal, we are told
by a contemporary,[2] "was like the return from banishment
of St Athanasius or St Chrysostom".

His deathbed declaration proclaims with dignity and
precision the principles he had followed so consistently and
firmly.

[1] He was evicted from his Welsh parish during the Cromwellian
régime, and was forced to teach for his livelihood in a village school
in Carmarthenshire.

[2] Dr Robert Jenkin, the Bishop's chaplain.

The Declaration of the Right Reverend Father in God,
John late Lord Bishop of Chichester, upon his Death-bed:

"Being called by a sick (and I think a dying) bed, and the good hand of God upon me in it, to take the last and best *Viaticum*, the Sacrament of my dear Lord's Body and Blood, I take myself obliged to make this short recognition and profession:

That, whereas I was baptized into the religion of the Church of England, and sucked it in with my milk, I have constantly adhered to it through the whole course of my life; and now, if so be the will of God, shall die in it: *and had resolved, through God's grace assisting me, to have died so, though at a stake.* And, whereas the religion of the Church of England taught me the doctrine of Non-Resistance[1] and Passive Obedience,[1] which I have accordingly inculcated upon others, and which I took to be the distinguishing character of the Church of England,—I adhere no less firmly and steadfastly to that; and in consequence of it have incurred *Suspension* from the exercise of my office, and expected a *Deprivation*. I find in so doing much inward satisfaction; *and if the Oath had been tendered at the peril of my life, I could only have obeyed by suffering*:

I desire you my worthy friends and brethren, to bear witness to this upon occasion, and to believe it, as the words of a dying man, and who is now engaged in the most sacred and solemn act of conversing with God in this world, and may, for ought he knows to the contrary, appear with these very words in his mouth at the dreadful tribunal.

Aug. 27. 1689.

Manu propria subscripsi,

Jo. Cicestrensis

This Declaration was read, and subscribed by the Bishop, in the presence of

> Dr Green, the Parish Minister who administered,
> Dr Hickes, Dean of Worcester,
> Mr Jenkin, his Lordship's Chaplain,
> Mr Powell, his Secretary,
> Mr Wilson, his Amanuensis,
> who all communicated with him.

I have quoted this somewhat lengthy Declaration of Bishop Lake, and likewise Bishop Thomas's letter to Dean

[1] I.e., to the lawful and even the unlawful demands of a lawful sovereign.

Hickes, because they express with such clarity the views held by those who were soon to be commonly known as Non-jurors—those who, having taken an Oath of Allegiance to a King who in their opinion had neither abdicated nor been legally deposed, found it incompatible with their sense of loyalty to take a further oath to that King's supplanter. Whatever we may think of the political theories upon which their attitude was largely based, there can be no doubt that to have acted in any other way would, to these men, have constituted a violation of conscience such as they could not for a moment contemplate. That they were prepared to suffer for conscience' sake, some of them had already had occasion to demonstrate. Thomas and Lake were old men, and death claimed them before any further sacrifice could be asked of them; but had they lived they would undoubtedly have gone out into the wilderness with Sancroft, Ken, and the other Non-jurors. Meanwhile, their deathbed testimonies to the truth as they saw it not only fortified those whose views were of a similar trend, but were at the same time regarded as a reproach to those who found themselves able to take the oath to William and Mary. The immediate consequence was a spate of pamphlets, letters, sermons, avowals, and defences from pulpit, press, and private pens. Once more, bitter controversy on a matter of highest principle threatened the somewhat tenuous unity of Church and State alike.

So far as the bishops were concerned, Sancroft and Ken on the one hand and Tillotson and Burnet on the other, represent fairly and typically the two opposing viewpoints. Yet so far was the question from being a clear-cut issue, even at this late stage, that we find Burnet in a long letter accusing Ken of inconsistency and Ken, by way of reply, reminding Burnet that he (Burnet) had himself for many years been a staunch upholder of Passive Obedience and that his change of heart was of somewhat recent origin.

Burnet's letter to Ken seems to have arisen out of a curious case where a priest, preferred to a living in the diocese of

Bath and Wells, had applied to the Bishop of Salisbury for institution. This request Burnet, very properly, had refused, sending the applicant back to Ken so that his Chancellor might perform the office on his behalf. He goes on to express regret at Ken's attitude with regard to the oath, particularly as he has been informed that Ken had advised others to take it. What is more, he has heard of a pastoral letter which Ken was alleged to have prepared for circulation in his diocese urging the clergy to take the oath. The industrious Doctor seems to have spent a considerable amount of time listening to hearsay. With his characteristic sly maliciousness, he permits himself to observe: "Your Lordship, it seems, changed your mind there, which gave great advantages to those who were so severe as to say that there was some-what else than conscience at the bottom."

This uncharitable innuendo provoked Ken into what, for him, was a retort of surprising trenchancy. It is dated 5 October 1689.

My Lord,

I am obliged to your Lordship, for the continued concern you express for me, and for the kind freedom you are pleased to take with me; and though I have already in publick fully declared my mind to my Diocese concerning the Oath, to prevent my being misunderstood; yet, since you seem to expect it of me, I will give such an account, which, if it does not satisfy your Lordship, will at least satisfy myself. I dare assure you, *I never advised any one to take the Oath*; though some, who came to talk insidiously with me, may have raised such a report. So far have I been from it, that I never would administer it to any one person whom I was to collate. And therefore, before the Act took place, I gave a particular commission to my Chancellor, who himself did not scruple it; so that he was authorised, not only to institute, but also to collate in my stead. If any came to discourse with me about taking the Oath, I usually told them I durst not take it myself. I told them my reasons, if they urged me to it, and were of my own Diocese: and then remitted them to their study, and prayers for further directions.

'Tis true, having been scandalized at many persons of our own coat,[1] *who for several years together preached up passive-*

[1] I.e., of the clergy; the allusion, of course, is to Burnet himself.

obedience to a much greater height than ever I did, it being a subject with which I very rarely meddled, and on a sudden, without the least acknowledgment of their past error, preached and acted the quite contrary, I did prepare a pastoral letter, which, if I had seen reason to alter my judgment, I thought to have published; at least that part of it on which I laid the greatest stress, to justify my conduct to my flock: and before I went to London I told some of my friends that, if that proved true which was affirmed to us with all imaginable assurance ... it would be an inducement to me to comply; but when I came to town I found it was false; and without being influenced by anyone, or making any words of it, I burnt my paper and adhered to my former opinion.

If this is to be called change of mind, and a change so criminal that people who are very discerning and know my own heart better than myself have pronounced sentence upon me, that there is something else than conscience at the bottom—I am much afraid that some of those who censure me may be chargeable with more notorious charges than that; whether more conscientious or no, God only is the Judge.

If your Lordship gives credit to the many misrepresentations which are made of me, and which I being so used to can easily disregard, you may naturally enough be in pain for me; for to see one of your brethren throwing himself headlong into a wilful deprivation, not only of honour and of income, but of a good conscience also, are particulars out of which may be framed an idea very deplorable. But though I do daily in many things betray great infirmity, I thank God I cannot accuse myself of any insincerity, so that Deprivation will not reach my conscience, and I am in no pain at all for myself. . . .

I heartily join with your Lordship in your desires for the peace of this Church, and I shall conceive great hopes, that God will have compassion on her, *if I see that she compassionates and supports her sister of Scotland.* I beseech God to make you an instrument to promote that peace, and that charity, I myself can only contribute to both by my prayers and my deprecations against schism and against sacrilege.

> My Lord,
> Your Lordship's very faithful
> Servant and Brother,
> Tho: Bath and Wells

Ken's reference in this letter to the Church of England's "sister of Scotland" is a reminder of the sufferings which the bishops, priests, and faithful laity of the Episcopal Church—Non-jurors to a man—were suffering at the hands of the triumphant Presbyterians. Assured of William's support and approval, the latter had expelled the clergy of the south-western counties from their homes and parishes with violence, inflicting upon them every conceivable hardship, humiliation, and insult. It is to the plight of these persecuted brethren that Ken is drawing the attention of Burnet, but unfortunately in vain.

The report which Ken says might have been an inducement to him to comply with the oath was to the effect that King James had made over the Kingdom of Ireland to Louis XIV of France. Had this report proved true, it seems, Ken might have felt no longer bound by allegiance to a King capable of such an act of treachery. In fact, however, it turned out to be yet another of the canards propagated in such profusion by James's enemies, and so Ken was able, no doubt with considerable relief, to destroy the pastoral letter which he had prepared solely as a precaution.

In spite of the explanation and disavowals so forcibly expressed in the letter quoted above, Burnet continued to misrepresent Ken's motive and actions: "Ken was a man of a warm imagination;" he says,[1] "and at the time of the King's [William's] first landing he declared heartily for him, and advised all the Gentlemen that he saw to go and join him."

Burnet, whose sole purpose here is to discredit the action of the Non-jurors (and incidentally to justify his own equivocal conduct), offers no evidence to support these charges, which are utterly at variance with Ken's behaviour when the invader's army was approaching Wells, and indeed with his whole course of action then and subseqently. Burnet's malicious mis-statements do not end here. Concerning the Convention debates on a Regency he writes:

[1]*History of My Own Time.*

But during the debates in the Convention, Ken went with great heat into the notion of a Prince Regent. And now, upon the call of the House, he withdrew unto his diocese. He changed his mind again, and wrote a paper persuading the Clergy to take the Oaths, which he showed to Dr Whitby, who read it, as the Doctor has told me often. His Chaplain, Dr Eyre, did also tell me that he came with him to London, where at first he owned that he was resolved to go to the House of Lords, and to take the Oaths; but the first day after he came to town he was prevailed on to change his mind: and he has continued ever since in a very warm opposition to the Government.[1]

Thus, by a judicious and unscrupulous blend of *suppressio veri* and *suggestio falsi*, Burnet of the uneasy conscience sought to impugn for posterity the motives of one whose self-sacrificing constancy was a continual reproach to his own elasticity of conduct. So might Pliable have blackened Mr Standfast to distract attention from his own shortcomings. The truth of the matter is, of course, that Ken had no hand whatever in bringing over the Prince of Orange, that he took no part in welcoming him, that he was all along opposed to the idea of offering him the crown. As for the Oath of Allegiance, his approach is entirely reasonable and consistent. His instincts are all against taking it, as were those of most men brought up to believe in a doctrine of Divine Right. The idea of Parliament hawking around the crown was abhorrent to him, particularly so long as the King was still alive. They had no more right, in his view, to offer the throne to William of Orange than they had to offer Ken's bishopric to, say, Burnet.

Yet, for good or ill, and irrespective of the means employed to bring it about, Ken and those who thought with him were compelled to recognize that William was *de facto* King. In certain circumstances it might be, not merely permissible, but a positive duty to accept the *fait accompli* and acknowledge an unlawful but *de facto* ruler as the lesser of two evils; the greater evil being the chaos and peril which

[1] Ibid.

might threaten the national life with no recognizable leader at the head of affairs.

What the Non-jurors, and indeed everyone else, had to decide was whether the existing circumstances were such as to justify such an acceptance and acknowledgement. It may have been possible for one so certain of his own rightness as Burnet to make up his mind in advance, as it were; it is not surprising if others less self-assured, and of perhaps greater moral sensitivity, took longer to reach a decision on this matter of supreme moment; and only in fact did so after profound consideration, the final dispelling of agonizing doubts, and ultimate and enduring distress of spirit. Had they approached the problem in any less sober and thorough-going way they would undoubtedly have incurred the reproach of frivolity and irresponsibility.

Ken's own hesitations and willingness to consider and reconsider the question from every viewpoint—as also his respect for the opinions of others, even when they ran clearly contrary to his own—are illustrated by what took place when he was staying at Lambeth Rectory with his old friend Hooper. The latter had already taken the oath to William and tried hard to convince Ken that he ought to do the same, employing in the process his not inconsiderable persuasive powers. "On parting one night to go to bed," we are told by Hooper's biographer, "the Bishop seemed so well satisfied with the arguments Dr Hooper urged to him, that he was inclined to take the Oaths."

The next morning, however, Ken greeted his host by remarking, "I question not but that you and several others have taken the Oaths with as good a conscience as I myself shall refuse them; and sometimes you have almost persuaded me to comply by the arguments you have used; but I beg you to urge them no further; for should I be persuaded to comply, and after see reason to repent, you would make me the most miserable man in the world."

There is no trace here of any harsh, unbending rigorism,

12

of arrogance, or self-complacency; no refusal to hear and consider an opposing point of view; no want of respect for the conscientiously reached position of others. Nor was Hooper any less tolerant and understanding. Seeing that his friend had reached a decision from which no further argument could more than momentarily detach him, he promised that he would mention the subject no more. The two men remained friends for life, each recognizing and respecting the deep sincerity of the other's convictions.

Another of Ken's old friends, Bishop Turner of Ely, seems to have feared the persuasive effect of Hooper's arguments. In a letter to Sancroft, headed "Ascension Day", he writes:

"I must needs say the sooner we meet our brother of B. and W. the better: for I must no longer in duty conceal it from your Grace (though I beseech you to keep it in terms of a secret), that this very good man is, I fear, warping from us and the true interest of the Church, towards a compliance with the new Government.... I apprehend your Parson of Lambeth has superfined upon our Brother of B. and W., and if he lodges again at his house, I doubt the consequence, for which reason I'll come over on Saturday morning, to invite him to my country house.

May it please your Grace, I am your Grace's most obliged and most obedient Servant,

Francis Ely

Turner need not have so distressed himself on this score. Ken's convictions were proof against all that the worthy Hooper could put forward as arguments for taking the oaths. Nevertheless, there seems to have been a general feeling, quite unfounded, that Ken intended doing so for we find, about the same time, another friend writing to remonstrate against such a course of action. This was the learned Henry Dodwell, Camden Professor of History at Oxford, a man of vast erudition and orotund literary style. He expresses his alarm at the rumours he has heard of his friend's impending apostasy and reproaches him in somewhat grandiloquent terms. Ken in reply, is surprised at Dodwell's readiness to

believe such rumours and suggests that he (Dodwell) ought
first to have inquired if there was any truth in them. This
provoked from the Professor a further letter so overwhelming
in its length, sonority, rhetorical profusion, and redundancy,
that it seems likely Ken had no heart left in him to continue
the correspondence. In any case, like Turner and the others,
Dodwell was battering at an open door. Ken was certain,
beyond all doubt, where the path of duty lay for him, and
nothing remained for him to do but to await with calmness
the inevitable outcome.

Although there was nothing more that he himself could
do, certain efforts were made on his behalf by others. As the
days of grace drew towards their completion, the people of
his diocese grew daily more distressed at the thought of losing
him. His inherent goodness, his mildness of disposition, and
untiring zeal for their welfare, had endeared him to all who
knew him and to a great many who did not. As so frequently
happens, this widespread affection only began to find expression when they were faced with the rapidly approaching
prospect of his departure.

The clergy of the diocese organized an earnest petition on
his behalf, and on behalf of all the other prelates and priests
who found themselves under a similar stress of conscience,
though it is doubtful if it was ever presented. In any case it
was now too late for anything to be done to check the march
of events. The Whig-dominated Government insisted that
the Act must be put into operation, a decision which was
hastened by the discovery of real or pretended plots to overthrow the régime, in which some of the Non-jurors were
believed to be implicated. Further delay was out of the
question and in the middle of April 1691, those bishops who
had not taken the oath were formally and finally deprived.

Steps were at once taken to appoint their successors, the
Queen, in her husband's absence in Holland, signing the
congé d'élire. Tillotson was appointed Archbishop of
Canterbury in place of Sancroft, Patrick was translated to

Chichester, Fowler succeeded Frampton at Gloucester, while Beveridge was nominated for the bishopric of Bath and Wells. The latter was a High Churchman of similar outlook to Ken himself, and though he had no scruples about taking the oath he was genuinely distressed at the thought of supplanting so pious and revered a prelate as Ken. He went to Sancroft to seek his counsel and was strongly advised to "say *Nolo*, and say it from the heart". To the general surprise, perhaps even to Sancroft's, Beveridge took the advice and declined the bishopric which, after three more weeks had elapsed, was offered to one Richard Kidder, Rector of St Paul's, Covent Garden, who accepted it. His consecration, and that of the other new bishops, took place at Bow Church on 30 August 1691.

Nothing now remained for Ken but to take his departure from Wells with a good grace, but not without a solemn protest, publicly made from his episcopal throne in the Cathedral, at the uncanonical manner of his deprivation. This was probably his last appearance as diocesan bishop in the Mother Church of the see which he had served so faithfully for six eventful years. There would be moving farewells to be said, of which no record has come down to us; partings from the Cathedral clergy with whom he had lived and worked on terms of warmest friendship; from the children he had baptized and catechized and confirmed, and to whom he had administered First Communion; from the poor and humble folk who had been guests at his table, Sunday by Sunday throughout the year.

His active episcopate was over; so short in point of actual years, yet so full of events of deepest consequence to the present and future of the English Church and nation. He had played his part and done his duty according to the light as he saw it. His reward, in a worldly sense, was loss of ecclesiastical office, employment, home, income, and the prominent place he had occupied for so many years on the stage of public affairs. Although he had twenty years of life

still before him, never again was he to hold any office or perform any function, ecclesiastical or civil. Ken and his fellow
Non-jurors went out, not accepting deliverance and not
knowing whither they went. Their world was not worthy of
them.

14

EXILE

THE "Glorious Revolution" was complete. William and Mary were declared King and Queen of England, and the measures of the "Convention Parliament" were endorsed by a more regularly constituted Assembly. Every attempt was made to give what was done an air of legality, yet in spite of everything it was indeed a revolution that had taken place and revolutions are not made by over-nice considerations of what is strictly lawful and what is not. Those who brought it to pass, as well as those who benefited by it, could claim the sanction of a necessity above and beyond the letter of the law, and given the circumstances, fears, and prejudices of the time, they were no doubt justified in doing so. If any further justification were needed, they could always subsequently point to the comparative internal stability and peace, as well as to the steadily increasing prosperity, enjoyed by the country in the years immediately after the revolution. The decade which followed it saw the foundation of the Bank of England, the launching of the National Debt, the formation of the East India Company, the beginnings of marine insurance at Lloyd's coffee house in London and the publication of Isaac Newton's *Principia*. Locke's *Treatise on Civil Government* had already appeared in 1689, the year of Revolution itself, and his *Essay on Human Understanding* in the following year. Thus the Revolution was fortified by the fruits of material success and the more shadowy support of a philosophical basis. A few years later still, it was to receive the military endorsement of Marlborough's victories and the posthumous triumph of William's single-minded foreign policy.

Meanwhile the Church of England had been deprived of nine of her bishops, over four hundred of her parochial clergy, and, in sympathetic support, the active allegiance of a small but influential section of her faithful laity. The bishops who found themselves unable to take the oaths included five of the seven who went to the Tower for their resistance to King James—Sancroft, Ken, Lake, Turner, and White. The other four were Cartwright, Frampton, Lloyd (of Norwich), and Thomas.[1] One Irish bishop (Sheridan of Kilmore), all the Scottish bishops, and practically the whole of the Scottish clergy followed their example. A lamentable, though perhaps inevitable, consequence of the Scottish clergy's attachment to their oath to King James, was the disestablishment of the Church, the intrusion of Presbyterian ministers into the vacant livings, and the ratification by William and the Scottish Parliament of the Westminster Confession (a Calvinistic statement of doctrine) and the setting up by the secular power of a Presbyterian system of religious worship and organization. The Highlands, it is true, made a brief but spirited resistance to the Revolution, led by the redoubtable James Graham of Claverhouse—"Bonnie Dundee" to his friends; "Bloody Clavers" to his Presbyterian foes. They won a resounding victory over William's forces at Killiecrankie, but Dundee himself fell slain in the moment of triumph, his army partially disintegrated, and a few weeks later the remnant was routed by the Covenanting Cameronians at Dunkeld. Calvinism was triumphant and speedily established; the Episcopal Church reduced to the status of a persecuted, Jacobite minority—albeit a large, and for a long time to come, an important one.

A contributory cause of the Scottish Church's sad eclipse

---

[1] Lake, Cartwright, and Thomas died before their actual deprivation could take effect.

and martyrdom was the fact that none of her bishops found himself able to take the oath to William, and so none remained to continue the principle of episcopacy. The Church of England was probably saved from a similar fate, not by the bishops who refused the oath, but by those who took it and remained at their posts. This is clear enough to us now; it was far from obvious to the Non-jurors or even, perhaps, to their conforming brethren. The new régime had not yet had time to prove its stability; it was by no means universally popular throughout the three kingdoms; and a Stuart counter-revolution and restoration was always a distinct possibility—though diminishing, after the Battle of the Boyne, the fall of Limerick, and the failure of King James's attempt to establish a bridgehead in Ireland for the reconquest of England and Scotland.

Those who refused allegiance to William and Mary, therefore, can be blamed only in retrospect for failing to see, as a logical outcome of their action, the disastrous situation which could have arisen had all their episcopal brethren been like-minded with them. They were too close in time to the confused and confusing trend of events to view them with the detachment and perspective which are possible to us. That their motives were utterly sincere and disinterested is beyond dispute. Men do not willingly abandon high office, homes, emoluments, careers, and prospects for a cause in which they have no profound belief. Their course was dictated by their consciences. There they stood; they could no other. Yet it cannot be denied that their going out from her fellowship and service immeasurably weakened the English Church, and left the field open to those Latitudinarian influences which were so sorely to diminish her spiritual potency and prestige in the ensuing century.

Of the Non-juring bishops, Sancroft, surprisingly, showed himself the least amenable to the sentence of deprivation. Whereas most of his colleagues contented themselves with a restrained and formal protest and then withdrew, as it were, in good order, the Archbishop exhibited a sudden and spirited recalcitrance. He had made up his mind he would not quit Lambeth until he was compelled to do so, and he proved a remarkably difficult man to shift. A letter of his to Bishop Lloyd of Norwich, dated 24 May 1691, shows him still firmly entrenched in Lambeth Palace and determined to remain in occupation till the last possible moment.

My deare Brother,
    It is very true I have been twice summoned to make way for the consecration of J.T. [Tillotson] here upon Whitsunday.... The sum of my answer was, that the warning was too short; that they might, if they thought good, turn me into the street by force; but that I could not be ready by that time to remove. I have been very busy, since I was warned hence, to put my *impedimenta* in order to an Ejectment or a Remove, and have made some pro gress in it; but it happens very well, that I had, before I heard from you, forbidden the workmen to come to-morrow; so that you will come most seasonably. In the interim, and ever, God keep you under his protection.
                              Yours in all love, W.C.

Even when he finally quitted Lambeth, on 23 June 1691, Sancroft left his Steward in occupation, with orders to stay put until the Under-Sheriff arrived to evict him. The Archbishop himself retired to his native village of Fressingfield in Suffolk, where he remained in peaceful seclusion until his death in November 1693.

Ken, at the time of his deprivation, was still only 54 years of age, and in the normal course of events would have had another fifteen to twenty years of active ministry before him. His immediate problem was where to live and how to occupy his time, now that he had, in good conscience, disqualified himself from serving the Church he loved so dearly and had adorned for so long. Here an old friend came to his rescue, his one-time fellow undergraduate Thomas Thynne, now Lord Weymouth. A devout Churchman, he and Ken had kept their long-standing friendship in good repair, and though one was a Non-juror and the other was not this caused no rift between them. Nor did it hinder Lord Weymouth from now offering his friend a permanent home at his noble country mansion of Longleat, midway between Frome and Warminster; an offer which Ken gratefully accepted.

Longleat, one of the great historic houses of England and now the seat of Lord Weymouth's direct descendant, the Marquess of Bath, was built for Sir John Thynne between 1558 and 1580 on the site of the ancient priory of St Radegunde. Macaulay refers to it as "the most magnificent country house in England", although, of course, in Ken's time it was a much smaller building. Many subsequent occupants enlarged the house and added to the grounds and outbuildings. "Capability" Brown himself, towards the end of the eighteenth century, replanned the gardens and provided a chain of ornamental lakes.

A suite of rooms on the second floor was placed at Ken's disposal, and here he housed the library of over a thousand books which he had brought with him from Wells; here he lived and prayed and worked for the remaining twenty years of his life. His other possessions he sold on leaving his episcopal palace, and these realized just over £700. To relieve him from any feeling of dependence, Weymouth suggested that Ken should hand him this sum of money, in return for which he would receive an annuity of £80. This, worth many times its modern value, provided for Ken's modest material needs, and removed from him all financial anxiety for the future.

It is difficult to see what else Ken could have done. Other deprived clergymen were able to find employment as private tutors, schoolmasters, or domestic chaplains in noblemen's households. Such employment, however, would have seemed unsuitable for one of Ken's distinction; one who was still regarded by many as the lawful Bishop of Bath and Wells. In the event of a Stuart restoration within his own lifetime, he would be required to resume his episcopate, perhaps to succeed to the primacy.

Meanwhile, thanks to Lord Weymouth's liberal hospitality, retirement with dignity was, not merely possible, but the most desirable immediate solution to Ken's problem. At the same time, it is sad to think of his outstanding gifts as preacher, teacher, spiritual director, and shepherd of souls being no longer available to more than a narrow circle of his Non-juring friends, and that the English Church should have suffered the loss of his fearless leadership, his penetrating judgement, his invariably wise counsel and general steadying influence, at such a decisive period in the national life. There is a strong temptation to exclaim, "The pity of it"; to demand impatiently, "To what purpose is this waste?"

Yet such impatience may well be misplaced. However mistaken the twentieth century may adjudge to be the motives which led the Non-jurors into the wilderness of privation, obscurity, and neglect, it may well pay the passing tribute of a sigh in deference to men who had the courage of their convictions, and who were prepared to face whatever might come their way of hardship, suspicion, and material loss. Is it too fanciful to suppose that by their example they may even have done more to inspire others than if they had remained securely in possession of their parishes and bishoprics? It is obvious that such a question transports us into the realm of the imponderables; that it can be asked at all is a salutary warning against over-hasty blame or lamentation.

Mention has already been made of the library which Ken brought with him to Longleat after his departure from Wells. These books, which he consistently refused to sell (though he gave many away to friends), were to be, next to his religion, the supreme consolation of his remaining years. He was that most fortunate of men, one to whom loneliness and exclusion from worldly affairs mean little so long as there are books around him. Ken was to live much with his books during the long, comparatively uneventful years at Longleat. He was not perhaps a scholar of the first rank as was, for example, his friend Hooper. Yet his learning was far from contemptible, the range of his reading was wide even for that age of scholarly divines, and he retained the tastes and instincts of a student to the end of his life.

Dean Plumptre, in his two-volume *Life of Ken*, has listed many of the authors whose works are to be found among the Bishop's books at Longleat and in the cathedral library at Wells. He begins by drawing attention to some of the more prominent, and therefore surprising, absentees. Shakespeare is not there, the Dean tells us; nor are Spenser, Bunyan, Dryden, Cowley, or the Elizabethan and Stuart dramatists. Amongst theological writers, we should look in vain for the works of the German and English Reformers—Luther, Calvin, Melanchthon, Tyndale, Cranmer, Latimer, Ridley, and the rest. The Puritan divines likewise find no place, and even the Anglo-Catholic scholars of the generation immediately before Ken's own are somewhat sparsely represented.

Classical authors appear in greater force, and though Homer, Herodotus, Demosthenes, and Aeschylus are not represented on his shelves, most of the other great names— Greek and Latin—are to be found there: Aristophanes, Sophocles, Euripides, Thucydides, Isocrates, Epictetus, Sappho, Theophrastus to uphold the glory that was Hellas; Horace, Livy, Ovid, Tacitus, Virgil, Juvenal, Cicero, Catullus, Petronius, Justin, Lucan, Martial, Terence, Plautus, and Pliny to reflect Rome's literary grandeur. In addition to Hebrew and Arabic books, the works of the Fathers fill many shelves, as we should expect in the library of a seventeenth-century Anglican bishop. Here are Athanasius, Athenagoras, Barnabas, Clement of Alexandria, Cyril of Jerusalem, Eusebius, Epiphanius, Justin Martyr, Gregory Nazianzen, Gregory of Nyssa, Origen, Dionysius the Areopagite, Ambrose, Augustine, Bernard, Jerome, Gregory, Hilary of Tours, Lactantius, Tertullian, Isidore of Seville, and Vincent of Lerins. The *Sententiae* of Peter Lombard and the *Summa Theologica* of St Thomas Aquinas represent the medieval Schoolmen.

Ken had collected a surprising (in the light of his anti-papalism) number of books by Romanist writers. Few of them, however, are of a didactic or controversial kind. What did appeal to him about the Church of Rome (as to many another convinced and completely loyal Anglican), was that Church's historic ritual, and the wealth of her ascetic and mystical theology. There are many Roman Catholic writings belonging to one or other of these categories in Ken's collection, and here it must suffice to mention as typical such famous works as the Life of *St Ignatius Loyola*, Molinos' *Spiritual Guide*, the works of Thomas à Kempis, the *Devout Life* and the *Love of God* of St Francis de Sales, and Rossignol's *Disciplina Christianae Perfectionis*. There are also copies of the Decrees of the Council of Trent, of Bossuet's *Doctrinae Christianae Expositio*, as well as of the Roman Missal and Breviary, Mabillon's *Liturgia Gallica*, the *Horae Diurnae*, and the *Rituale Romanum*. To Bath Abbey Ken left a remarkable collection of books by Spanish authors. Contemporary or near-contemporary writers whose works he had acquired included Sanderson, Sancroft, Thorndike, Cosin, Pearson, Boyle, Jeremy Taylor, Hobbes, Toland, Dodwell, and Field. In this group, too, it is interesting to notice that there were three of the works of Gilbert Burnet— a *Vindication of the Revolution*, *The Rights of Princes* and *Deaths of the Primitive Persecutors*—as well as a book *On the Pentateuch* by Ken's successor at Wells, Richard Kidder.

English literature outside the range of religious writing is, as we have already noted, somewhat sparsely represented among Ken's books, and is almost entirely confined to the poetical works of Milton, Crashaw, Herbert, and Donne. There are, however, many works of history, among them the *Chronicles* of Speed, Hollished, and Froissart respectively, Bede's *Ecclesiastical History*, Ussher's *Brittanicae Ecclesiae Antiquitates*, and Buchanan's *Rerum Scoticarum Historia*.

Such was the substance upon which the mind of Ken was nourished during the years of enforced retirement and obscurity. It is perhaps strange that with so much of other men's thoughts to stimulate him he produced no major literary work of his own. His writing during this final period of his life seems to have been mainly confined to the composition of verse, for which he had a certain facility but no outstanding talent. Apart from his morning, midnight, and evening hymns, hallowed and esteemed through long familiarity and usage, his verses have achieved no immortality, though there is evidence that he himself felt that they had a certain merit. It is true that he wrote very largely to take his mind off the controversial issues of the day and his own conflicting emotions occasioned by them,[1] and not for immediate publication. Yet it is clear from the care with which Ken preserved them that he had some hope of their posthumous public appearance.

Ken's principal product in verse is the lengthy epic *Edmund*, written in a manner faintly reminiscent, now of Abraham Cowley, now (and far more faintly) of Milton's *Paradise Lost*. The poem, based on the life and death of the East Anglian Prince who suffered martyrdom at the hands of the Danes in the year 870, is of interest mainly because of the partly autobiographical character of certain of its passages and the expression which can be detected therein of some of Ken's views on matters political or religious. *Edmund* itself has received little approbation from Ken's sundry biographers, and there is little enough that can be said in its favour. It was fashioned in the artificial style then in vogue—a style which when employed by a Cowley, a Dryden, an Addison, or a Pope was capable of exhibiting polish, grace, and wit sufficient to charm the reader into forgetting the stilted mannerisms, the allusiveness, and the excessive use of personification; in the hands of less skilful practitioners its effect could be pedestrian and banal to a degree.

[1]One group of his poems bears the title of *Anodynes, or Alleviations of Pain*.

Perhaps the fairest appraisal of Ken as a versifier is that
of one who, himself no mean poet, admired without reserve
the heroism and holiness which marked Ken's life. John
Keble, author of *The Christian Year*, sometime Professor of
Poetry in the University of Oxford, and one of the founding
fathers of the nineteenth-century Catholic Revival, wrote of
the man whose ecclesiastical and theological opinions he
shared:

We shall hardly find, in all Ecclesiastical history, a greener
spot than the later years of this courageous and affectionate
Pastor; persecuted alternately by both parties, and driven from
his station in his declining age; yet singing on with unabated
cheerfulness to the last. Whoever in earnest loves his three well-
known Hymns, and knows how to value such unaffected strains
of poetical devotion, will find his account in turning over his
four volumes, half narrative, and half lyric, and all avowedly on
sacred subjects; the narrative often cumbrous, and the lyric
verse not seldom languid and redundant; yet all breathing such
an angelic spirit, interspersed with such pure and bright touches
of poetry, that such a reader as we have supposed will scarcely
find it in his heart to criticize them.[1]

Perhaps we do well to echo this charitable judgement
passed by one saintly man upon another, and content ourselves with observing that, while as a maker of verse Ken
undoubtedly had his moments, his greatest achievements
and claims upon the veneration of posterity do not lie within
the rarefied realms of Poesy.

It is not to be thought that he spent the whole of his remaining years in virtual seclusion at Longleat, alone with his
books and his versifying. He was not yet, as we shall see,
entirely finished with the world of public affairs nor did he
intend that his retirement should turn him into a recluse.
Furthermore, grateful and devoted as he was to his friend
and benefactor, Lord Weymouth, there may well have been
times when he felt his position acutely as a permanent lodger
in another man's house and, out of consideration to his host

[1]*Quarterly Review*, Vol. XXXII, p. 230.

as well as to his own self-respect, was ready to absent himself awhile from the felicity of Longleat.

There were other houses where the homeless Bishop was a welcome and honoured guest. A few miles away, at Poulshot in Wiltshire, his nephew, Izaak Walton junior, was Rector, and, as we have seen when William's army was approaching Wells, Ken was at least an occasional and more probably a frequent visitor there. Visits were also paid from time to time to London, to his beloved Winchester, to Bath, in order to take the waters, and to the hot springs at Clifton for a similar purpose. On his journeys to the two last-named places he sometimes spent a night with a certain Colonel Phillips; at Winchester he stayed with the Headmaster, Dr Cheyney, who had once been his chaplain. Other houses which were open to him were those of a Mr Cherry at Shottesbrook, of Mrs Thynne[1] at Lewesdon near Sherborne, of Archdeacon Sandys, and of the Misses Kemeys at Naish House near Portishead. These last were two maiden ladies, of great piety and generosity, to whom Ken acted as a kind of spiritual director, and beneath whose hospitable roof he found refuge and tranquillity when Lord Weymouth was away from Longleat, as well as at Christmas when he found the festivities and fashionable assemblage of guests at the great house more than he could adapt himself to with any degree of contentment.

[1] Lord Weymouth's widowed daughter-in-law.

15

THE NON-JURORS

EVEN AFTER they had been deprived, the more extreme Non-juring bishops considered themselves to be the only legitimate holders of the sees from which they were ejected, and, consequently, that they were entitled to the obedience of the clergy of those dioceses. The prelates who had replaced them were regarded as intruders and schismatics. They, the Non-jurors, were the true Catholic Church of the country, the faithful remnant who alone had not bowed the knee to the usurping Baal.

To those of them who thought thus, it became increasingly important that the apostolical succession of "true" (i.e., Non-juring) bishops should be carried on. Sancroft began to fail rapidly in health and vigour after his deprivation, and on 9 February 1692, he delegated all his archiepiscopal powers to Lloyd, formerly Bishop of Norwich. In the following year it was decided that, in view of the fewness and age of the surviving Non-juring bishops, others should be consecrated to continue the line. This decision led to a split within the ranks of the body. Frampton strongly disapproved and would have nothing to do with it; Ken, a moderate like Frampton, disliked the idea and only with reluctance gave it his sanction.

The extremists did what they could to lend their proceedings an air of legality. As no sort of election was possible they were forced to fall back on an Act of Henry VIII, which made provision for the appointment and consecration of

13

suffragan bishops by the King and Primate acting together. A list of suitable candidates was drawn up and Dr Hickes, the former Dean of Worcester, was despatched to St Germains, in May 1693, to seek King James's approval. It is said that the exiled monarch treated even this ardent loyalist with studied and insulting neglect, keeping him waiting in ante-rooms for weeks on end while he, the King, consulted first the French bishops and finally the Papal Curia about the course he should pursue.

Evidently their verdict was favourable, for at length His Majesty was graciously pleased to approve the Non-jurors' plan, and from the submitted list of names selected those of Hickes himself and of Thomas Wagstaffe, lately Prebendary and Chancellor of Lichfield. These two men were consecrated with great secrecy by Lloyd, Turner, and White, on 24 February 1694—Hickes as Suffragan Bishop of Thetford and Wagstaffe as Suffragan Bishop of Ipswich.

George Hickes was a man of prodigious learning; an acknowledged authority on the Anglo-Saxon and Icelandic languages, as well as an accomplished theologian and patristic scholar. He had been sent down from Oxford, in 1659, on account of his openly flaunted Royalism. In 1684 he had been offered, but had refused, the bishopric of Bristol. When, after his refusal of the oath to William and Mary, he was deprived of his deanery, he fastened with his own hands a strong protest to the gates leading into the cathedral choir, a demonstration which made it necessary for him to go into hiding for some considerable time. After Bishop Lloyd's death in 1709, Hickes became the acknowledged leader of the Non-juring body, to whom he was affectionately known as "the good Father Hickes". He died in 1715, the year of the first Jacobite rebellion, and was buried in St Margaret's church, Westminster.

Wagstaffe, before his ordination, had studied medicine, and after he was deprived of his benefices he supported himself by practising as a physician, but "still wearing", we are told, "his canonical habit". He was with Sancroft when that good old man died, and wrote a moving account of his passing. His second son, Thomas, was ordained as a Non-juring priest and lived much of his life at Rome, where he became Anglican chaplain to the "Old Chevalier" (*de jure* James III), a devout Roman Catholic, and subsequently to that Prince's son, Charles Edward—a rather less devoted one.

It was perhaps because of these clandestine consecrations that the Non-jurors, for the next few years, were under suspicion of plotting with other known Jacobites to overthrow the régime. As early as the spring of 1691 a conspiracy to this end had been unmasked by Government agents, who had arrested at Tilbury three men travelling as envoys to the Court of St Germains on behalf of a numerous and influential group of London Jacobites. Amongst the documents seized from them were various letters to the exiled King over the water, one of which bore the signature of Ken's sometime school-fellow, Francis Turner, the deprived Bishop of Ely. It was addressed to James and his Queen under the pseudonym of "Mr and Mrs Ridding", and was full of expressions of loyalty and of devotion to their cause. As Turner professed to be writing not in his own name only, but also "on behalf of my elder brother, and the rest of my nearest relations", this was taken to imply that Sancroft and the other Non-juring bishops were, if not implicated in the plot, at least privy to it. A strict surveillance was placed upon them for a time, while a warrant was actually issued for Turner's arrest. This he avoided by escaping abroad in disguise.

The other bishops, who almost certainly knew nothing whatever of the plot until it was unmasked, were in considerable danger of apprehension, and were reduced to writing to each other under assumed names. Ken, for example, communicated with Bishop Lloyd by addressing his letters to "Mrs Hannah Lloyd", while his own correspondence was directed to "Mr Jones". Poor Turner, whose ill-considered dabblings in conspiracy must have been a source of deep sorrow to his lifelong friend, was compelled to spend the rest of his life with the threat of seizure hanging over him; a virtual fugitive, with continual recourse to assumed names and continually changing disguises. He died in 1700 on All Souls' Day, and was buried beside his wife at Therfield, the single word *Expergiscar*[1] being inscribed upon his tomb. Ken, writing of him four years later, refers to him as "our brother of Ely, now with God".

These disturbing events, tended not only to bring the Non-jurors under the suspicion of seditious activities, but also served to accentuate the growing cleavage in their own ranks. To moderate-minded men like Ken, Frampton, Kettlewell, Dodwell,[2] and the charitable layman Robert Nelson, the attitude of the extremists became increasingly distasteful. They deprecated any course of action which tended to perpetuate the schism, and Frampton and Ken in particular were anxious to find some means of ending it. Writing to Bishop Lloyd some years after the consecration of Hickes and Wagstaffe, we find Ken remarking: "I am willing to allow all degrees of excusability to those who are of a different persuasion from myself, in the business of clandestine Consecrations, against which you know I always declared my judgment. I foresaw it would perpetuate the schism, which I daily deplore: . . . but I was forced at last to tolerate what I could not approve of."

To Hickes he writes, concerning the schism: "I need not tell you what pernicious consequences it may produce, and I fear has produced already; what advantage it yields to our enemies, what irreligion the abandoning of the public assemblies [i.e., the Church of England services] may cause in some, and what vexation it creates to tender consciences in the country, where they live banished from the House of God."

[1]"I shall awake."

[2]As we have seen, Dodwell had been as violent as anyone against taking the oaths, but the spectacle of the bishops' self-sacrifice seems to have mellowed his outlook.

It is not clear whether Ken himself attended the public services of the Church or not. There was always the difficulty of the State Prayers in which William and Mary would be mentioned and interceded for by name. It is more than probable that during William's lifetime Ken was content to attend only such services as he himself conducted in Lord Weymouth's private chapel at Longleat, or those conducted in private chapels and houses elsewhere by other Non-juring bishops or priests. After the accession of Anne it seems likely that he may have felt able to worship once more, at least on occasion, in the fellowship of the Church which he loved as a most devoted son and from which he had no desire to separate himself.

Archbishop Sancroft died in 1693, and his successor Tillotson in the following year. Within a few weeks of Tillotson's passing Queen Mary, who had grieved deeply over the Archbishop's death, herself caught smallpox and died, on 28 December 1694, at the early age of 32. Her funeral oration was preached by the new Archbishop, Tenison, and was immediately the cause of no small stir.

Mary's comparatively brief life had scarcely been a happy one. Brought up for reasons of state in a religion to which neither her father nor her step-mother subscribed; married, again for reasons of policy, to a Prince whose religion also was not hers, and who was cold, austere, cynical, and unfaithful; poor Mary had small cause for cheerfulness and, dominated as she was by her masterful husband, one is not disposed to blame her over-much for her share, whatever it may have been, in her father's downfall and supercession. Many of the Non-jurors, however, adopted a more censorious attitude towards her.

Her behaviour towards her father savoured to them of heartlessness worthy of a Regan or a Goneril. They could not overlook the childish glee with which she took possession of the royal palace and apartments after the King's flight; nor could they pardon the want of affection and duty they considered she showed in permitting her father to live the rest of his life dependent upon the charity of Louis of France. Even Sancroft permitted himself an uncharacteristic dig at the "virtuous ladie" into whose private treasury went the confiscated revenues of the forfeited and unfilled bishoprics. It has been suggested, however, that the Archbishop may have intended here a sardonic reference to William's mistress, Elizabeth Villiers, whom the Queen on her death-bed begged the King to put away.[1]

Tenison's funeral sermon, being wholly adulatory, moved the Non-jurors to tremendous indignation, and some of their criticism found expression in privately printed and widely circulated pamphlets. One of these in particular, bearing the title, *A Letter to Dr Tenison on his Sermon preached at the Funeral of her late Majesty*, was generally attributed to Bishop Ken. The available evidence as to authorship is inconclusive. One of Ken's early biographers (Anderdon) thought it unlikely that Ken wrote the *Letter*, and quotes from a letter, written by Tenison to Evelyn and dated 20 April 1695, in support of his belief: "There is come forth an answer to it [the Funeral Sermon], said to be written by Bishop Ken; but I am not sure he is the author: I think he has more wit and less malice."

A later biographer, Dean Plumptre, inclines to the view that Ken did write the pamphlet and quotes, to offset the above remarks of Tenison, a manuscript, now in the Library at Lambeth, upon which is endorsed, "Dr Knighton's Answer to Kenn", and underneath, in Tenison's hand, "I would not have it published. T.C.". From the letter itself the Dean professed to find sufficient evidence to convince him of Ken's authorship, but whether he was correct or not in his conclusion, it is certain that the *Letter*'s publication did nothing either to diminish the religious tensions of the time or to endear further the Non-juring bishops and clergy to the King and his Ministers.

[1]Overcome with remorse, he did so—for a time!

A further opportunity for the Government to discredit the Non-jurors seemed to offer itself as a result of a suggestion made by Kettlewell in a letter to Bishop Lloyd written on 20 December 1694. In it he proposed that a fund should be started to relieve the dispossessed, and frequently distressed, Non-juring clergy: "When my Ld. Bp. of B. and Wells, in great charity and kindness was pleased last to call here, I was proposing to him the setting up of a Fund of Charity, for regular collection and distribution of the same among the poor suffering clergy."

Kettlewell went on to suggest that the bishops might send out a circular letter inviting contributions to such a fund, adding, after their respective signatures, the word "Suffering", "Displaced", "Ejected" or "Deprived". In conclusion, he says that a friend authorizes him to say that he will give £100 and collect as much more as he can. Although he himself did not live to see it put into operation, Kettlewell's suggestion met with a ready response from Lloyd and the others, and in the following July the appeal was issued. It bore the heading "The Charitable Recommendation of the Deprived Bishops", and was addressed "To all Christian people, to whom this Charitable Recommendation shall be presented. Grace be to you, and Peace from God the Father, and from our Lord Jesus Christ".

After outlining briefly the poverty and distress which existed amongst many of the deprived clergy and their families, the circular continues:

Now We, in compliance with their Intreaty, and with all due regard to their Suffering circumstances, have thought it our Duty (*as far as in law we may*) heartily to recommend their necessitous condition to all pious, good people; hoping and praying that they will take their cause into their serious consideration, and putting on the bowels of Charity, extend their Alms to them, and their needy families.

And we will not cease to pray for a Blessing upon such their Benefactors: and remain in all Christian Offices,

Yours

William, Bishop of Norwich ⎫
Robert, Bishop of Gloucester ⎪
Francis, Bishop of Ely ⎬ Now
Thomas, Bishop of Bath and Wells ⎪ Deprived
Thomas, Bishop of Peterborough ⎭

July 22nd, 1695

Two points in this appeal are worthy of note. It went out above the signatures of those who had been diocesan bishops and had suffered deprivation; neither Wagstaffe nor Hickes, the newly consecrated Suffragans, signed it. Secondly, the clause, "so far as in law we may": this was probably added on legal advice, to guard against the possibility of a prosecution on the grounds that the signatories were acting *ultra vires* or under false pretences.

For a time no notice was taken of the circular letter, except by those for whom it was intended. Kettlewell had died on 12 April 1695, at the early age of 42, fortified by the Holy Sacrament of the Altar administered to him by Bishop Lloyd. It was Ken, however, who officiated at his funeral in the parish church of All Hallows, Barking,[1] conducting both the Burial Office and Evensong, robed in his episcopal habit.

This, of course, tended once more to draw attention to those anomalous and highly inconvenient persons, the Non-juring bishops and priests. Then came the "Charitable Recommendation". Neither of these reminders, however, would have led to any official action had it not been for a plot, on the part of Sir John Friend, Sir William Perkins, and others, to assassinate William. Both of these men were condemned to death and were attended on the scaffold by one of the most prominent and able of the Non-juring priests, Jeremy Collier. Sir William Perkins was a penitent of Collier's, and the latter publicly absolved both of the condemned men before they died. This was taken by many people to imply condonation of the plot and Collier, sternly

[1] Where Archbishop Laud lies buried.

censured for his injudicious action by the two archbishops and most of their suffragans, narrowly escaped arrest.

This incident thoroughly alarmed the authorities, who were rapidly becoming confirmed in their view that Non-juror and Jacobite were practically synonymous terms. It was decided that action must be taken, and on 14 April 1696, warrants were issued by order of the Privy Council for the apprehension of all the bishops who had signed the "Charitable Recommendation", with the single exception of Frampton. For some strange reason his motives alone appear to have been regarded as above suspicion.

On 28 April Ken was called before the Privy Council for questioning. Once more his loyalty was being impugned; once more he found himself arraigned before a secular tribunal and required to clear himself of charges of a political character.

He was first asked whether he had subscribed to the charitable appeal, a copy of which was handed to him. He readily admitted that the document bore his signature. To further such a work, he said, was no more than an effort to fulfil the will of him who bade his followers feed the hungry, clothe the naked, tend the sick, and visit the captive. He trusted that he would not be blamed now for doing what at the Last Judgement he would be condemned for leaving undone.

No one, he was told in reply, would condemn charity, but the method by which it was proposed to procure it was illegal. To this Ken had an adequate answer. The promoters of the appeal had taken the precaution of obtaining legal advice, and they had received an assurance that what they had done was perfectly legal. Their position had been fully safeguarded by the clause which they had inserted in the "Recommendation"—"as far as in Law we may".

The inquisitors now decided that this line of approach had better be abandoned, and someone raised the objection that the money had been misused, that it had been given to immoral and undeserving persons and, in particular, to a cleric "who goes in a gown [i.e., a cassock] one day, and in a blue silk waistcoat another". To this somewhat frivolous complaint Ken replied that it might be mistaken to give money to an unworthy or undeserving person, but hardly criminal—unless given for him to use for some wrongful purpose. Even an unworthy man may be lacking the necessaries of life, and so long as God grants him space for repentance it is a Christian duty to help him support the life which he is permitted to retain. Ken went on to remind his interrogators that after the Monmouth rebellion he had tried to relieve the misery of as many of those who were imprisoned for their part in it as he was able. Many of these, he had no doubt, were unworthy and irreligious men, yet he had visited amongst them night and day, doing what he could to ease their sufferings and encouraging others to do likewise. King James, he added pointedly, had found no fault with him for so doing.

There seemed to be little purpose in pursuing this equally unprofitable line, so once more the court of inquiry reverted to the point of legality. Someone had discovered that the appeal had the nature of a "brief", an official publication which normally could be published only by persons able to claim some measure of royal authorization. For private persons to issue such briefs constituted an usurpation of the royal prerogative. This nice point of constitutional law Ken respectfully, and wisely, declined to contest. He might well have been worsted in such an argument, and if he were to be charged on such a technical point it would obviously be advisable that he should engage competent counsel to defend him.

Next it was alleged that in putting his name to the appeal Ken and the other signatories had usurped ecclesiastical jurisdiction. His rather acid rejoinder to this was that he had never heard that begging was a part of ecclesiastical jurisdiction. It was clear from the document that they (the signatories) were only beggars, a privilege which he trusted they might be permitted to retain. He had no doubt that their Lordships had received a good deal of strange and misleading information in connection with the appeal, but, having honestly and sincerely explained the part he had in it, he humbly submitted himself to their Lordships' justice. One request he would make. In view of the fact that he had answered the summons to appear before the Council, even before the warrant was served on him; and as he was in somewhat indifferent health, he begged that he might be permitted to return to his sister's house, there to await whatever might be their Lordships' pleasure. This not unreasonable request their Lordships were graciously pleased to grant.

The result of the examination was entirely satisfactory to Ken and the other bishops. No evidence of treasonable intent could be proved against them, and by an Order in Council dated 23 May 1696, they were released from custody. Once more, after enforced and unwelcome publicity, Ken was able to retire into the quiet obscurity of his life at Longleat.

Two years after this affair he lost by death yet another of the famous "Seven". Thomas White, deprived Bishop of Peterborough, died in May 1698. Since being ousted from his see he had lived quietly in London, emerging only to attend on the scaffold Sir John Fenwick, another of those tried and condemned for treason in January 1697. About the same time one of the oldest of Ken's friends, Lord Maynard, also passed away; followed shortly after by yet another, dearly loved by Ken, Dr John Fitzwilliam. One by one the men who had been the friends of his youth and of a lifetime were being taken from him, leaving him more and more alone with his memories of better and happier times. Fitzwilliam had appointed Ken as his executor and by the terms of his will had left him the life interest on a capital sum of £500, which sum was to revert at Ken's death to the Library of Magdalen College, Oxford. This kindly and timely legacy no doubt provided him with a little more money with which to practise the charitable pursuits in which his soul delighted. One feels that not the least of his sorrows occasioned by his reduced circumstances must have been the inability to do what he once had loved to do in the matter of entertaining and assisting the needy, whose necessities weighed so much more with him than their deserts, whose vices were forgotten in their woe.

The last decade but one of Ken's eventful existence closed with the deaths of the two men with whose lives and destiny his own had been so fatefully and inextricably interwoven. On 6 September 1701, at the Palace of St Germains, James II's sad, frustrated exile ended, as that unhappy and unfortunate monarch breathed his last. In startling contrast to his earlier looseness of life, his latter years had been passed in most exemplary piety. He had paid frequent visits to the monastery of La Trappe, sharing in the austerities practised there as a result of De Rance's reforming zeal. In his death-bed message James besought the pardon of all whom he might in any ways have injured. Was he, one wonders, thinking of Ken and others who had received so little kindness at his hands, and yet had demonstrated their loyalty to him at such remarkable personal cost? At the same time he forgave all the world; the Emperor who, he felt, had so basely deserted him in his time of need, despite their common religious faith; the Prince of Orange who had taken away his place and nation; his daughter Anne who, in his darkest hour, had driven away to join his foes. And so, dying better than he had lived, this figure of tragedy, this King without a throne, passed quietly from the scene of human affairs upon which he had played so controversial a part; leaving under the benevolent care of his good friend and benefactor, Louis XIV, the 13-year-old "James III" to continue his line and to provide a rallying point for Jacobite hopes and activities for half a century to come.

Six months later he was followed to the grave by the son-in-law who had not scrupled, in pursuit of his grand design, to take by threat of force the position and power which James had no longer the nerve to maintain. On 9 March 1702 William III died from the effects of a fall from his horse when it stumbled over a mole-hill as he was riding from Kensington to Hampton Court. "The little gentleman in black velvet" succeeded where so many clumsy, would-be assassins had failed, and thus earned his place in the remarkable assortment of Jacobite toasts.

William had never been successful in winning more than the respect of his English subjects, and not all of them even respected him. In Ireland after the Treaty of Limerick, and in the Scottish Highlands after the Massacre of Glencoe, his name was held in execration. It is doubtful if even the Covenanting Lowlanders, or the fanatical Ulstermen who held out so valorously for his cause in Londonderry, felt real affection for this aloof, unlikeable foreigner. It is equally doubtful whether he ever desired that they should. Although his mother was an English princess, his heart was in Holland —and no one can blame him for that. And although, at his own insistence, he was offered and accepted the English crown, it is only fair to say that this was purely in pursuit of his one unwavering purpose—the overthrow of Louis and the French hegemony of Europe—and never to satisfy personal ambition or a craving for power and glory.

His wider political aims were ultimately triumphant, though it was Marlborough who, playing Joshua to William's Moses, was to bring them to their final fruition. As a factor in English domestic politics it is not remarkable that William's touch was less certain, his influence less decisive, his interventions less successful. That certain long term benefits resulted from his reign cannot be denied, but it is not to William himself that we owe them. Nor can his influence upon the destinies of the English Church and her sister Church in Scotland be regarded as other than disastrous, though here again not all the blame must be laid at his door. An indifferent English monarch he may have been; but a great European statesman he undoubtedly was. In defence of the liberties and independence of small nations, in opposition to over-towering ambition and lust for power, he remained constant, fearless, and inflexible. He burned himself out in the cause to which he had dedicated his life until, at the early age of 52, such terrestrial matters ceased to concern him. Worn out and sick in mind and body, not even news from Holland of the successful progress of his latest diplomacy could draw from him more than the weary whisper, *"Je tire vers ma fin"*, and then he, too, passed within the sphere of a higher protocol.

It must have been with distinctly mixed emotions that Ken, in his retirement at Longleat and with ten years of his own life still before him, heard of the deaths of the two sovereigns whose conflicting aims, ambitions, and actions had led to the untimely curtailment of his own career. Whatever he may have thought or felt at the passing of two men to whom he owed no debt of gratitude, it cannot reasonably be doubted that for *de jure* and *de facto* monarch alike he offered up prayers to God for the rest and refreshment and salvation of their souls.

16

THE CLOSING YEARS

THE DEATHS of James and William, coming as they did within a few months of each other, might have led to an ending of the schism within the English Church. Many of the more moderate Non-jurors, Ken among them, would eagerly have grasped at any proffered olive branch put out by the authorities. The accession of the easy-going Anne, with her High Church background and preferences, encouraged the exiles to hope that some *rapprochement* might be attempted, some encouraging gesture made of a kind which could lead to their early reconciliation.

They were speedily and sharply disillusioned. With a lamentable lack of consideration and statesmanship, Parliament proceeded to pass by Statute a new oath in which all who held office were required, not merely to attest their loyalty to Queen Anne, but also to repudiate the rights of succession of her half-brother, the young Prince of Wales. This crass piece of legislation was only passed by narrow majorities and after strenuous opposition and protests on the part of some of the most influential of the peers, among them Lord Weymouth. Not only did the new oath close the door to any return of the Non-juring bishops and clergy to the active service of the Church, it in fact produced a fresh crop of secessions. Those who now felt impelled to leave the National Church became known as "Non-abjurors", on account of their refusal to abjure the rightful heir to the throne, as they conceived him to be—all of Anne's children having died in infancy.

To her credit it must be recorded that Anne herself did all she could to ease the unhappy situation. The Church of England was very dear to her, and it distressed her to contemplate its sundered state and to see it robbed of so many of its most able and learned men. Furthermore, amongst the deprived clergy she numbered some of her oldest and most esteemed friends. Soon after her accession the bishopric of Carlisle fell vacant and she conceived the plan of translating Bishop Kidder to the vacant see. This would have made Bath and Wells available for Ken to resume his interrupted episcopate, an arrangement which would have given great satisfaction to many, and not least to the Queen herself. It would also have deeply gratified Lord Weymouth, now a member of Her Majesty's Privy Council, who had been assiduously pressing upon his Sovereign the claims of his old friend and honoured guest.

To this proposition Kidder expressed himself as agreeable, but when it was put to Ken he gratefully but regretfully declined. No doubt the Abjuration Oath was more than he could swallow, but independently of this he was determined not to return to public life. Ambition had never burned strongly within him and now, approaching his three-score years and ten, he doubtless considered himself no longer capable of vigorously administering a mainly rural diocese. So Kidder stayed where he was—a fact of fatal consequence to himself—and one Nicolson was sent to Carlisle.

St Asaph was the next bishopric to fall vacant. Anne refrained from again attempting to lure a Non-juror back to the fold, but she did the next best thing by offering the see to Ken's old friend Hooper, already Dean of Canterbury. Although he had not felt conscientiously constrained to refuse the oath either to William or Anne, Hooper had been no subservient place-seeker, in spite of Burnet's characteristic description of him as "reserved, crafty and ambitious". Indeed for him to be so stigmatized by Burnet is a reasonably safe guarantee that he was none of these things. On the contrary, his biographer assures us, Hooper proved himself remarkable independent of thought and action, and utterly unconcerned with creating good impressions or with jockeying for high position after the prevalent fashion of the day. As an instance of his independence of mind, it is said that William had given orders that all who preached before the Princess Anne should refrain from bowing towards her as they began their sermon. Bowing had hitherto been the accepted custom, but the suspicious William feared that it might provide or suggest an outlet for the expression of feelings disaffected towards himself. But to Hooper the Princess, as daughter of the late King and next in succession to the throne, had the fullest claim upon his respect and he consistently disregarded the command which forbade him to show it.

Ken was delighted at his friend's elevation to the episcopate and in a letter to Lloyd, written from Poulshot and dated 30 October 1703, he describes Hooper as "one of the best understandings I ever knew [who] if he will exert himself, will do excellent service to this sinking Church".

In the same letter we are given a glimpse of the disabilities which now increasingly assailed him. He would, he says, regard it as "one of the best excursions I could make to pay you both a visit, but besides my aversion to the town [London], I am afflicted with such pains, that I am by no means fit for travelling—they are rheumatic, and lie within my joints, and never come to the extreme parts, and at this present my left arm is in a great measure disabled."

Ken seems to have grown closer to Lloyd in these latter years. The divergences of view which had tended to their estrangement now appeared of less significance in the face of their common and continued sojourning in the ecclesiastical wilderness. Letters passed frequently between the two men, those of Ken to Lloyd, still addressed for security to "Mrs

14

Hannah Lloyd", invariably being couched in terms of warmth and even of affection. In another communication, dated "Nov. 13th, 1703", we find Ken again writing to Lloyd with reference to Hooper's appointment.

You have a very true apprehension of your brother of St Asaph. He is of an excellent temper as well as understanding, and a man of sincerity though he may be of a different judgment;[1] and I much desire that you may often meet, and consult how to moderate things as much as may be, *salva veritate*, for I fear that many of our friends run too high, and that the Church of Rome will reap advantages of excesses in that kind.

One is almost tempted to look again at such a letter as this, to make certain that the date is not 1845, that it is not addressed to, say, Dr Pusey and signed by John Keble. *Plus ça change.* . . . Nearly a century and a half before the Oxford Movement it was necessary for the Catholic Ken, loyal to Anglican and Prayer Book principles, to appeal to his friend to use his influence in restraint of ill-considered extremism which might merely serve to pull Rome's chestnuts out of the fire for her.

It is clear from letters such as these of Ken's to Lloyd that, irrevocably divided though they might be over the question of the oaths, there was no sundering of old friendships, no irrevocable breach of courteous and kindly communication between at least the more moderate-minded Non-jurors and the less Erastian of their conforming brethren. They indicate, also, a mellowing of Lloyd's own attitude and a corresponding growth of confidence and fellow feeling on the part of Ken towards him. "Your letters," writes Ken, "are a great consolation to me in this solitude, and therefore I intreat the continuation of them."

Less than a month after Hooper's consecration and enthronement, there occurred the event which was to lead to important modifications in Ken's relationships with the National Church. On the night of 26 November 1703, the

[1] I.e., on the question of the oaths.

greater part of the country experienced a gale of unparalleled ferocity. Defoe vividly describes some of the results of this tornado, estimating that damage was done to the extent of some four million pounds sterling:

The loss is universal, and its extent general: not a house, not a family that had anything to lose, but have lost something. The sea, the land, the houses, the churches, the corn, the trees, the rivers, all have felt the fury of the winds. In the New Forest in Hampshire above 4,000 trees, some of prodigious thickness, were blown down: and above 450 parks and groves lost from 200 to 1,000 trees each. Twelve ships of the navy were totally wrecked: the Eddystone Lighthouse was destroyed, and the people within it perished. It is impossible to describe the general calamity. About 8,000 persons were supposed to have perished.[1]

Ken was staying with his nephew at Poulshot on the night of the storm, and in a letter to Lloyd he describes his experience of it.

Nov. 27th, 1703

My good Lord and dear Brother,

I return you my thanks for both yours. I have no news to return, but that last night there was here the most violent wind that ever I knew; the house shaked all the night; we all rose, and called the family to prayers, and by the goodness of God we were safe amidst the Storm. It has done a great deal of hurt in the neighbourhood, and all about, which we cannot yet hear of; but I fear it has been very terrible at sea, and that we shall hear of many wrecks there. Blessed be God who preserved us. I hope that your Lordship and your family have suffered no harm, and should be glad to hear that you are well. I beseech God to keep us in his holy fear.

Your Lordship's
Most affectionate Friend and Brother,
Tho: B. & W.

The same day as that on which the above letter was written an examination was made of the vicarage roof, which revealed that all who had slept beneath it the previous night had had

[1]Daniel Defoe, *The Storm*, 1704.

a remarkably narrow escape. In a further letter to Lloyd, Ken says,

I think I omitted to tell you the full [story] of my deliverance in the late storm, for the house being searched the day following, the workmen found that the beam which supported the roof over my head was shaken out to that degree, that it had but half an inch hold, so that it was a wonder it could hold together; for which signal and particular preservation God's holy name be ever praised! I am sure I ought always thankfully to remember it.

This deliverance of Ken's takes on an even more remarkable and dramatic aspect in view of the tragic happening that same night in his old residence, the Bishop's Palace at Wells. There, too, the storm struck with relentless fury, finding less resistance in its ancient structure. That part of the palace where Bishop Kidder and his wife lay sleeping collapsed upon them: when rescued from the ruins in the morning they were both dead. No one else in the Palace or in the town of Wells suffered any hurt. Well might the more superstitious and less charitable among the Non-jurors feel that in this grim tragedy was to be seen the retributory finger of Providence. Well might Ken himself feel that there, but for the grace of God and his own unaccommodating conscience, went he, *de jure* Bishop of Bath and Wells.

The vacancy caused by Kidder's untimely end was the signal for the customary lobbying at Court by or on behalf of several would-be successors to the dead man's mitre. The Queen, however, had her own ideas on the subject, as indeed she had about most of the episcopal appointments she was called upon to make. Unlike her successor, she was neither willing nor obliged to delegate the duty to her principal minister. Although it is still the custom for such nominations to be announced according to the formula, "The King (or Queen) has been pleased to approve the appointment of A. to be Bishop of B.", yet Anne was probably the last English sovereign whose nominations were for the most part her own free and unfettered choice, whatever advice she may have been pleased to seek and ponder.

Now, faced with the sudden vacancy in the see of Bath and Wells, she sent for Hooper—only recently installed at St Asaph—and told him that she meant him to transfer to the West Country diocese.

Hooper was taken completely by surprise. To be consecrated to one bishopric, and then within a month or two to be translated to another, was so sufficiently rare as to be virtually unheard of. Furthermore, he was considerably embarrassed. In expressing his gratitude to Her Majesty he asked permission to decline the appointment, explaining the diffidence he felt in occupying the throne which had belonged, and in the views of some still belonged, to his old and valued friend, Dr Ken. Greatly daring, in view of Ken's earlier refusal, he begged leave to propose that the Queen should again offer to restore Ken to his bishopric.

The proposal did Hooper credit, and the good natured way in which Anne agreed to it did equal credit to the Queen. Nothing would have given her greater satisfaction had Ken seen his way to accepting her kindly intentioned offer. It would almost certainly have led to a healing of the schism, and Hooper did all he could to induce his old friend to return to Wells. There is little doubt that Ken was deeply touched by these moves on his behalf, perhaps greatly tempted by them. But there was still the difficulty of the oaths insisted upon by Parliament, and there was the added drawback of his own increasing infirmities. This happy ending to his story of heroic sacrifice in the cause of conscience was not to be. He expressed his gratitude for the Queen's offer and desired Hooper to return his deepest thanks for her kind and gracious remembrance of him, at the same time explaining that he was unwilling to "return into the business of the world again". He desired only to see his former flock in safe hands, and he knew none to which they might be better entrusted than Hooper's.

When it was plain that no further persuasions would avail to make Ken change his mind, Queen Anne again offered the vacant bishopric to Hooper. It was while Hooper still hesitated that Ken wrote to assure his old friend that not only need he have no scruples about accepting it, but that he, Ken, would willingly relinquish all his claims in Hooper's favour.

December 6th, 1703

My very good Lord,

I am informed that you have an offer of Bath and Wells, and that you refused it, which I take very kindly, because I know you did it on my account; but since I am well assured that the Diocese cannot be happy in that degree in any other hands than in your own, *I desire you to accept of it*, and I know that you have a prevailing interest to procure it.

I told you long ago at Bath how willing I was to surrender my canonical claim to a worthy person, but to none more willingly than to yourself. My distemper disables me from the pastoral duty, and had I been restored I declared always that I would shake off the burthen and retire. I am about to leave this place, but if need be, the Archdeacon can tell you how to direct to me. My best respects to your good family.

God keep us in His holy fear.

My good Lord, your Lordship's

most affectionately,
T. B. and W.

Thus generously and eloquently urged by Ken, and in view of the latter's promised act of resignation and renunciation, Hooper wrote to the Queen formally accepting translation to Bath and Wells. At the same time Ken wrote to Bishop Lloyd to notify him of the step that he had taken. In a further letter to Lloyd, written some twelve days later and perhaps in response to some doubts expressed by the latter, Ken amplifies the motives which had prompted him.

I, hearing that the Bp of St Asaph was offered Bath and Wells, and that on my account he refused it, wrote to him to accept of it. I did it in charity to the Diocese, that they might not have a

Latitudinarian Traditour imposed on them, who would betray
the baptismal faith, but one who had ability and zeal to affect it;
and the imminent danger in which religion now is, and which
daily increases, ought to supersede all the ancient canons. I am
so disabled by rheumatick and colick pains that I cannot in
conscience return to a publick station, were I restored; and I
think none ought to censure me, if in such perilous times I desire
a coadjutor, for which I have good precedents, as well as reasons.
It is not the first time I dissented from some of my brethren; and
never saw cause to repent of it. The ladys here send you their
duty.

There is a curious air almost of defiance about the latter
part of this letter, and the reference to a coadjutor appears
rather odd in the circumstances. But it seems for the time
being to have satisfied Lloyd, who wrote in return to con-
gratulate Ken (!) on the choice made of Hooper. Ken, not
unreasonably, took this to imply that Lloyd approved of his
cession of his canonical rights, an implication which Lloyd
later denied could or ought to have been read into his words.
There is small doubt that Lloyd's indignation was stimulated
by the noisy expostulations of some of the more extreme
Non-jurors, who complained bitterly that Ken had sold the
pass, that his "lapse" was an occasion of lamentation for them
and of laughter to their enemies, that he had undone more
with one word than the others were likely to have done with
ten thousand.

Ken was deeply pained by the attacks made upon him and
traces of uncharacteristic asperity may be discerned in his
references to them. He writes to Lloyd protesting that "the
Jacobites at Bristoll, fomented by those at London, are
thoroughly enraged against me for my cession to one whom
all mankind besides themselves have a high esteem of"; and
again: "The ferment against me rises higher and higher,
insomuch that when the neighbours at Bristol come hither[1]
they manifestly insult me." Lloyd, in his reply to this letter,

[1] I.e., to Naish Court, the home of the Misses Kemeys, where he was
staying.

deplores the unmannerly attacks made upon Ken but is plainly disconcerted and put out that Ken should have acted in the matter without prior consultation with himself and his other Non-juring brethren.

> I was sensibly grieved [he says] for the noyse and outcryes, made both at Bristoll, and here above, upon the account of your Cession. How a sudden passion may carry and transport some men at Bristoll I know not; but I am sure I have not heard any of the brethren here say anything disrespectful to your person, or your character, unless what amounts to no more than this, viz. that they seemed offended because your conduct in and about the Cession, was not managed *communi consensu*.[1]

Lloyd, in fact, found himself in some difficulty. His veneration and love for Ken had led him in the first place to approve the action he had taken; at the same time, as ostensible head of the Non-juring party he could not altogether dissociate himself from their subsequent attitude of dismay. If we may judge from two further sharply worded communications to him from Ken, Lloyd would seem to have joined more openly, if somewhat belatedly, in the general outcry. Such an apparent *volte face* wounded Ken deeply, and we find him giving vent to his feelings in that forthright manner which he was apt to assume when writing or speaking in self-defence. It is strange to find the gentle, affectionate Ken expressing himself with such bitterness, and yet one more indication of the strength of the feelings which these unhappy controversies could arouse in the most charitable and peaceable of men.

> Though I wrote to your Lordship last, yett I am in a manner bound to write again, to let you know that the ferment against me rises higher and higher ... and though you are pleased to tell me that others kindled the flame, and not yourself, I must take the freedome to tell you that it is yourself have most contributed to it. For 'tis still vehemently urged against me that I acted quite contrary to your earnest remonstrances, which you know to be false. If I did, I do not remember that I ever put myself into

[1] Anderdon, *Life of Ken*, p. 719.

your keeping, and was to do nothing but by your direction; but you yourself can acquit me in that particular, by only relating matter of fact.[1]

There is much more to the same effect, culminating in the reproach that Lloyd had shown some of Ken's letters to those of the Non-jurors who were among his fiercest accusers. This Lloyd denied having done in a reply quite as angrily phrased as Ken's letters to him—if not more so—in which he charges Ken with "pettish heat", comments roundly, "what stuffe is this", and concludes by declaring that he will not be concerned in any further *brouilleries*.

Ken was not the man to let the sun go down upon his wrath. His passion was quickly spent, no malice was nursed, and a few days later we find him writing once more to Lloyd, this time full of contrition and his accustomed humility.

Your Lordship's was sent to me to Poulshot last night. I confess when I wrote my last I was heated, and provoked to a great degree, and if my provocation transported me to any indecent expressions, I beg your pardon, which you will I hope the more readily grant, because you seem to have been in the like passion when you wrote, and because I intend to give you no further trouble. You must give me leave to be sensible[2] when I am insulted, which I can very easily forgive. Every day increases the satisfaction I have in providing so well for my flock. God keep us in His holy fear, and make us wise for eternity.

Your Lordship's very affectionate
Friend and Brother, T.K.

From these words the true and lovable Ken looks out at us. The man who cannot for long stand upon his dignity or harbour resentment; to whom friendship and good relationship mean more than points scored in debate; who is not ashamed to confess himself as having been in the wrong, nor to ask pardon where he had offended; who is human enough still to enjoy the sly suggestion that Lloyd, too, had said more than he intended, and to insist that what he himself had done

[1]Ibid., pp. 724–5.
[2]I.e., sensitive.

about ceding his canonical position still seemed to him entirely right; yet, greater than all these, his essential, abiding, unself-seeking charity. Such a man is bound to have his critics, for genuine goodness, by its silent reproach to spiritual and moral mediocrity, inevitably attracts disparagement and depreciation; but his real enemies must be few indeed.

In the letter to Lloyd just quoted, and dated 1 May, Ken for the first time since his consecration abandoned his episcopal signature and signed himself simply "T.K." This was to be his usual practice thenceforward, although occasionally he added the phrase "late Bishop". The change was indicative of the renunciation he had made in favour of his successor, and of his resolve to devote what years might remain to him in the pursuit of inward peace and preparation for the inevitable hour of his departure—in the medieval phrase, to making his soul.

These last years were made materially easier for him by the grant of a royal pension of £200 a year. Hooper, when accepting the bishopric of Bath and Wells, had asked and received the Queen's permission to retain, *in commendam*, the Precentorship of Exeter, that he might hand over the annual revenue of the post—£200—to Bishop Ken by way of compensation. Anne was pleased by the proposal, but Trelawney, Bishop of Exeter and one of Ken's companions in the Tower, objected on the grounds that the patronage, upon Hooper's consecration, should fall to him. A deadlock ensued which was only ended by the good offices of Godolphin, the Lord Treasurer. It was at his suggestion that the pension of £200 was granted to Ken from the Privy Purse, on condition that Hooper resigned the Precentorship.

Ken expressed his gratitude to the Queen, to Godolphin, and to Hooper, in a letter to his old friend assuring him that, while his (Ken's) sense of her Majesty's favour towards him is deservedly great, yet even greater is his satisfaction in the Queen's choice of his successor at Bath and Wells. It was fourteen years since his deprivation, yet the well-being of his beloved diocese still occupied a central place in his prayers and affections. With Hooper to be its shepherd and ruler, he felt that its future was in sound hands, doctrinally and spiritually, and that he could with an easy mind murmur his own *nunc dimittis*.

As for the addition to his income, that would doubtless have gone the way of all money in Ken's always liberal hands had not Hooper intervened to see that he spent some portion of it at least upon modest comforts for himself. He would not allow Ken to give it all away, "which he was so charitable as to be always doing: so that his habit was mean, and a poor horse to carry him about, which made Hooper entreat him to lay out something for himself; and from that time he appeared in everything according to his condition."[1] It is pleasing to think of the good old man, after so many years of enforced economy, at the insistence of his friend discarding his shabby cassock and worn-out mount in favour of ones more fitting to his station.

It was in this great year for Britain of 1704, and shortly after the capture of Gibraltar by Rooke, and Marlborough's even more famous victory at Blenheim, that Ken paid a visit to the aged Bishop Frampton, the cheerful, courageous, deprived Bishop of Gloucester. Frampton would have been one of the prelates sent to the Tower by James but for the fact that, living so far from London, he had arrived too late to sign the Bishops' Petition. He was a Non-juror of the type of Ken himself—firm in refusing the oaths, but equally firm in declining to regard those who remained within the Church as schismatic. Queen Anne offered to make him Bishop of Hereford but he respectfully declined, observing humorously that he could not hold two bishoprics, and that he had always found one more than enough to manage. If he had had to accept one he would have preferred his old one; but he could

[1]Anderdon, *Life of Ken*, p. 731.

no more take a new one than hold the old one, for "that which put me out when in will keep me out when out".

Ken describes his visit in yet another letter to Lloyd, with whom he is once more on the most cordial terms.

I made, as I told you I intended, a visit to our good Brother of Glocester, who was not a little joyed to see me. He is very cheerful, and being past eighty, does not only daily expect, but, like St Paul, longs for his dissolution. He has many infirmities of old age, but his eyes are very good, and he uses no spectacles. With all the tenderness imaginable he remembers your Lordship. . . .[1]

A little later we hear of Ken, while staying in Gloucestershire, calling at Badminton to pay his respects to the Duke of Beaufort. Ken being an early riser, his Grace was still abed and the visitor was entertained to breakfast by the chaplain, who was unaware of his identity. While they were still at table the Duke came in and, seeing Ken, at once knelt and asked for his blessing, to the profound astonishment and confusion of the chaplain, who immediately began to apologize for the casual way in which he had received him. Ken, however, cut short his protestations, declaring that he had been most hospitably entertained.

Bishop Frampton died in 1708, after a long life of many vicissitudes but of unexampled fortitude and acknowledged piety. Both Pepys and Evelyn express their admiration of him, particularly remarking upon his eloquence in the pulpit. The former, as ever, is the more exuberant in his praise.

I to church, and there beyond expectation find our seat, and all the church, crammed by twice as many people as used to be: and to my great joy find Mr Frampton in the pulpit; and I think the best sermon for goodness and oratory, without affectation or study, that ever I heard in my life. The truth is, he preaches the most like an apostle that ever I heard man; and it was much the best time that ever I spent in my life at church.[2]

Evelyn is characteristically more restrained, but no less admiring.

[1] Ibid.
[2] *Diary*, 20 Jan. 1667.

27th October, 1673. I went to hear that famous preacher, Dr Frampton, at St Giles's, on Psalm XXXIX.6. This divine had been twice at Jerusalem,[1] and was not only a very pious and holy man, but excellent in the pulpit for moving the affections."

Frampton's death meant to Ken the severing of yet one more link with those difficult but devoted days when they had taken their stand together for the things they prized above place and favour. On 1 January 1710, he lost the last of his deprived colleagues when William Lloyd, sometime Bishop of Norwich, also died. This left Ken as the last survivor of the original Non-juring bishops, and with the knowledge that his own call could not, in the nature of things, be long delayed, he felt that while he was still able he must do all in his power to urge the return of as many as possible of the Non-jurors to the Church. Already in 1705 Dodwell had expressed the opinion, in a work entitled *The Case In View*, that upon the death or resignation of each of the deprived bishops the intruded occupants of their sees would automatically become the rightful and canonical holders of them. Where no altar was set up against altar, there could be no schism. The more extreme Non-jurors, such as Hickes, Wagstaffe, Collier, and Brett, strongly dissented from this point of view, holding that those who had accepted the sees of the deprived were guilty of the sin of Schism, from which neither the death nor resignation of the lawful holders could absolve them.

The all-important question was: what would be Ken's attitude, as the last of those who had suffered deprivation? Dodwell now wrote to him to inquire whether he still insisted upon his episcopal claim in such a way as to justify the continuance of the schism. Ken's reply was prompt and unambiguous.

My answer is that I do not, and that I have no reason to insist upon it, in regard that I made a Cession to my present most

[1] In earlier life Frampton had been chaplain to the English factory at Aleppo.

worthy Successor, who came into the Fold [i.e., the bishopric of Bath and Wells] by my free Consent and Approbation. As for any clandestine Claim, my judgment was always against it, foreseeing that it would perpetuate a schism, which I found very afflicting to good people scattered in the Country....

In response to a similar inquiry from the distinguished Non-juror and philanthropist, Robert Nelson, Ken returned the same unequivocal answer. This entirely dissolved the doubts of the moderate party, and they resolved forthwith to make their submission to the Church from which, in all sincerity and at great cost to their personal feelings and spiritual comfort, they had seceded. At Shottesbrook in Berkshire, on the First Sunday in Lent, 1710, Dodwell and Cherry, with their respective families, once again received the Holy Sacrament in their parish church, a joyful peal on the bells in the tower being rung to mark their return to fellowship. Robert Nelson followed their example soon afterwards.

The subsequent history of the Non-juring Movement lies outside the scope of this book. Their story is a fascinating but a sad one, in that very soon, owing to differences over questions of ritual, there was a schism within the schism and the two conflicting branches were fated to compete for the allegiance of an ever-diminishing band of followers, although the last of the Non-juring Bishops, Charles Booth, actually lived on until 1805. But so far as any threat to the internal unity of the Church of England was concerned, this ceased to exist with the submission of Dodwell, Cherry, Nelson, and the rest, on the firm and sincere advice of Ken. And if it be asked why he did not himself set an example in this respect, he pointed out to Nelson the different situation he was in as "a public person". On the other hand, he expressed himself as perfectly willing to communicate at the altar with his successor, and on 21 April he wrote to Dodwell to this effect.

My very worthy Friend,

I return you many thanks for the caution you gave me that my Example should not be mistooke, lest it have an ill influence on others, which is very far from my intention; and as soone as I am fitt for travelling, I shall, God willing, goe to the Cathedral on purpose to communicate with my Successor; that being the most conspicuous, and the Communion Office has nothing exceptionable.

It was a brave resolve on the part of an old man, but whether he was able to implement it is not known. His health about this time was beginning to cause him considerable distress and in Easter week, when his letter to Dodwell was written, he had been "seas'd with a very severe fitt of the rheumatism". He proposed to go to Clifton to take the hot wells treatment, but he was unable to move from Longleat until later in the summer. In May he writes to Lord Weymouth, "I thank God the violence is over, and I recover my strength, but my pain still continues, and is most raging when I am in bed".

That summer he spent at Bristol, from which place perhaps he was able to journey the short distance to his beloved Wells and to receive Communion, as he had desired and intended, at the hands of his old friend and successor, Bishop Hooper. This is only surmise, for no more letters are known to exist from his once prolific pen. The voyage of his life was nearing its end and he was soon now to enter harbour.

In November he went to stay at the house of Mrs Thynne at Lewesdon and there he sustained a stroke which left him partially paralysed. He remained at Lewesdon until early in March of the following year when, against the pleadings of his hostess, he set out in an attempt to go as far as Bath, where he hoped to obtain relief from his afflictions. He reached Longleat on Saturday 10 March 1711, and spent that evening "adjusting some Papers". The following day he kept to his room—that hospitable chamber where, on and off for the past twenty years, he had lived amongst his books, reading, praying, writing his hymns and poems and singing them to his own accompaniment on the viol. On Monday he was unable to leave his bed, and two physicians, one from Bath, the other from Devizes, were summoned to attend him. It was plain, however, that there was little they could do for him, and when they told him that he had only two or three more days to live he contentedly murmured, "God's will be done". He had already clothed himself in his death shroud, which for many years he had carried with him in his travelling case.

He dozed fitfully during the next two or three days, as they plied him with opiates to deaden his pains. Perhaps he was back once more in the Winchester of his boyhood and of the early years of his ministry; or at Wells, where he had known such brief and intermittent happiness. Once he was heard to murmur Hooper's name, but the watchers by his bedside were unable to distinguish anything more. He lingered on until the shadows fled at daybreak on the morning of 19 March. Then, released from the weary, pain-racked flesh his gentle spirit passed to where all those he had loved on earth had gone before him; his sister Anne and good kind Izaak Walton, the saintly Bishop Morley, the Lady Maynard and her Lord, brave old Sancroft, gentle Frampton, the impetuous, restless friend of his schooldays, Francis Turner.

It was his own expressed wish that he should be buried "in the Churchyard of the nearest parish within my Diocese, under the east window of the Chancel, just at sun-rising, without any manner of pomp or ceremony, besides that of the Order for Burial, in the Liturgy of the Church of England". And so it was that he was laid to rest in the churchyard of Frome-Selwood, a few miles from Longleat and just within the bounds of the diocese of Bath and Wells.

To the parish of Frome he bequeathed "the little Patin and Chalice guilt" with which he had so often celebrated the Holy Mysteries on behalf of the living and departed. And in the will where he made this and other bequests known, he declared the Faith by which he had tried to live and in which he died:

I die in the Holy Catholick and Apostolick Faith, professed by the whole Church, before the disunion of East and West; more particularly I die in the Communion of the Church of England, as it stands distinguished from all Papall and Puritan Innovations, and as it adheres to the doctrine of the Cross.

Over his grave, instead of the plain stone slab for which he asked, they placed a curious iron grill-like monument, in the shape of a coffin and surmounted by an iron mitre and crozier. It is strange that Ken's wishes in this matter should have been disregarded or misinterpreted, and no attempt made to set upon or near his final resting-place the inscription which he had himself composed and which shall therefore serve here as epitaph and aspiration:

May the here interred Thomas, late Bishop of Bath and Wells, and uncanonically Deprived for not transferring his Allegiance, have a perfect consummation of Blisse, both in body and Soul, at the Great Day, of which God keep me allwaies mindfull.

15

APPENDIX A

THE PETITION OF THE SEVEN BISHOPS

To the King's Most Excellent Majesty.

The humble Petition of William, Archbishop of Canterbury, and of divers of the Suffragan Bishops of that Province (now present with him) in behalf of themselves and others of their absent brethren, and of the Clergy of their respective Dioceses,

Humbly sheweth;

That the great averseness they find in themselves to the distributing and publishing in all their churches your Majesty's late Declaration for Liberty of Conscience, proceedeth neither from any want of duty and obedience to your Majesty, (our holy mother the Church of England being both in her principles and in her constant practice, unquestionably loyal; and having, to her great honour, been more than once publicly acknowledged to be so by your gracious Majesty), nor yet from any want of due tenderness to Dissenters, in relation to whom they are willing to come to such a temper, as shall be thought fit, when that matter shall be considered and settled in Parliament and Convocation; but amongst many other considerations, from this especially, because that Declaration is founded upon such a Dispensing power, as hath been often declared illegal in Parliament, and particularly in the years 1662 and 1672, and the beginning of your Majesty's reign; and is a matter of so great moment and consequence to the whole nation, both in Church and State, that your Petitioners cannot in prudence, honour or conscience, so far make themselves parties to it, as the distribution of it all over the nation, and the solemn publication of it once and again, even in

God's house, and in the time of his divine service, must amount to, in common and reasonable construction.

Your Petitioners therefore most humbly and earnestly beseech your Majesty that you will be graciously pleased not to insist upon their distributing and reading your Majesty's said Declaration.

And your Petitioners (as in duty bound) shall ever pray, &c

Signed

W. Cant.	Tho. Bath & Wells.
W. S. Asaph.	Tho. Petriburgens.
Fran. Ely.	Jon. Bristol.
Jo. Cicestr.	

APPENDIX B

The Original Versions of Bishop Ken's
Hymns for Morning, Evening, and Midnight

A Morning Hymn

Awake my Soul, and with the Sun,
Thy daily stage of Duty run;
Shake off dull sloth, and early rise,
To pay thy Morning Sacrifice.

Redeem thy misspent time that's past,
Live this day, as if 'twere thy last:
T'improve thy Talent take due care,
Gainst the great Day thy self prepare.

Let all thy converse be sincere,
Thy Conscience as the Noon-day clear;
Think how all-seeing God thy ways,
And all thy secret Thoughts surveys.

Influenc'd by the Light Divine,
Let thy own Light in good Works shine;
Reflect all Heaven's propitious ways,
In ardent Love, and chearful Praise.

Wake and lift up thy self my Heart,
And with the Angels bear thy part,
Who all night long unwearied sing,
Glory to the Eternal King.

I wake, I wake, ye Heavenly Choire.
May your Devotion me inspire,
That I like you my Age may spend,
Like you may on my God attend.

May I like you in God delight,
Have all day long my God in sight,
Perform like you my Maker's Will,
O may I never more do ill.

Had I your Wings, to Heaven I'd flie,
But God shall that defect supply,
And my Soul wing'd with warm desire,
Shall all day long to Heav'n aspire.

Glory to Thee who safe hast kept,
And hast refresht me whilst I slept.
Grant God, when I from death shall wake,
I may of endless Light partake.

I would not wake, nor rise again,
Ev'n Heav'n itself I would disdain;
Wert not Thou there to be enjoy'd,
And I in Hymns to be imploy'd.

Heav'n is, dear Lord, where e'r Thou art,
O never then from me depart;
For to my Soul 'tis Hell to be,
But for one moment without Thee.

Lord I my vows to Thee renew,
Scatter my sins as Morning dew,
Guard my first springs of Thought and Will,
And with Thy self my Spirit fill.

Direct, controul, suggest this day,
All I design, or do, or say;
That all my Powers, with all their might,
In Thy sole Glory may unite.

Praise God, from whom all blessings flow,
Praise Him all Creatures here below,
Praise Him above ye Angelick Host,
Praise Father, Son, and Holy Ghost.

An Evening Hymn

Glory to Thee my God, this night,
For all the blessings of the Light;
Keep me, O keep me King of Kings,
Under Thy own Almighty Wings

Forgive me, Lord, for Thy dear Son,
The ill that I this day have done,
That with the World, my self, and Thee,
I, e'r I sleep, at peace may be.

Teach me to live, that I may dread
The Grave as little as my Bed;
Teach me to die, that so I may
Triumphing rise at the last day.

O may my Soul on Thee repose,
And with sweet sleep mine Eye-lids close,
Sleep that may me more vig'rous make,
To serve my God when I awake.

When in the night I sleepless lie,
My Soul with Heavenly Thoughts supply,
Let no ill dreams disturb my Rest,
No powers of darkness me molest.

Dull sleep of Sense me to deprive,
I am but half my days alive;
Thy faithful Lovers, Lord, are griev'd
To lie so long of Thee bereav'd.

But though sleep o'r my frailty reigns,
Let it not hold me long in chains,
And now and then let loose my Heart,
Till it an Hallelujah dart.

The faster sleep the sense does bind,
The more unfetter'd is the Mind;
O may my Soul from matter free,
Thy unvail'd Goodness waking see!

O when shall I in endless day,
For ever chase dark sleep away,
And endless Praise with th' Heavenly Choir,
Incessant sing, and never tire?

You my blest Guardian, whilst I sleep,
Close to my Bed your Vigils keep,
Divine Love into me instil,
Stop all the avenues of ill.

Thought to thought with my Soul converse,
Celestial joys to me rehearse,
And in my stead all the night long,
Sing to my God a grateful Song.

Praise God, from whom all blessings flow,
Praise Him all Creatures here below,
Praise Him above ye Angelick Host,
Praise Father, Son, and Holy Ghost.

A Midnight Hymn

Lord, now my Sleep does me forsake,
The sole possession of me take,
Let no vain fancy me illude,
No one impure desire intrude.

Blest Angels! while we silent lie,
Your Hallelujahs sing on high,
You, ever wakeful near the Throne,
Prostrate adore the Three in One.

I, now awake, do with you joyn,
To praise our God in Hymns Divine:
With you in Heav'n I hope to dwell,
And bid the Night and World farewell.

My Soul, when I shake off this dust,
Lord, in Thy Arms I will entrust;
O make me Thy peculiar care,
Some heav'nly Mansion me prepare.

Give me a place at Thy Saints' feet,
Or Some fall'n Angel's vacant seat;
I'll strive to sing as loud as they,
Who sit above in brighter day.

O may I always ready stand,
With my Lamp burning in my hand.
May I in sight of Heav'n rejoyce,
When e'r I hear the Bridegroom's voice.

Glory to Thee in light arraid,
Who light Thy dwelling place hast made,
An immense Ocean of bright beams,
From Thy All-glorious Godhead streams.

The Sun, in its Meridian height,
Is very darkness in Thy sight;
My soul, O lighten, and enflame,
With Thought and Love of Thy great Name.

Blest Jesu, Thou on Heav'n intent,
Whole nights hast in Devotion spent,
But I frail Creature, soon am tir'd,
And all my Zeal is soon expir'd.

My Soul, how canst thou weary grow
Of Ante-dating Heav'n below,
In sacred Hymns, and Divine Love,
Which will Eternal be above?

Shine on me, Lord, new life impart,
Fresh ardours kindle in my Heart;
One ray of Thy all-quickening light
Dispels the sloth and clouds of night.

Lord, lest the Tempter me surprize,
Watch over Thine own Sacrifice,
All loose, all idle Thoughts cast out,
And make my very Dreams devout.

Praise God from whom all blessings flow,
Praise Him all Creatures here below,
Praise Him above ye Angelick Host,
Praise Father, Son and Holy Ghost.

APPENDIX C

BISHOP KEN'S PROSE WORKS

A Manual of Prayers for the use of the Scholars of Winchester College, and all other Devout Christians. (To which are added Three Hymns, for Morning, Evening and Midnight.) Charles Brome: London (n.d.).

An Exposition on the Church Catechism or The Practice of Divine Love Composed for the Diocese of Bath and Wells. Printed for Charles Brome, at the West End of St Paul's; and William Clarke in Winchester. 1685.

Directions for Prayer for the Diocese of Bath and Wells. 1685.

Prayers for the Use of all Persons Who Come to the Baths for cure. 1685.

Articles of Visitation and Enquiry. 1685.

A Pastoral Letter from the Bishop of Bath and Wells to his Clergy concerning their Behaviour During Lent. 1688.

A Letter Exhorting the Clergy of the Diocese of Bath and Wells to collect in behalf of the French Protestants. 1686.

(His verse was published, after his death, in four volumes.)

BIBLIOGRAPHY

"A Layman" (J. L. Anderdon), *The Life of Thomas Ken.* 2 Vols. 1854.

F. A. Clarke, *Thomas Ken.* 1896.

Dictionary of English Church History (ed. Ollard and Crosse). 1948.

Dictionary of National Biography: Article, "Thomas Ken", by W. Hunt.

W. H. Hutton, *The History of the English Church from the Accession of Charles I to the Death of Anne.* 1903.

J. H. Overton, *The Non-Jurors.* 1902.

E. H. Plumptre, *The Life of Thomas Ken.* 2 Vols. 1878.

The Prose Works of Thomas Ken D.D., and a Short Account of his Life by W. Hawkins Esq. The whole Collected by J. T. Round. 1838.

J. W. C. Wand, *The High Church Schism.* 1951.

INDEX

Summoned before Privy Council, 193–5; Death of friends, 195; Deaths of James II and William III, 196–8; Declines to return to Wells, 200; Hooper's elevation to Episcopate, 201; Letters to Lloyd, 202; The great storm and death of Bishop Kidder, 203; Again declines to return to Wells, 204–205; Pained by attacks from Non-jurors, 207; Further letters to Lloyd, 206–9; Grant of Royal pension, 210; Visits to Bishop Frampton and to Badminton, 211–12; Death of Lloyd, 213; Letter to Dodwell on ending of schism, 213–14; Deterioration of health, 215; Last illness, death and burial, 216–17.

Keroualle, Louise de, 69

Kettlewell, John, 188, 191-2

Kidder, Bishop Richard, 172, 200, 204

Kirke, Colonel, 59–61, 80, 82, 100

Knox, Alexander, 28

LAKE, JOHN, BISHOP OF CHICHESTER, 120–1, 162–3, 175

Langley, Sir Roger, 133

Lamplugh, Thomas, Archbishop of York, 121, 145, 148

Legge, Colonel, 55

Lloyd, William, Bishop of St Asaph, 45, 120–1

Lloyd, William, Bishop of Norwich, 66, 120–1, 175, 185–8, 191, 201–4, 206–10, 213

Louis XIV, 29, 50, 88–90, 148, 167, 196

MACAULAY, LORD, 131, 134

Markland, Dr, 35

Mary of Modena (Queen), 76, 87–88, 107, 130, 148

Mary (Princess, later Queen), 41–42, 44, 48, 107, 154, 180–90

Mary, Queen of Scots, 100

Mary, Countess of Warwick, 18

Maynard, Lord, 16, 101, 195, 216

Maynard, Lady Margaret, 16, 49, 216

Mews, Peter, Bishop of Winchester, 65, 120

Monk, General, 12

Monmouth, Duke of, 70, 78–82, 122, 144

Morley, George, Bishop of Winchester, 3, 13, 16–17, 20, 32, 43, 63–5, 119, 216

NASH, JOHN, 87

Nelson, Robert, 92, 188, 214

OATES, TITUS, 32, 150

Osborne, Sir Thomas (Earl of Danby), 31, 146, 154

Owen, Dr John, 6, 8, 10

PATRICK, SIMON, BISHOP OF ELY, 76, 119, 171

Pearson, John, Bishop of Chester, 32

Penn, William, 109, 110, 115

Pepys, Samuel, 14, 31, 35, 53–61, 78, 143, 212

Perkins, Sir William, 192

Petre, Father, 109, 125, 148, 150

Petty, William, 8

Pink, Dr, Warden of New College, 7–8

Plumptre, Dean, 124, 180, 198

Powis, Lord, 148

QUIN, JAMES, 11

ROCHESTER, EARL OF, 102, 146

Rooke, Admiral, 53, 211

SANCROFT, WILLIAM, ARCHBISHOP OF CANTERBURY, 32, 43, 47, 66, 68–9, 75, 89–90, 101, 104, 110, 119, 120–1, 125–7, 131, 135–7, 139–42, 146, 148, 151, 153, 164, 175–7, 185, 189, 216

Sanderson, Robert, Bishop of Lincoln, 13

Sheldon, Gilbert, Archbishop of Canterbury, 99

Sheridan, William, Bishop of Kilmore, 175

Sherlock, Thomas, Bishop of London, 32, 119

Shrewsbury, Earl of, 131, 154